365 DAYS OF
good morning
good life

AMY SCHMITTAUER LANDINO
Bestselling Author of Good Morning, Good Life
& SARA MITCHELL MCCAIN

This book is for:

_____

Here's to making every morning a good one.
Please accept this gift and all the exciting
opportunities that will come with it.

From:

_____

Find out how you can order gift or bulk copies
at www.GMGL365.com.

reader praise for Good Morning, Good Life

"*Good Morning, Good Life* is not about waking up early. It is a way of thinking about how you can achieve what you want while keeping your mental sanity in a tumultuous world."
—*Cristina Sirbu*

"Before *Good Morning, Good Life* I believed the myth that in order to have a morning routine you have to get up really early and spend two hours doing it. With my work schedule and lifestyle, that isn't realistic. *Good Morning, Good Life* opened my eyes to understanding that every person can craft a morning routine that works for them - the point is to begin the day on your terms. It doesn't fundamentally matter if that is at 5:00am or 8:00am - whatever works for you in the season of life you are in. By learning how to start the day on my own terms, my 'Good Morning' helps me create my 'Good Life' my way."
—*Julie Sieron*

"It helped me gain the mental clarity I longed for. I knew I hated feeling like a hot mess mom but I just didn't know what to do about it. Keeping my morning, my life, and my mind organized and intentional allows for so much more peace and love in my life."
—*Miranda A. Clarke*

"I honestly feel happier. I definitely think I'm more productive which gives me way more energy than the extra sleep ever could. I feel more present with my family because I'm not rushing as much. And I feel proud of myself which is invaluable."
—*Gianna DeMedio*

"[After *Good Morning, Good Life*] I started to wake up with awareness, not just because I had to. I started to really choose in which direction I wanted to make my day go—and then my life."
—*Elisa Furiglio*

"Before *Good Morning, Good Life* my mornings were hectic, unorganized and I felt like I started each day in a panic. Now, my mornings are calm and peaceful. I start each day with a clear mind, am happier and less focused on what needs to be done urgently as I have a clear plan for each day. *Good Morning, Good Life* is not just a book, it's a daily guide."
—*Marice Young*

"Now my mornings give me something I never understood I needed: time to be thoughtful and space to process reality."
—*Jessica Eden*

"My mornings have always been a struggle as a mom of four kids, but *Good Morning, Good Life* changed my mindset! My mornings have functionality and rhythm now!"
—*Samantha Martinez*

"*Good Morning, Good Life* taught me to find what works for me and to not ask for permission to do what works in my life right now."
—*Brittany Clift*

"I thought I only had to do things only the popular way and I can't stick to it then I am not good at morning routines. So I tried to keep like the most popular morning routine that I knew and after a very short amount of time I gave up. I loved the freedom and empowerment [*Good Morning, Good Life*] gave me. I created my own space for success."
—*Velislava Yoncheva*

"You helped me alter the trajectory of my life, but more importantly to be a model of consistent successful behavior for my daughter...absolute tragedy struck my family and everything fell apart. That said, [*Good Morning, Good Life*] kept me pushing forward. The grief was devastating and I honestly believe without the year prior of implementing your strategies, habits, and suggestions... I would NEVER have made it. It was the first time in my life I continued to persevere through personal hardship, basically alone. I could have reached out for help, but [*Good Morning, Good Life*] already laid the foundation."
—*Ada Napolitano Garcia*

365 DAYS OF
good morning good life

AMY SCHMITTAUER LANDINO
Bestselling Author of Good Morning, Good Life
& SARA MITCHELL MCCAIN

Copyright © 2023 GATLUW House LLC All rights reserved.

Printed in the United States of America Published by GATLUW House LLC

2000 PGA Blvd. Suite 4440 Palm Beach Gardens, Florida 33408

www.amylandino.com

ISBN: 979-8-9851331-0-3

Library of Congress Control Number: 2022918668

For Bianca & Roy

contents

Introduction   12

7 pillars to go after the life you want   18

1 | JANUARY   21

2 | FEBRUARY   55

3 | MARCH   87

4 | APRIL   121

5 | MAY   153

6 | JUNE   187

7 | JULY   219

8 | AUGUST   253

9 | SEPTEMBER   287

10| OCTOBER   319

11| NOVEMBER   353

12| DECEMBER   385

Conclusion   418

Acknowledgments   420

Suggestions for further reading   426

References   427

About the authors   430

introduction

Three years ago, I was clinking glasses with my husband, celebrating another successful year of business. That year, we closed on our first home together, opened a physical office to grow operations, expanded our team with additional full-time employees, and capped it all off with the massively successful launch of my second bestselling book.

It was more than a proud moment. It was the culmination of all the hard work and focus I put in—day after day—to get my life to reflect exactly what I wanted. As I think back to that time, there's one thing I know for sure: None of it would've happened without a daily sacred step, my morning routine.

The power of a good morning is more than just something I'm passionate about. It's been critical to both my success and my happiness. No matter how unpredictable life can be, I've found that the key to a good life is starting each day on my terms.

Whether I'm waking up in a city on the other side of the world or in the comfort of my own home, I know what my first actions of the day will be—and, more importantly, why I'm doing them. I could be starting my day in Riyadh, getting ready to speak at an entrepreneurial summit put on by the crowned prince of Saudi Arabia, waking up in a New York City hotel room preparing to deliver an interview on the Tamron Hall Show, or opening my eyes to the familiar scene of my bedroom, gearing up for a creative video shoot for my YouTube channel. Where I'm physically located doesn't make a difference. My body is my home and I can take the necessary steps to stay mentally present and grounded.

Once you engineer the first moments of your day to support you, your life inevitably transforms. The decisions you make for the rest of the day shift. You begin to try things that you used to avoid for fear of failure. And every single time you follow through, you demonstrate to yourself what you're capable of accomplishing. You emulate the version of you that you deeply believe you're destined to become.

This is what inspired me to write my last book, *Good Morning, Good Life: 5 Simple Habits to Master Your Mornings and Upgrade Your Life*. I felt that by sharing my morning philosophy I could help others find theirs as well. I saw that book as an opportunity to create the ultimate morning routine manual—but not in the ways other books claim to do. Rather than giving you a rigid list of arbitrary tasks to do each morning and declaring they'll (somehow...magically?) be the perfect formula for you, I created a framework for you to identify what works for your ideal life. I wrote about comprehensive building blocks that you can customize for the day ahead. (Spoiler: There isn't one "right way" to wake up each day. We're all different!)

No, you don't have to be a "morning person" or wake up before the sun (unless you want to). Yes, you can still have an effective morning routine even with your abnormal schedule, home full of young children, devout love of sleep, or any other challenge you suspect to be a total roadblock. When you take the steps that energize you first thing in the morning, you set yourself up for a fulfilling day.

How? By proving to yourself that you can be proactive rather than reactive—even when stress is high, motivation is lacking, life is unpredictable, or, quite frankly, you'd rather stay in bed. If you can take initiative in those moments, you can do it anytime, anywhere.

The *Good Morning, Good Life* method is both straightforward and completely unique to you. It consists of the three morning moments: movement, mindfulness, and mastery. If you fill these three buckets, you'll have done everything you need to start the day on your terms. Your ritual could be as short as 15 minutes or as long as you like. I've seen routines on both sides of the spectrum, and the results are the same: accelerated confidence, refined decision-making skills, and a heightened sense of ownership that spills into the rest of your life.

I know this because so many of you told me so! I could not have fathomed how incredible it would feel to hear the stories from real people who decided to take their mornings into their own hands (flip to page 4 for some of these testimonials!). Witnessing the radical changes you've made for yourselves has made that book one of the most important things I've done in my career.

Without a doubt, the most fulfilling part of sharing *Good Morning, Good Life* was watching many of you arrive at the same epiphany I had: Mornings don't have to be the way they've always been. Rushed, chaotic, devoid of purpose. Or even just...there. Instead, they can be the foundation you fall back on when life happens (and it will). I also witnessed you have another revelation: Once you experience the feeling of starting the day on your terms, there's nothing you can't do. When you take control of the first moments of your day—no matter how tired, stressed, unmotivated, or distracted you might feel—you become unstoppable. You demonstrate mastery.

Yet, even when we take ownership over our lives, not one of us is immune to being human. No matter how much we plan or optimize, so much of life still consists of working through universal experiences like needing validation, overcoming perfectionism, feeling like an imposter, lacking inspiration, doubting your capabilities, or being stuck in a rut. Yes, the routine centers us. But, at the same time, life doesn't always go as planned.

It's that discovery that inspired the pages of this book, 365 Days of *Good Morning, Good Life*. (And, yes... there are actually 366 entries. But "365" looked better on the cover. Hehe.)

When I first sat down to start writing this daily reader, my life felt far from routine. My husband, Vincenzo, and I were struggling, like many families do, to have a child of our own. We were also adjusting our business to a new normal in a post-pandemic world. And (because why not make all the changes at once?) we sold our first house for an offer we couldn't refuse and found ourselves temporarily between homes. Routine? Yeah...it was pretty hard to come by—or to even say with a straight face.

I'm certainly not the only one who has seen their life change these last few years. Many of us have been grappling with the surprises of life and all they entail, including my co-author. One thing's for sure: When it comes to life's plot twists, it's important to feel like you have someone in your corner.

a note from Sara Mitchell McCain

Here's a simple truth: The majority of life exists beyond our control. The well-being of the world? That's a bit above your pay grade. Other people, their opinions, and their feelings? They own those. Circumstances at work? Occasionally, but not always. As a recovering perfectionist, it took me many years to accept this reality around control. And yet, once I released the assumption of unattainable ownership over everything, I was able to embrace the power I held over the significant things—my purpose, my motivators, my time. The outcome? Clarity—and most importantly—sanity.

While you'll never be able to script your entire existence, you can set the stage and have a say in the production of things. You may not be able to cast every actor, but you get a say in who holds leading roles. Direct your life, trust the power you do hold by focusing on the well-being of your world, understand your feelings, and choose your circumstances. It can all start in one day, with one resonating reflection, on one intentional morning. In the pages of this book, I invite you to find your "aha!" moment, to join us as you set your stage, and to start your journey of reflection.

✶✶✶✶✶

The decision to co-author this spinoff book was an easy one. I knew exactly who would do it with me. As my best friend for over a decade, Sara has been my sounding board, unending ear, mommy colleague, shoulder to cry on, career mastermind partner, everything in between, and now, co-author. When we connect, it's not about gossip or boring chats filled with small talk. We share ideas. We think about what it means to make life better. We support each other. And we do that by telling the truth, whether the answers are what we want to hear or not. This book was an incredible labor of love to write together. I know I couldn't have made it as amazing as it is for you without her prolific writing skills and wisdom.

Sara and I want to be that voice for you when the noise threatens to rattle you. Through this book, we hope to remind you of the force that you are and speak to you as an honest friend in your mindfulness moment each morning.

In the midst of all of those life changes, writing this book became the greatest therapy I could've ever received: sharing all of the principles and motivation that helped me throughout my life and career, collaborating with Sara and a spectacular team, and reading the words every day for members of the Shine Squad community on our private podcast. What a journey this has already been—and now it's finally in your hands!

Whether you've read *Good Morning, Good Life* or not, you know that the struggle of maintaining a morning routine is real. The feeling you get when things finally click and you discover what works for you is exhilarating. You want it to last forever. You can't imagine ever going back to life before you achieved what you know now.

But then, you have a late night (or two). The kids wake up one too many times. The news infiltrates your peace. The coffee gets spilled. You end up snoozing the alarm, scrolling on Instagram, and the hits just keep on coming.

It's inevitable. Life is going to happen. When it does, you can let it throw you off balance, or you can be the action-taker we both know you are and stop the spiral.

That's what this book is all about. We're not going to pretend our mornings are all sunshine and rainbows. We know obstacles will pop up. We know we won't always be on top of our mindset game. We know there will be days we wake up feeling unconfident, uninspired, or ill-equipped (or all of the above) for the day ahead.

When you wake up to start your day, the last thing you need is a chorus of limiting beliefs playing in your head. Fill your mind every morning with an assurance of your vision, confidence in your capabilities, and wisdom to take on the inevitable challenges ahead.

Finally, a quick disclaimer: As you flip through these pages, you'll encounter advice that may or may not be right when taken out of context. As you run into challenging ideas or questions that stretch your way of thinking, keep in mind that everything written in this book is framed around our 7 Pillars of GATLUW (Go After The Life yoU Want): Mindset, Career, Wealth, Health, Relationships, Spirituality, and Legacy.

These are the areas we consider when we go after the life we want. They're the foundation of the inspired and purposeful lives we're working toward. They're essential to a life well-lived, which is why every entry you read is grounded in one (or more) of these pillars. Flip to page 18 for more insight on each of these guiding principles and the conversations you'll encounter about them in this book.

Now entering a new stage of my life as a mother, the twists and turns continue. No matter what's in store for me next, this book offers guidance that gives me the confidence I need—not only to start every day on my terms but also to own the tone I'm setting for life. Equally, I know it's going to be the game-changer you need to gain that same clarity in your life, regardless of the opportunities or challenges in front of you at this moment.

If you're ready to take it up a notch, I recommend joining us for the *Good Morning, Good Life* 30-Day Challenge. It's a series of videos with ideas, strategies, and inspiration to help you start the day on your terms. To sign up and enjoy this and more premium content, visit www.goodmorninggoodlife.tv.

No matter where you are in your journey, what day it is, if all is going well, or if things feel pretty rough right now, I hope you'll open today's page and receive what you need to go after the life you want!

7 pillars to go after the life you want

mindset

How you think is who you become. It's vital to have a mindset that supports you because we can't expect fulfillment to begin anywhere else. Every page of this book is meant to inspire your mind so you can think differently, positively, objectively, and most importantly, with forgiveness. We offer grace to you and those around you with these ideas. With that mindset, you can weather anything.

career

Everyone's career has a different significance to their lives. Many of us are seeing our professional lives differently, especially throughout all the world changes that have taken place in these last years. But ambition needs an outlet, and our careers are often where that takes place. Channeling the right energy into this space so you won't burn out is critical, and these ideas are meant to serve you so you can thrive in your career.

wealth

Money. Such an important subject, yet no one wants to talk about it. If only the conversation were being had, we could stop blaming a lack of financial literacy for the problems that persist in people's lives. The subject of wealth in this book is not about becoming "wealthy" as much as it's about creating your own idea of what wealth could be. If you're open to that possibility for yourself, we offer these ideas to empower you toward it.

health

When was the last time you checked on how you feel? Do you even know? We get so caught up in our minds that it's easy to lose track of what the body is going through. Without your health, everything becomes that much harder. To encourage a healthier lifestyle, we offer ideas for how you can get better tuned in to what you truly need.

relationships

There are so many people that we interact with on any given day that directly impact how we feel, what we think, and what we do. You could say that our relationships are as vital to our well-being as a good mindset because of how often the two intertwine. We offer you suggestions for how to grow fulfilling relationships, nurture the ones you have, and seek the ones you're lacking.

spirituality

Knowing that there's something greater than oneself at work is the ultimate feeling of hope. No matter what your personal beliefs are, we offer ideas in support of a world where there's always someone in our corner, cheering us on as we live this human experience.

legacy

Some might remark that a "brand" is what people say about you when you're not in the room. If that's true, then maybe your legacy is what people feel when you're no longer on Earth. Does it matter? Probably not, but leaving this world a better place in your own way is certainly worth shooting for. We offer these thoughts to give you small (but impactful) ways you can do just that.

january

You can call it "making resolutions." Or you can call it "making changes."
In the end, it's the performance that matters.

The new year is undeniably a special time. In one moment, you get to experience both an ending and a beginning. You can say goodbye and release what no longer serves you while leaning into hope and possibility.

With the tick of a clock, you see (and believe) that your life can change in a matter of minutes.

...and yet, can't this be true at any time?

Why do you need the guise of a new year to discover a new you? Or, better yet, do you really need a new you? The notion of resolutions can be polarizing. Many kick the idea around only to become defeated and ultimately label them as arbitrary and dumb. Others find the concept to be a refreshing invitation—a permission slip, if you will.

Whatever your relationship with resolutions is, the time of year you decide on them is irrelevant. Whether the day itself feels like a milestone or not, when you work to achieve something different, better, or new in your life—the effort required to make the change is on you.

Resolving to change is something we choose when the time is right for us. That time is yours to determine—be it today, tomorrow, or three months from now. However, we're not promised any space of time and must show our dedication by making the most of what we have.

What matters most is the intention beyond your resolution. Make sure you line up your intent with any changes you call into your life because that's what will propel you into action.

2

"I'll start tomorrow" is an impossible guarantee.

Today is all we have. Read that again. *Today is all we have.*

It doesn't mean that more can't be done tomorrow—there's just no way to promise that. But what a beautiful day it'll be when you wake up again tomorrow! Good morning! Good life! Another opportunity to seize the day is here.

That mentality only works if you have it today. Right here. Right now.

Recognize that the long list you carry with you is an accessory of choice. If you're annoyed by all the things you *have* to do, ask yourself: "Who's really mandating this of me? Am I putting all this pressure on myself today?"

What would you do for the next 24 hours if that was all you were promised? What's stopping you from doing those most important, urgent things right now?

Decide to live a life that maximizes every single day rather than counting down to the next day. Here's a hint: if you keep nudging that one nagging task over to the next day again and again—there's a reason for it. Either it doesn't need to be done by you, or it just doesn't need to be done. Figure out which it is, and either delegate it or delete it.

Step 1: Embrace today as your guarantee.
Step 2: Actually live like it.

january

3

When we're given the opportunity to live a human experience,
we must take care of the only body we're given to fully experience it.

We've all shown up to work on little sleep and immediately started counting down the hours until we're back in bed again. We've all hit the theoretical wall after forgetting to fuel ourselves properly for a marathon-like day of commitments. We've all planned that perfect trip only to find ourselves feeling diminished from the stress and pressure that built up before it even began.

How we show up physically is a direct reflection of where our attention is—or, in most cases—where it's not. Our bodies are our biggest allies, but they're also our biggest tattletales. The minute they feel spent, broken down, or overlooked—they let us know (whether the timing is ideal or not).

We tend to take our bodies for granted. Some of us have become accustomed to our bodies always doing what we expect. For others, your mind and body are never on the same page.

Your body deserves to be noticed. With all it does for you, the least you can do is to make sure it's properly hydrated, nourished, rested, and prepared for the plans you've made ahead.

When was the last time you stopped everything you were doing and took inventory of how your body felt?

Do it now, from head to toe. Check in and respond accordingly. The pause will definitely be justified when you head into your next activity more physically present than your last.

4

Happiness only happens in the present. Not in the potential future.
Not even in the nostalgic past. It's right now or it's never.

How much of your day is spent looking from one minute to the next, living in anticipation of the coming moment without ever feeling the moment you're in?

Guilty as charged? No sweat. We all need a little help growing out of this habit of the rush.

Our days are made up of patterns. These mini routines have comforted us, shaped us, and continually defined our time. They're our safe spaces. They're our home base and foundation. Most of us rely on them instinctively without any real reflection. This is how we wind up blurring minutes and moments until slowly—day by day— we lose the concept of intention with our time. Then when we find ourselves frustrated for days and weeks, we wonder why.

The chipping away of our happiness happens little by little, not always all at once.

So, next time, what would it look like if you caught yourself?

Just for today, notice yourself as you rush. Don't push to the next hour. Instead, see this second for what it is, for all it holds. It's already so much more than you're giving it credit for.

A life on your terms cannot begin until you learn to let outside disappointment coexist with your choices.

How many times have you found yourself coming up with an exciting and beautiful plan for your future only to feel the tug of reality at your side? That tug comes from the fear of all the people who won't approve and how brutally open they'll be when they remind you of that fact.

We often decide (without any actual confrontation) to hold ourselves back and avoid the chance of an uncomfortable conversation.

When we start to open up, people instantly assume a platform to share their opinion on the matter, whether it's welcome or not. Whether they're *qualified* or not. But there's also a chance that the conversation could go better than expected.

Regardless, we make an early decision to side-step the whole event. We don't even bother with our well-made plans, in an attempt to avoid potential friction with others.

How is this helpful, and to whom?

Sure, you get to skip a challenging initial exchange (and likely many more questions in the future that feel a lot more like wisecracks), but how else is this helping you?

When you people-please at your own expense, not only are you taking away from your future, but you're not presenting your true and authentic self. You're ultimately lying to the world about who you are and what you have the potential to do. This only happens because you haven't found a way to let outside disappointment coexist with your decision-making process.

You serve others when you start with yourself. You're better for them when you're best to yourself. What plan would you pursue today if you were unafraid of disappointing someone else?

To achieve mastery, focus on consistent progress.

We all want to feel like we have our *thing*. Something that makes us feel special. Something we can own.

Wouldn't it be amazing if we could just instantly be great at what we want to do? Of course, it doesn't work that way. We can't be an expert from the outset because there would be no value in gaining experience or the journey to that final, daydream-worthy destination.

The journey is precisely what offers you fulfillment.

Mastery-seeking is an opportunity to seize that eye-opening journey. It's also what helps you determine how you'll bring value to the world. To achieve mastery, you must be disciplined and dedicated. It's about showing up often and letting the process teach you, no matter how hard it gets. You must have an unwavering ability to forge ahead so you might someday see what mastery looks like for you.

When you were little, you mastered tying your shoes after many frustrating attempts. When you got a little older, you mastered driving a car after hours of painstaking practice behind the wheel.

Mastery isn't knowing it all. Mastery is the ability to steadily improve without deviating. If you take one step every day for 100 days, you'll still go further than the person who took a huge leap on their first day and quit the next.

Something extraordinary exists there. Let yourself start the journey so you can fully experience it.

7

Turning a wish into reality begins with a powerful daydream.

Did you ever play dress-up as a kid?

For just a little while, you pretended to be someone or something else—anything you could imagine. Just to get a taste. But, when playtime ended, it was back to reality.

Now that we're all grown up, there seems to be no time *except* for reality. Even if you wanted to be someone else or try something new, is it productive to daydream when there's so much else to do?

Just because childhood has come to a close doesn't mean your mind has to grow out of exploring possibilities. Let your imagination play today. You don't have to change your wardrobe to try on new ideas. Pretend you chose a different career path or that your home is located in another state. What does it look like? How does it feel? How would your life be different? How would it be *better*?

Be willing to give something new a try, even if it starts in the safety of your unlimited imagination. Everything begins with your mindset.

January

8

Building wealth isn't about making more money.
It's about making money do things differently.

It's time for a mindset shift—and this one is for your bank account.

Many people feel that talking about money is taboo, but talking about building *wealth*? Well, we avoid that even more actively. Want to ditch the conversation around cash? Go right ahead. The only catch is that when we don't talk about what we need help with, we definitely won't receive it.

Here's an easy first step: stop thinking about achieving wealth as an obsessive path focused only on making more money. This pattern of thinking is a trap to make you feel guilty about wanting solid financial health in your life.

Ultimately, we need to view financial gains more holistically. To do this, we have to get creative. Rather than narrowly thinking that the only way to build wealth is to make more money at your job (whether hourly or salary) challenge yourself to consider things from a new angle.

What investments can you make in other aspects of your life? What fees are you paying that could be paying *you* instead? How are you letting debt define you to the point that you feel unworthy of making exponential changes in your life?

The answer to better financial wellness has less to do with the constant need for more and *everything* to do with how you utilize your time and money.

How will you choose to pursue wealth?

january

9

Only the average are happy with being comfortable.
Pursue the uncomfortable to discover the extraordinary.

No one *wants* to be uncomfortable. The idea of discomfort is far from tempting and maybe even anxiety-provoking. What exists on the other side of discomfort is a place very few will go.

Learning to flex the muscle of doing what feels impossible at first will help you find confidence in the unknown. Suddenly, discomfort becomes curiosity. A once risky move dwarfs into a predictable hurdle. It catapults you into a new zone of certainty you never even knew could exist.

Being uncomfortable not only directs you toward your next move but simultaneously shows you how capable you *already* are at achieving whatever it might be. Meanwhile, those who are comfortable continue their search in all the wrong places for those very same answers to no avail. No experience equals no explanations.

Get comfortable being uncomfortable so that you can discover the version of yourself you've never been more comfortable with.

january

10

Your first victory of the day is a start that's defined by you.

Your superpower is your ability to set the tone for your life, and it starts every morning of each new day. Choosing to own your day packs way more strength than all those cups of coffee you reach for. (Don't worry. You're more than welcome to have both.)

Start to navigate a powerful day by building small, positive habits in the morning:

- Greet your reflection with a smile instead of the usual sleepy frown.

- Ignore your phone for the first 30 minutes of the day.

- Practice a tall and confident posture on the way to the kitchen for your daily caffeine fix.

- Take just five minutes to sit in stillness and meditate before you open your mind to the rest of the world.

- Embrace the usual traffic jam as a chance to feel all the good feelings that come with singing your favorite song.

Small habits create big changes.

If you believe the version of you who does these things consistently is too good to be true, you'll never start. Just try something. See how it works for you. If you like it today, do it again tomorrow.

Good morning. Good life.

11

No one will give you the permission you seek. You must offer it to yourself.

When it comes to absorbing others' opinions, we often tell ourselves that their thoughts don't matter to us. We do this to comfort ourselves, but by negating their thinking, we're still giving more space to their opinions than to our own.

We fixate. We dwell. We find ourselves questioning every crucial decision because we're consumed with the effect it might have on others. We consider the outcome for them before considering why we're having this internal debate at all.

We want to feel better. We want to be reassured. We want permission. We may not admit it right away, but validation would *just* hit the spot. It feels good to be approved of, to be given the go-ahead from someone you value. It feels safe.

Most of the time, we don't get that permission—even when we directly ask for it.

Why wait for someone else to offer the acceptance we need from ourselves?

Instead of waiting for the light to change, let's reroute. Look for how you can give yourself the affirmation you're seeking. Stop waiting to get that permission slip and write it to yourself.

january

12

Small steps bring big results.

Here's something exciting: It's *completely* within reason for you to achieve everything you want in life.

You're capable of accomplishing as many giant milestones as you determine. If you can dream it, you can do it. And you deserve to know that.

One thing you may consider as you venture out today to take on the world is to take baby steps. Rather than trying to take huge leaps in the right direction, crawl before you walk. Walk before you run. The momentum will come, no matter how slow you think you're going.

The reason why you should think small when going big is so you can beat your biggest, scariest obstacle: the start.

Remember the dread of starting a school project that felt impossible when first assigned? Or the constant dragging of your feet when you dressed for a gym class but had no desire to go?

You don't have to run a marathon today. All you have to do is walk a mile. You don't have to cut out all your favorite foods. You just need to make one healthy swap.

The start is the hardest because it's your first sign of being able to change. That's why even the small steps will help you win.

january

13

*Have as much gratitude for those who choose not to
follow your path as those who do.*

Self-improvement is an opportunity to do just that: to improve yourself. And, it can be thrilling too, if you let it. The more open you are, the more "aha!" moments and mindset shifts you'll discover. You won't be able to help yourself from brimming with excitement or sharing what you've learned.

Unfortunately, disappointment quickly settles in when those closest to you don't find themselves as riveted by improving themselves in the same ways you might. *Especially* when you've become the preacher they never asked for.

Remember this saying: "When the student is ready, the teacher appears."

Stay obsessed with being a lifelong learner because your curiosity will lead to immense happiness. But—even more importantly—don't lose your gratitude for your loved ones just because they're not receptive to your valuable lessons yet. When they're open, they'll see your incredible progress and ask how you might be able to show them the light they need.

14

Today is an opportunity to be better than yesterday.

If you can do one thing better today than you did yesterday, you're already ahead of the game. Challenge yourself to answer this question: "What would I do today if I were a grown-up version of who I was yesterday?"

When we're young, people constantly ask us what we want to be when we grow up. Then, we grow up and realize there never really was a definitive benchmark of being a "grown-up" after all.

It's not some milestone you suddenly reach or status you finally earn after a specific accomplishment. It's a daily choice to do something just a little better than you did the day before, learning from experience and making inches of progress in the different corners of your life. Ideally, you're never *really* grown up because you're always willing to grow forward.

Let's bring it back to today. What does it look like for you to be a grown-up version of who you were yesterday?

Maybe you lost your temper a little too quickly yesterday, so today, you're going to remember not to take yourself so seriously. Or, you might have indulged in too much binge-watching last night, so you're setting a limit tonight to get to bed on time. Today, agree to let go of judgment and try to choose a positive thought when you need to reclaim that space.

This is growing up. This is adulting. This is self-care. This is raising your standards. And it happens one small step at a time.

Look at the standard you held yourself to yesterday. Recognize what worked and what didn't. You always retain the permission to change your mind. To try something new. To drop what just doesn't serve you anymore, no matter how much it's become expected of you (or how much you expect it from yourself).

Take what sparked in you yesterday and use it to ignite you today.

january
15

The ground is shaky beneath those who cannot decide.

What would it look like to confidently know that *every* action you took was grounded in accountability? That your self-belief meant more than the explanation of your actions to others?

The choices you've made are significant. The actions you've taken to get where you are matter. You fought for a reason. You dug in and decided with intention. You deserve the credit—with no need to justify it to anyone.

Even if the outcome doesn't meet your expectations, that doesn't mean you shouldn't have tried in the first place. Don't backtrack your choice by second-guessing what moved you initially. Don't minimize your accomplishment of decisiveness and action. Doubt has a way of worming its way into your mind and out of your mouth faster than you can acknowledge what worked.

What worked is that you chose with confidence. What worked is that you were motivated to do and not just *say* you might. What worked is *you*.

Stand your ground. Own your decisions by actually making them.

16

*Self-awareness is completely owning who you are,
no matter how uncomfortable it makes others.*

How often do you step into a new space and filter out pieces of yourself without a second thought?

Maybe you feel hesitant to be vulnerable in a new environment. Perhaps you're holding your breath with the uncertainty of what's expected of you. Or maybe you prefer to observe before you interact. Whatever the cause, the outcome will be the same: If you aren't *all* there, you won't be all in.

What if you showed up without the filter? If you stepped *out* of the box you've put yourself in?

What would happen?

What *could* happen?

Imagine what living boldly and without hesitation could feel like. No, you won't be everyone's cup of tea. And, yes, observing social cues is appreciated. But that isn't really the point, is it?

Eventually, you'll need to show the world who you truly are. Until then, the worst thing you can do is make people believe that they've been in a room with an entirely different person.

Be fully expressed now and always, or you'll miss the only life you get to be truly and authentically your best self.

january

17

When you affect one, you have the power to affect many.

We all aspire to matter. We desire to create real impact on a life beyond our own.

Consider what you're pursuing right now. The big thing. Your life-giving, ambitious, fulfilling passion. Ask yourself how many people would need to be impacted for this thing to be a success.

How big is your answer? Is it thousands, maybe hundreds?

How about twenty?

What about just five?

Or—what if all your work and dedication changed the life of just one person? Would it be worth it then?

If you could change just one person's life with the good you do, it wouldn't just be a success—it would be *extraordinary*. The true definition of a legacy left.

When you do something so well that it changes the world of another human being, you have unlimited potential to spread that influence far and wide. You don't need to do it all to create something big, but you must do something so it can begin to ripple out on its own.

Who are you doing it for?

Whoever they are, they motivate and ground you. They're the point of confidence you seek out when everything feels like complete chaos. They amplify your drive and accelerate your desires. They're your North Star.

Think of just that one person today and take every step with extra intention in their honor. Do it for them so you can truly live life fully for yourself.

18

*You can't overanalyze your way to the truth,
but you can try anything else.*

Have you ever noticed what you're doing when you're feeling the most stressed? How about the most anxious? Or the most insecure?

For a moment, step outside of your overthinking mind. You're probably going to look down and see that you're doing a whole lotta nothin'.

When you're in this place, it may not *feel* like nothing. Maybe you're watching television or scrolling social media on your phone (or possibly even doing both at the same time).

Not only is that *nothing*—it's nothing with some scripted drama and a serving of comparison sprinkled on top.

We so desperately want to choose the path that's right for us. But, we get stuck in thinking rather than doing, caught up in all the scenarios that *could* play out rather than leaning into what we *want* to play out. That's analysis paralysis at its best.

You're more ready to act than you're willing to admit. Taking one simple action today will move you forward, if for no other reason than allowing you to escape your usual state of overthinking for awhile.

Nothing takes down over-analyzation faster than moving toward your dreams.

january

19

*True focus comes from believing in yourself. When you're unsure,
you welcome distractions. Trust that you're on the right path.*

Do you like where you are in your life right now?

You can answer quietly so that no one hears but answer honestly. Fight the urge to sugarcoat it. Get real and genuine as you level set with your present reality. Are you content moving forward on this path?

If the answer is a fast and easy yes, lean into that space and keep going. Don't hold back. However, if you find yourself ready to follow that yes up with a "but" or a series of other paths you'd maybe choose instead—you're rolling out the red carpet for an endless maze of surface-level progress. It's going to get you absolutely nowhere.

Confidence grows with time and experience. No one's asking you to have a lot of confidence if that time and experience isn't there. Just don't confuse this skill with the prerequisite of having self-belief. You don't need time and experience to know that you're capable of something more.

If you can imagine it and see it for yourself, don't let the millions of other things you could or should do keep you from making your dreams a reality.

Whether you said yes or no to being on the right path, the real takeaway is that you *knew the answer*. Trust yourself and follow that faith with steadfast focus and self-belief.

january

20

Success is not a limited resource.
There is enough success available for all.

Not everyone had the luxury of being raised with the advice, "You can do anything you put your mind to." Still, you might have heard it in movies and storybooks, or maybe you knew someone whose family saw things that way.

More often than not, we're introduced to the world as a cold place with little opportunity. Before you know it, you're recovering from a scarcity mentality you didn't realize was wrong to adopt in the first place.

What *is* a scarcity mindset? It's an obsession over the lack of a critical resource. For most people, the fixation is on how little time or money is available. This is a real rampant mental health issue for so many, but we struggle to come to terms with it and instead convince ourselves it's an effective form of self-preservation.

Think about all the times that you...

- Heard someone's exciting news and immediately felt a twinge of internal disappointment

- Attended a special event to honor someone and got stung by a bit of jealousy

- Congratulated a friend or colleague who decided to pursue their passion while secretly hoping they'd fail (even just a little)

Of course, we aren't our thoughts. That said, we *are* responsible for the mindsets we choose not to shift. Instead of letting the harmful habit of comparison linger, challenge it.

Success isn't a pizza with a limited number of slices. Success waits for you at the pizza shop, always making more and offering options to all who enter. The only way there won't be enough for you is if you never venture out to grab your slice.

One person's win isn't your loss. Instead of allowing others' success to become a measurement of yours, create the life you want and define your own success.

january

21

If not now, then when?

Welcome to this moment. Stop and notice it.

What are you doing? Where are you? What time of day is it? What do you hear? Who surrounds you?

There it goes.

The moment has passed, and another has arrived. Before you can fully appreciate one, it's already gone. Forever.

Time is the most precious thing we will ever have. There will be precious people we'll cherish. Precious items we'll hold dear. But nothing will truly be ours except the time we have right now.

What will you do with it today?

January

22

There's no such thing as overnight success.
Success is a one-night stand that won't be there in the morning.

As immediate as social media makes everything seem, success has never been instantaneous.

Millions of views on yesterday's post? A sold-out product launch? A brand new expert born from the validation of thousands of fans?

The hype will confuse you. But when it all dies down—reality sets in.

Instant success doesn't exist. In fact, it never has. The success that finds you comes from all the progress you make along the way. All the research. All the connections. All the *years* of work!

Your staying power and your will to succeed *will* culminate into something. It always does. And, when the outside world agrees, you'll feel like you never felt before.

But people will always move on. And, just like that, it'll feel like everything you worked for resulted in one little blip on the radar.

Success falls out of style just as quickly as it shined the spotlight on you. She's fickle, she's flighty, and as soon as she sees something else that catches her eye—she's gone.

The only way to proceed is to remember one thing: Whether or not you're a success is up to *you*. Appreciate it, acknowledge it, and move on to the next.

january

23

To find your happy is to be happy.

You are worthy of joy over sorrow.

You are capable of living in bliss instead of distress.

Living a life with more glorious moments begins when you challenge the darker ones instead of letting them take over.

Take back your happiness by:

- Noticing the good. What would your past self never be able to believe about how wonderful your life is right now? Gratitude is the source of all things happiness.

- Opening up. It may feel like the scariest idea of all—being vulnerable and raw to another person—but it'll tether you. Who will you call upon to be reminded of the light?

- Releasing judgment. If you just aren't feeling it today, that's okay. Let those emotions be what they are—nothing more, nothing less.

It might not be easy, but a mental shift *is* possible. Is it worth it? You certainly are.

january

24

If you want the right people to know you, let them in.

It's time to get vulnerable.

Building bonds with the right people will require you to do a little extra lifting in the emotion department.

This can be a daunting task for some, but it's also the only thing that's going to pull your tribe toward you. Being your true, authentic self attracts the relationships you need to thrive.

If the word "vulnerable" alone scares you, think about the people you feel the most connected to in your life. Those bonds likely formed because someone was ready to be exposed and authentic. They were ready to take a leap of faith.

Perhaps you have a friend who emulates this. Maybe you're drawn to them for their boldness and commitment to being themselves. Let them inspire you. As you think about them, picture what it would feel like to lean into all your relationships with that level of fierce authenticity.

Letting someone in is as easy as showing them exactly who you are.

january
25

Listen to your body when it tells you what it needs.

It might be sleep. It might be less sugar. It might be a little sunlight and Vitamin D. It might be all of the above. It might be none of the above. Only *you* will know the answer, and only *when* you start paying attention to yourself.

Go beyond just listening. Really sit in that space. Get in tune with how your body feels—the good, the bad, and the uncomfortable.

When was the last time you asked yourself what your body needs? If you're in the minority of those who have this conversation with themselves regularly, are you a person who actively listens?

As you sit and ask these challenging questions, allow yourself to scan your mind and body. Assess what feels aligned and register what needs to be recalibrated. Instead of assuming what will work for you based on trends and outside conversations, recognize the simple lingering desires that come from within.

There's no one-size-fits-all. Your body is unique, and it requires personalized attention. Fortunately for you, you're the best expert for the job!

Take note, and your body will thank you. Most of all, your body will be *restored.* Balance is only attainable when you're willing to take a good, honest look inward.

What do you hear? What do you feel? What will you *do*?

january 26

The steps to take will reveal themselves when you're clear on where you're headed.

Do you know what you want?

Really think about it. Is there something you desire deep down in your being? What's that lingering idea that keeps you up at night? What would you desperately like to see come true for you?

No matter how laborious the objective you have in mind, it's not as far away as it might seem. Your perspective is only skewed by the assumption you've made of how out of reach it seems.

Change your mind. Decide that it's possible. Focus on the why without worrying about the how.

Once you've proclaimed it, there's only one thing left to do: Let the vision carry you forward to make it happen. Stay focused. Fixate on what you desire, where you want to be, and who you want to become. When a thought from scarcity or imposter syndrome tries to get in the way, let it know you're not available for feedback at the moment. Sorry not sorry.

Once you know your destination, every intentional step forward will expose itself. It will give you more understanding, awareness, and knowledge than you had before. You don't need to know every twist and turn along the way. You'll take them as they come, and you'll be prepared when they reveal themselves.

As long as you know exactly where you're headed, you can do nothing but make progress.

Life isn't about the world understanding you,
but you understanding the gift of your life.

A big part of what's wonderful about life is getting to spend it with other people. It's an extraordinary thing to experience, and each of us has the opportunity to experience it. The challenge is keeping ourselves from being too consumed with what everyone else is thinking about us *all the time.*

Look in the mirror. The only one questioning you is *you.* Everyone else is far too busy worrying about themselves.

The only person in the room that needs to understand you is *you.* The only person who needs to approve of what you're doing is you. The only person who needs to know your *why* is you. At the end of the day, what drives you only needs to make sense to you.

Today, let's keep it simple. Where's your head at? And, if it's focused on someone else's head, why do their thoughts deserve more consideration than your own?

january

28

The loudest person in the room is rarely the most interesting.

Have you ever entered a room where it seemed all eyes were on just one person?

How have they attracted that attention? Maybe because they're a captivating storyteller? Or because they have enough jokes for days?

Getting attention is a skill, no doubt. The loudest person in the room may seem like a talent with all that they have to say, but those who talk more often than they listen reveal something else about themselves. Meanwhile, those who are listening may be revealing something even more interesting about who *they* are.

Who you choose to be as a member of the crowd must be considered with great intention. Your role will be memorable not because of the quantity of your words but the quality of your conversation. People who ask questions and opt to be an engaged audience are those with whom real relationships are formed.

Instead of trying to prove something, be the one genuinely interested in elevating the ideas of others.

When we see money as a support system instead of just a means to an end, we become more comfortable talking about it.

Money talks—*unless* we actively avoid talking about it. (And, let's be honest, we tend to avoid anything that could potentially be labeled as "taboo.")

It's time to demystify your wallet. If we're truly going after the life we want, we must discuss the meaning we put on money. Even more so, we need to acknowledge the power we allow it to have over us. Only then can we can go from a power struggle to a power play.

There's not one person alive who doesn't need money to survive. We need it for the car that gets us to work, the chicken nuggets on our kids' plates, and the cozy home that protects us after a long day. Money provides stability and support in every aspect of our lives. Admitting that truth doesn't make you selfish or greedy—the opposite, actually. It makes you objective and honest about what needs to happen for you and your family to thrive.

We can't be afraid to discuss finances. It's the only way we learn, improve, and grow so we can truly live a life. When the alternative is hiding from the truth and staying silent to avoid rocking the boat, you do a disservice to no one but yourself.

Saying nothing will get you nowhere. Speak up! Get a sense of how to talk about your dollars and cents. You just might find you inspire others to do the same, and there you have it: a real productive conversation that lifts everyone up.

When it comes to discovering and discussing your money goals, what conversation do you wish to have?

january

30

The highs and lows don't define you. Your reaction to them does.

If we're not careful, we spend too much of our lives in reaction mode. Life is beautifully muddied with loads of other people whose ambitions, pursuits, setbacks, and disasters can clash with our elegantly-made plans. We want to defend the good we're trying to do, and thus the temptation to react appears.

Our desire to be in control combined with unvetted, momentary emotions tempts us to resort to inappropriate reactions. But remember, those actions aren't inappropriate because of how they make you look but because of how they make you *feel*. There's a simple and direct formula that'll help you let go of your default negative reaction when it tries to sneak in.

First, ask yourself how you wish to feel. It's easy to let a multitude of flooding emotions take you whitewater rafting away from your desired state of mind. How you wish to feel is 100% within your control.

Next, fully embrace that positive feeling and remind yourself of three things:

1. You don't control others, just as they don't control you.

2. Discredit negative thoughts and instead choose one that support your desired feeling.

3. This isn't about you.

Pausing gives us the fortitude to acknowledge what we need. You may not have anticipated the situation you find yourself in, but you can always regain control over the impact it has on you (and those around you) by evaluating what's still within your power.

Choose the reaction that echoes who you want to be—for you and all the lives you touch.

31

*Getting clear on your goals and knowing what you want are
two different steps in the process.*

Knowing what you want out of life is a pretty tall order, but when you can close
your eyes and escape to that place—really *see* yourself in it—it's an incredible feeling.

Your vision is powerful, and it's only the beginning. It's still merely a dream until
we give it agency to become real.

Defining your goals helps activate the life you want. The word "goal" can feel heavy
and daunting, perhaps because goals carry expectations and responsibilities with
them. Or because they make it very clear how to define failure.

But we're not going to think about that. What we're going to focus on is that goals
help us do things that increase strength. Strength cannot be fabricated; it can only
be built by hand. Strength gives us confidence, something that can only be earned
when collected through consistent action.

What do we need to reach for the goals that bring our vision to life?

- A clear vision
- A measurable result
- A deadline

These details will help you realize a completed mission. It's that simple. When you
set a goal, you must also know the indicators of success and failure.

When you close your eyes to see your vision and watch yourself in that space, the
goals you set (whether you achieve them or not) should add color and story and
smell and ideas that make it all feel like an inevitable possibility.

Ready. Set. Goal.

february

february

1

A leader doesn't measure themselves by how many followers they have but by how they make an impact in a life of their own design.

When you know you're winning, how do you keep score? Does your metric come from an outside source or a feeling of contentment from within?

The capabilities we have for communication and connection today easily distract us from what truly reflects a life well-lived. Each highlight we share on social media seems to contribute to our greater cause, but little reflection occurs after pressing the post button.

Your effort to share your message is an opportunity to connect with the hearts and minds of others. You diminish the impact you have on the world when you try to put an arbitrary number on it. Define your own metrics so you can ultimately do life on your own terms.

Know your worth. Share it with the world. Repeat.

february

2

*No matter what's top of mind today, your health is
your top priority every day.*

You know the feeling. You're down for the count and can't remember the last time you actually felt *good*. You're worn out, overextended, exhausted, and overwhelmed. Physically, you just can't.

Is that how it's been for you recently? Or, worse, regularly?

When you're at your breaking point, it's unlikely that living your best life is top of mind. At this point, you'd probably be fine with just operating at a *somewhat* normal level.

It doesn't have to be that way, starting *right now*. The first step to realizing you deserve better is recognizing that you've been burning the candle at both ends to the point that it's permanently engulfed in flames.

You deserve to be taken care of. You deserve to take care of yourself. You deserve to live a long, full life. When you show care to your physical, mental, and emotional health, you're doing everything in your power to make your health your top priority. This is what we must do to give ourselves the opportunity to experience all the other wonderful aspects of living our best life.

The life you want revolves around taking care of the body that'll get you there. Take a step in that direction today.

3

A to-do list is incomplete without the slow and important task of rest.

There are always a million things to do and get done. We check items off, add items on, and the cycle never ends—day in and day out. Our lives are consumed by to-do lists, defined by what we have *yet* to accomplish.

The next time you start to number your tasks, make a note to pause. Give yourself the assignment of a break.

A moment for clarity.

A moment for you.

At that moment, allow yourself to fully rest. It'll lead to relief, and from relief comes insight, and from insight comes purpose. Every running list of tasks needs to have alignment with your purpose.

Let's assign ourselves fewer ways to check a box and *more* ways of discovering what truly fills us up.

Turn the habit on its head. What would your "Done List" look like if you wrote it at the end of a fully-expressed and inspiring day?

february

4

Remove the qualifiers from your speech,
and you'll remove the need to be qualified to speak.

"Just" "Sorry" "Maybe..." "I think..."

You've likely used these words and phrases recently, more often than you realize.

They're the fluff we mindlessly add to our email correspondence to make ourselves sound—what? More playful? Easy to work with? Less bossy? We use these qualifiers as a coping mechanism because being bold is hard.

Upon reflection, you can probably think of the ones you lean on the most. Our language is padded full of words that we *think* help us appear kinder, softer, or more agreeable. But for the sake of what? Who are you really serving when you water yourself down?

These words weaken delivery. They make you appear unsure of yourself. They open up possibilities for confusion—almost guarantee it, actually—even though you knew what you *really* meant to say all along.

Instead of pumping your thoughts full of qualifying words, recognize that you're *already* qualified to be at the table.

- Replace "Does that make sense?" with "Let me know if I can help clarify that for you."

- Forget predicting others' struggles with prefaces like "I know you're super busy..." and get straight to the point.

- Don't apologize for your presence or think of something to say in an awkward exchange. Our sorries are so much less powerful when we waste them in a meaningless moment.

Language is a tool. How are you using it?

february

5

We are only able to help others because we have been helped ourselves.

You are not alone.

Let that truth sink in. Repeat it if you need. Then, repeat it again. *You are not alone.* Some days we all need to hear this one.

None of us were born having it all figured out. We all showed up to this life fully unprepared, unaware, and completely uncertain about what would come next.

It sounds pretty terrifying, doesn't it? But you did it. You got through. And here you are, still standing strong!

Why?

Because of a person. Or a few people. The ones who saw you, saw what you needed, and took action to offer you help.

Some of us were lucky enough to have met that person from day one, our mother's comfort creating a foundation of security and support. Others waited longer to feel that safety, discovering it in that first friend who taught them what loyalty means. You may have battled through more struggles until you connected with a partner who held your hand and showed you unconditional love.

People exist to help one another. Remember who helped you when you needed it most. Have gratitude for them. Let that feeling carry you into helping someone else when you see they need it.

february

6

When you say yes to one thing, you're saying no to something else.

It's no surprise that many of us grapple with anxiety and overwhelm when we consider all the commitments we've signed up for without a second thought.

In a moment that you're encouraged to commit to something or go somewhere, it's hard to think of anything else but the confrontation before you. It's so much easier to be easy-going. "Sure!" you say with a smile.

Was your last yes actually for you? Or was it for someone else?

Why worry about my homework when I could go out to eat with friends instead? Why do I need to have some alone time to recenter myself if I can show up to one more event for my child and prove I'm the best parent ever? Why bother with that important task when I could let this new show on Netflix distract me for now?

What you say yes to directly reflects your commitment. Over time, those yeses add up. The wrong ones will chip away at you, while the best ones will take you to new heights.

When your motivations are strictly for the sake of praise and not for your own desires, your yes is coming from the wrong place. While that doesn't mean you should ignore the needs of those in your life, it does mean giving yourself the consideration you deserve first.

february

7

*The question is not what you'll do with your life
but what you'll decide to be known for.*

Starting young, we're continually asked what we want to be when we grow up.

For some people, that answer comes naturally as their talents soar. To others, it's paralyzing. How are you supposed to know what all your years will be like before you've had even a moment of real experience?

This socially acceptable line of questioning has contributed to a sad status quo that does anything but help people find their place in life. It's not about what you'll do or how you'll make it happen. Those tactics and how tos may give you some momentary feelings of relief, but those will be short-lived.

To find the meaning you crave and obtain the knowing that your time during your human existence is well-lived, spend more time pondering what you want people to remember you for.

What will they say when you're not in the room? What will they tell their friends? What will they speak about upon your passing?

The details of what you *did* will be lost in comparison to how you made people *feel*. This is what we should truly be asking our youth to consider as they pave their own path.

Don't get lost in the minor details of how you'll make an impact. Focus on the impact itself and then reverse-engineer who you'll become.

february

8

Be careful with what fills your mind.
What you consume is what you become.

Who do you want to be?

We all enter this life with a body and a soul. The former is how you appear on the outside as you make your way through the external world. It gives you the ability to act, to move, and to cause change in the environment around you.

The latter is your highest self—who you were created to be.

We're all on the same lifelong mission: to align our outward expression in the world with the inner stirrings of our souls and mind. To match our internal convictions with external reality.

The attributes you accept as truth about yourself, the thoughts you adopt as belief, and the actions that make up your daily existence—all of these elements culminate into the person you become.

february

9

Make each moment for you, by you.

How have you been reacting in your life recently?

When things don't go your way, do you look around for something to blame? Do you check in with yourself during moments of frustration?

Be honest. Instead of judging your responses, decide if you want to see more of them in your future. For the reactions that don't feel like a true representation of yourself, there's always time to adjust.

Here's your new mantra: For me. By me.

You always get a say in how you show up. Your own influence over yourself is all you need. When you believe that it's all for your good and in your favor, you can emulate the person you know you truly are.

Each step you take, every moment you react, and all the thoughts you think— they're all for you, by you. Remember the intention you wish to come from and proceed accordingly.

For you. By you.

february

10

Action brings peace.

Have you ever felt like you're trapped on a ride you never intended to be on?

You get caught up in the spinning of your thoughts, and suddenly you're wrapped up in a mind that won't stop. Without consciously choosing to buy a ticket, you're stuck in a spiral and can't seem to find a way off. Every new thought dominos into the next until you have a stack of limiting beliefs with no sign of relief in sight.

Instead of waiting for something to change, be that change right now. Choose to take action. Pick a direction and follow it through. Scrap overthinking and *just go.*

You can continue to question and fight new ideas, but then again, didn't you want off that ride?

Whatever you do to make a move will initiate a series of other actions. The choice to act in and of itself will be accompanied by its own series of questions and the fear of the unknown. Getting out of your own mind and taking a step in the right direction will evoke the calm you didn't know you could feel.

You deserve to feel and embrace that calm. Confidence in where you are and where you're headed will show you how much fun the ride can actually be.

february

11

Let it be what it is. Not better. Not worse.
Awareness will show you the difference.

Have you ever found yourself in a financial situation that made you feel as if you were underwater? Whether this is the case today or if it's a distant memory for you, the feeling is likely very easy to recall.

No one wants to feel the effects of scarcity, and yet, we all suffer through them constantly. Plus, with scarcity comes assumptions. When you assume the worst, you simply can't be at your best. Decide to make a change by taking one simple step: Make an honest assessment.

What do the numbers *actually* say? What's really working for you right now? What's *not* working? How negative is the reality of the situation, grand storytelling aside? You don't need to be an expert at math to know exactly where you are in your financial situation. Ignorance is not bliss. Naivety only holds you back from creating your destiny.

And women in the room aren't excused. On the contrary, it's time to step up. For far too long, the female race has been conditioned to stay silent when it comes to money. Let's rewrite that rule and own our space a little more boldly.

No matter how wonderful, challenging, or unknown the state of your finances may be right now, make the change that heads toward self-awareness.

When you know your numbers, you'll know your next steps.

february

12

Your body is the vehicle that can take you anywhere.
Care for it like you have somewhere important to go.

The task list in front of you. The errands you must run. The big things you still hope to accomplish. We're so eager to get going on checking these boxes that we forget they're only feasible as our body allows them to be.

When you sacrifice a sufficient night of sleep to gain a few more hours of preparation for that big presentation, you hinder your body's ability to show up with vitality and focus the next day. When you neglect to hydrate yourself or take a much-needed lunch break to fuel up, you impair your body's ability to carry you through the rest of the day.

Your health is all-encompassing: mental, emotional, and physical. If one aspect of your overall wellness is suffering, it won't be long before the others begin to falter.

As tempting as it is to test the waters of how far your body can carry you, when you do so without healthy boundaries you're simply racing towards burnout. While others tote around their tales of all-nighters, missed meals, caffeine quick fixes, and the like—simply nod at them from your much-deserved pit stop as they whiz by.

You know it'll all catch up to them, anyway. It's only a matter of time. Choose the route of longevity, investing in care for yourself that'll serve you for the length of a marathon rather than just a sprint.

The feeling that comes will be worth the short-term sacrifices.

february
13

Who you see within you reflects who you see around you.

People are our greatest influence.

Motivational speaker and bestselling author Jim Rohn put it best when he reminded us of a critical factor of who we become. He said, "You are the average of the five people you spend the most time with."

We're never truly alone. We also can't go it all alone.

In living a human experience, it's natural for us to look around at those close to us to see how they're navigating it all.

Take note: Who's physically in your presence the most often every day? What do you notice about yourself when you're with them? What do they bring out in you? What do they make you want to suppress? Who lights a fire in you to make you want to be a better person? Who simply makes you smile?

When you reflect on these moments with these specific people in your life, do you like who you see blossom from within? Pay close attention to these dynamics and how they contribute to who you're becoming.

february

14

Unconditional love is possible, and it starts with you.

They say you cannot truly be loved until you love yourself. Yet, as we navigate the circumstances around feeling and offering love, we place our hope in destiny, assuming it's going to have our back someday.

The good news is that it's destiny's *entire* job to bring you exactly what it's supposed to. However, we can't merely count on the inevitability of destiny to connect us to who we're meant to love without any additional effort.

Destiny is *not* as predetermined as many would assume. Your effort influences everything about how your destiny arrives. Destiny is empowered entirely by you.

In order to manifest the destiny you hope to see for yourself, you must open yourself to unconditional love—not just for those you welcome into your life, but for yourself.

Without unconditional love, you're not a free-thinking individual. Without unconditional love, you're fueled primarily by ego. Without unconditional love, you're blocked off from even the most desirable outcomes because of the many conditions you've decided will get in your way.

Many mistakenly believe unconditional love entails ignoring all foolishness and settling for mistreatment. This conflict comes from your ego and not your higher self. True unconditional love becomes possible when you separate a person's thoughts and actions from their heart and essence. A person is still lovable no matter what their human experience displays.

This is *especially* true when that person is you. Manifestation of true, unconditional love starts within you.

15

Success doesn't come to you. You need to go out and get it.

This is your time. This is your moment.

That milestone you've been dreaming of, that achievement you've been waiting to reach—it's here. The recognition is all yours for the taking.

While accepting these truths may feel like a stretch (especially if you feel like you've been dreaming, wishing, and waiting forever), know that it's not. Everything that feels in your way right now is just ordinary resistance, ready to trip you up when you lose your focus.

Don't lose your focus.

Success can only be defined by you, and therefore, it can also only be achieved by you. Of course, there will be help along the way—and please do seek it out—but that moment of vindication will only feel truly yours if you go out and get what you want.

Take ownership of all of it, and it'll be yours.

february

16

Confidence is built by the practice of ignoring the irrelevant.

We all have a tendency to get fixated on flaws, especially our own. Naturally, we assume everyone else is seeing and talking about them too.

They must be watching. They must be noticing. They must be as consumed as we are with everything that isn't quite right.

But are you consumed with what isn't right in someone else's life? Do you lie awake at night wondering how Suzie is ever going to create the life of her dreams or why Andrew made the decisions he did?

Even if you did find yourself questioning another person's life today, those thoughts certainly weren't more than a blip compared to the inner monologue each of us listens to 24/7. We can't help it—it's simply in our nature to assume that others must see, feel, and pay attention to the same things we do. The next time you assume everyone else is looking at you and *only* seeing flaws, challenge that thought.

It's time to stand up to your inner critic with a much-needed reminder of who you are rather than fixating on what you're not. Instead of worrying about what other people think is wrong with you, decide what you want them to see. Show it to them. Show who you truly are. And while doing so, practice ignoring the irrelevant factors that happen throughout the process. They're simply small tests of whether the real you is here to stay.

Next time the mirror gets cruel, give it a reality check.

february

17

Your higher self is always waiting to say hello.
Stop and make them feel welcome.

Your mind is incredibly powerful.

And yet, that power can be easily overlooked or forgotten. Things like grocery lists, birthdays to remember, and texts to answer take up so much precious mental real estate that we forget how incredible the influence of our imagination can be.

Your mind has unlimited capabilities. If you want more for your life, you have the ability to visualize it in a space that's completely controlled by you. If you don't start rerouting your thought patterns, you risk losing control of your actions.

The power is all yours as long as you choose to take it.

When you make that choice, you level up to your higher self: a person of purpose and passion. Immerse yourself in the visualization of this life coming to fruition, to the point where you feel it up, down, and throughout your whole body. When you see yourself becoming the person you know you have the potential to be, you start to believe it. And those beliefs will change your life.

If all the day's mundane tasks are going to take up space in your mind, ensure that they don't take *over*. Always make time for the chance to see your higher self in action. That vision will move you in ways you didn't know possible.

february

18

Admit failure to begin a journey of success.

Envisioning an incredible achievement becoming possible is easy. Even easier? Picturing a cringey misstep along the way.

The idea of failure is enough to debilitate even the most promising of minds. But is this really where our deepest fears come from?

The world is a cruel place when it comes to failure. One error can trigger any number of obstacles, from becoming the butt of a brand new joke to getting "canceled" from society altogether.

All of the potential pitfalls are scary because they're entirely out of our control and only happen because of the court of public opinion.

At the end of your journey, you'll see just how much you have to offer others in the form of both your achievements and your lessons learned. The truth is, in the end, failures are celebrated as much as victories. It just depends on what's happened since. For those who push through to greatness and see their vision come to life— even with a couple of unfortunate lessons along the way—the journey to success always ends with a hero's welcome.

Heroes are only made possible by the confrontations and failures they survive. Those stumbling blocks are what remind everyone of what's truly possible.

Instead of being crippled by your fear of failure, master the vulnerable territory that comes with acknowledging that you're worthy of great success.

february

19

Every morning is a good morning if you decide it is.

Morning routines, when crafted perfectly to your liking, are a complete delight.

The small things we make an effort to do every day contribute to our positive mental health. Starting the day on your terms is just one way to feel empowered to start heading in the right direction.

But every morning isn't going to go perfectly. Actually, it rarely will. Perhaps some outside circumstance has prevented you from being able to focus on your lovely morning, or maybe you took a couple of wrong turns before it could even begin.

A couple of morning curveballs don't have to cause a domino effect, but we often let them take their toll. When you let that one-off moment spiral into more, it can feel difficult to stop the negative momentum.

The last thing we want to see is a bad day turning into a crappy week, evolving into a wasted month, and snowballing into a bad year. We're far more powerful than to fall victim to this.

Breaking the cycle begins when you acknowledge where the day took a wrong turn. Find where things got off track and acknowledge how it could have immediately been rerouted.

We're all allowed to miss the mark now and again. Just remember that you don't have to take yourself so seriously to the point that one mishap leads to total self-sabotage. Life is too short, and we just don't have time for that.

Good morning! Good life! It's all up to you.

february

20

Choose to grow. Choose to learn.
Choose to ask questions and have challenging conversations.

From a young age, many of us are taught to be quiet—to keep our silly questions to ourselves. But who does that serve?

Without asking questions, we forfeit receiving real answers. And we absolutely cannot become more financially literate. Money only talks if you do.

It's up to you to be bold and start the conversation. When you do, you'll see just how much you can change the game for yourself and for those who will mimic your actions.

The energy you put out is transformational.

Money is one of those topics we tend to avoid. Usually, because someone told us it's not polite table talk, or perhaps because you've observed others make a tactless attempt at it (which, of course, inevitably gets awkward). Just because you've seen it be uncomfortable doesn't mean it always will be, especially when you're clear on what you stand to gain.

- How will better money management help you achieve your goals?
- What does a day of feeling confident with your bank account look like?
- Where can you picture the home of your dreams, and what will it take to create it?

If you're coming from a place of genuine interest, you'll ask for guidance, produce an open dialogue, and learn something new.

Isn't that result worth taking a chance on?

february

21

Don't get discouraged when someone doesn't understand you.
Clarity comes from understanding yourself.

We tend to seek out people who will understand and embrace us. There's no escaping our human desire to be seen and known. Yet, it's a lofty expectation and a demanding need to place on others.

How often do you find yourself simply wanting to be understood?

We all go to great lengths to achieve this. We explain. We emulate. We put on a display—all in an effort to get the outside world to truly see what's within us.

But, will they? Will they actually see the real you? Before you ask this of someone else, have you grasped it first? Do you truly know and understand *yourself*?

If you're missing the clarity of who you are and what purpose you serve for the world around you, you must be able to discover it on your own. What you're known for is guided by you but *decided* in the eyes of others. Who you *truly* are is completely up to you in your own eyes.

What do you know for sure about yourself?

february

22

Trusting the process means having patience with all of it.

Every step you take is a part of the process: the good, the bad, and the ugly. No matter which step you're on in your journey right now, remember the saying, "Patience is a virtue."

Do you have the audacity to go down this road that could very well change your life? If so, you must have complete trust in the process—no matter what happens or how long it takes.

You must accept that every move won't be perfect. You must live through the mess when it arises. And you must work your way to the next step even when everything feels as clear as mud.

Patience is accepting that you may not be able to control every circumstance that blows its way through your plans. It's knowing that each moment will pass. The good will pass. The uncomfortable will pass. And it'll all come back around again in time.

When you combine patience and trust in your process, you're building a solid foundation for the good that'll come.

february

23

If you want to know the secret to success,
be willing to listen to the whispers of your heart.

The difference between someone who loves what they do and someone who clocks in and out is a simple notion of whether the work matters to them, deep down.

Passion doesn't just come from how excited we are about what we pursue but also from the people we help. We go to work not to grind but to feel some kind of purpose and see the improvement we've made in the world.

We're all looking for that secret to success—the golden ticket that'll unlock our passion and inspire us every day. But, the more we search outside of ourselves, the less we'll feel a connection to the work work that brings the passion we're looking for.

Listen to what your heart says about what matters and do that job like it's your life's work.

february

24

The applause will come after the work is done.

You have access to all the motivation you need.

So, hold your applause. Or, more accurately, stop waiting for everyone else's—because it may not be coming. Whether or not the roaring sound of recognition happens for you, that can't be your only source of motivation.

You've pursued a passion before. It may have been a job, a title, or a relationship. Whatever the achievement, odds are good that at some point in your journey, you held your breath and waited to be recognized for the work you put forth.

But did the validation make it all worth it? How did you feel after the quiet quickly returned?

You deserve celebration, and it has an important place for your self-reflection. Even so, it eventually dissipates to ensure that you've cared for the one and only cheerleader who will be with you until the end.

Never stop saying cheers to you, even when it feels like a party of one.

february

25

You're not stuck. Your back is against the wall.
Head in the opposite direction.

It's hard to believe that you're not stuck when you find yourself in a situation that feels all-consuming. You search and stress to find ways to get out, but the box that surrounds you is closing in faster than it's offering a reprieve.

That's the funny thing, though. There's no box at all. There never is.

We force ourselves inside one based on limiting beliefs and previous negative experiences that feel louder than anything else we can imagine. We forget about the vast world of possibility and that, in all actuality, the world isn't so absolute.

When you feel stuck in a box, tune out all distractions and sit there for a moment. Let it be. Yes, your back is against the wall. You feel cornered with nowhere to go. But there's always a way out.

If you strip away the imaginary walls (built on lies and limiting beliefs) that you think are in front of you, you'll see that all you have to do is walk in the opposite direction from where you stand right now.

New doors will open. New perspectives will reveal themselves. You'll no longer be stuck right now, and maybe you'll never be stuck again.

Be courageous enough to question the validity of the limits that surround you.

february

26

When you serve your body you serve your life.

Our physical selves embody how we're doing at every level. But, more than anything, tuning in to how you feel goes far beyond your reflection in the mirror.

If you're tired, your yawn gives you a heads up that it's time to start winding down for bed. If you feel energized by endorphins, your body gives you a spark of happiness. If you're dragging, your body asks for nourishment to prevent a total shutdown. At every turn, your physical state reminds you of what you need.

The problem is that somewhere along the way, we stop remembering to listen.

Today, reassure your body that you're in this together. Drink a little more water. Stand up and stretch every hour. Get that extra hour of sleep.

Help your body so it can help you, too—for the rest of your long, amazing life.

february

27

Our greatest weakness lies in giving up.
The surest way to succeed is to just do one more.

You've fought for this moment.

You are who you are, here and now, because you chose to keep showing up. Even when you were tempted to quit, here you are *still standing*. It might not feel like a big deal—but it is. That deserves to be celebrated.

It's totally human to want to quit. In fact, it's normal to want to quit *frequently*. You could do just that and chalk it up to not being the right fit for you. But you haven't yet because you know in your gut that you'd be lying to yourself, that you'd always ask yourself: "What if?"

When you look back at your life with a microscope, rather than cringing at your mistakes, congratulate yourself for every last misstep.

Consider those frustrating (and potentially devastating) mistakes. Now, remember what the days and weeks after them felt like. You were likely hard on yourself. You likely raised the bar for your expectations and criticized who you'd become. But, after you sat in that anger and annoyance, you did something about it.

The greatest superpower of anyone who ever became anything is *staying power*. Will you do one more? Will you continue to push through the challenges because you know it's hard for a reason? Will you be the last one standing?

february

28

*Taking the time to explain is just a fancy way to
excuse, complain, and blame.*

We all have the best of intentions, don't we? And, we simply want those intentions to be well known, especially in the case that something doesn't go to plan.

But while we're preparing a story that'll demonstrate how our innocent efforts were rudely interrupted by some outside source—we avoid the truth.

The truth is that none of that matters now.

There's simply no excuse for living a life filled with excuses. One becomes two, two becomes three, and soon you're blaming, complaining, and fixating. You're transfixed, stuck in a vicious cycle, and consumed by shifting responsibility.

As a result, you take ownership of nothing. Making excuses is a thought stopper, not a thought starter. We need new thoughts right now to move us forward in this moment. We need *progress*.

The sooner you remove your addiction to explaining and replace it with a desire to problem-solve, the sooner you'll become an asset to all and, most importantly, to yourself.

february

29

Seek out the listeners, then follow their lead.

Have you ever noticed how wonderful you feel when it appears that someone is genuinely listening to you? Isn't it glorious to not hurry to get to your point so you can earn the next bit of attention in a conversation?

The people who wow us are the ones who make an effort to listen. Beyond just that, they're also the ones who have the most to share. They understand more, have achieved more, and their security in their own voice means they don't have to beg for attention. They choose to listen.

The conversation gets a lot more interesting when you remember to pay attention.

Think back to some unfortunate first impressions you remember. Who stands out? Was it the person who cut you off as you tried to introduce yourself or the person who jumped in with an unrelated personal anecdote whenever they had the opportunity?

What about the people you remember for the right reasons? Maybe you met someone who was genuinely curious and asked questions that excited you. Their authentic interest in getting to know you likely provoked more depth and led to greater understanding. You certainly valued their desire to know you.

Now, ask yourself, did their inquisitiveness inspire you to return the favor? Let others speak. There's more wisdom found in hearing than in being heard.

march

1

Solving problems means being a great listener,
even when that conversation is one you're having with yourself.

Can you remember a time you felt someone was talking *at* you rather than *with* you?

Step back into that moment. Did the conversation feel good?

These exchanges happen constantly. We could all use help being more active listeners. Maybe when you look back, you recall that unproductive conversation as a giant time suck (or maybe it was just another unextraordinary interaction in your day).

Now, let's try a different approach. Have you ever caught yourself talking *at* your problems? You might not have even noticed you were doing it. It may look like you have a lot of self-awareness about what's happening in your life. You may feel a sense of pride that you know what's going wrong.

You talk about your problems and know them like the back of your hand. You also find yourself talking to yourself in circles on repeat about them. But does *talking* nonstop about your problems solve them?

When we're having critical conversations with ourselves, we need to step up our listening skills. Think about a problem you're facing, then try talking *with* it rather than at it. What would an alternative argument be?

When you shift your approach, you shift yourself toward a potential solution.

march

2

Your mind can limit or propel you. The power is all in your head.

What challenges are playing on repeat in your mind right now?

You owe it to yourself to release them. Just because you don't have all the answers right now doesn't mean you should feel limited by the situation. You're more than the unanswered seed of doubt planted in your head. You have the power to address it head-on and move forward from it.

The thoughts that keep repeating in your mind are asking for attention for a reason. When you leave those lingering thoughts and questions unanswered for too long— or assume the worst case must be the only way—they keep their power over you.

You define the limits that exist, which also means you have the power to *redefine* them. The real question is if you'll decide to do so. Harness your power. Be limitless. The choice is yours.

march

— ③ —

That feeling you get about the challenge ahead is your gut telling you it's not a matter of if but when.

The simple, hard thing is always the answer.

Or, to quote Ryan Holiday in his studies of ancient stoic teachings: "The obstacle is the way." It's frustrating at times, but it's true.

You want to take action toward retirement, but you think you don't have enough money to start. Begin setting aside a small amount every time you get paid so you can start to grow your investment while practicing the power of saving.

You feel ready to start your business full-time, but you don't have enough clients to replace your current paycheck. Dedicate your spare time to the ones you have now. Find ways to adjust your lifestyle so you might sooner support yourself without the crutch of your full-time gig.

You have a mountain of debt that debilitates you, even on payday. Make a list of everything you owe, and slowly (but consistently) chip away at it. Show yourself how a little progress makes a big difference.

Picture the end goal and keep it in mind. Then, be brave enough to do the *hard* thing. It'll change your life.

march

(4)

When you connect, people connect to you.

We all know (and have maybe even personally experienced) the fable of the princess and the frog. In case you missed it, the gist is that the princess had to kiss a whole lot of frogs before finding the one who'd become her prince.

Beyond the fairytale, this analogy is a beautiful illustration of what it's like to find and discover your people. To make new connections, you'll first stumble upon many who aren't *quite* a fit.

Every new acquaintance won't necessarily become a lifelong friendship. Not everyone at the networking event is a potential client. And, of course—not every date has the potential to be your future significant other.

So, you keep trying to connect. Sometimes one meeting will lead to another that you never saw coming. Sometimes a wrong fit actually leads to the right one! You keep making introductions, knowing that every once in a while, one will come along that sticks. Before you know it, one connection changes the entire course of your life.

Think about the people in your life that matter most to you. How did those bonds come to be? Try to thoroughly understand the pieces that make each relationship differ from the hundreds of people you've met. They're rare. They stand out for a reason. When you realize their uniqueness, you can better understand how to seek out more just like them.

Don't worry about the frogs. Remember that the people that count will show themselves when the time is right to truly connect with them.

march

— ⑤ —

You can do it all, just not at the same time.

When you think about the legacy you want to leave behind, what person do you see?

As you ponder your greatest self, you might see an incredible individual who's lived an accomplished life. Not only is that a completely valid aspiration, but you really *can* be all that you're imagining.

We never want to lose that vision because it's vital that we push every day to make our desired impact a reality. However, we tend to *underestimate* what we can do in a lifetime and *overestimate* what we can do in a day.

You can be all things. It's absolutely within your power. Even what you haven't been able to imagine for yourself yet is possible.

But, to get there, you must avoid trying to achieve everything you want all at the same time. Living an overwhelming day will always result in the pain of feeling your goals are impossible. It'll burn you out. You'll lose faith.

No goal is impossible with unwavering determination and focus.

Try thinking about "having it all" in a new way. Look at it with the knowledge that to really appreciate something, it deserves your undivided attention. Over time, the "somethings" you saw through to the finish line will add up to *all* the things you did to make the world better when you're gone.

march

6

Some people work to live, while others live to work. A select few discover that you're only doing a job when you aren't delivering on your life's work.

When did Mondays become the enemy? Why do we look forward to the weekend or vacation more than every other day?

Too often, we do what we think we're *supposed* to do in life, only to end up (maybe?) satisfying outside sources while we count down the minutes to contentment.

You can embody vacation energy without buying a plane ticket. You can love your weekdays just as much as your weekends.

It starts by analyzing how you spend your time and being honest about how you got here. Today, reflect on whether the unhappiness you're choosing is more important to you than a bit of uncertainty.

You get a say in what you look forward to. Beyond that—you also get a say in the hours you devote to wishing time away rather than embracing the time you have.

Time isn't within our control, but how we spend our time *is*.

march

(7)

When you have clarity of your will, you are powerful.

Finding willpower when we need it always seems to be a challenge. Why isn't it a simple resource to call upon the moment we feel stuck or challenged?

Instead of focusing on an arbitrary signal of motivation to come your way, try reframing the idea of it altogether. Let's break down the Power of your "WILL" instead.

W stands for your *Why*. Your why is yours and yours alone. It motivates you so much that you'd be fully willing to make changes in your life for it. Think of it as the vehicle for getting you where you're going. It's the persistent feeling that makes everything possible.

I stands for your *Initiative*. The first step is yours to take. Think of it as the gas in your vehicle. No one will hold your hand to get you started without you putting skin in the game first. This is your time to act. Big or small, take the initiative for the sake of your why. Show your willingness to take charge to get what you want.

L stands for your *LOW* (*or the Life that's Over With*). When you decide to take action, start by reflecting on what you want to leave behind. Your Life that's Over With is a starting point you won't be returning to. Call to mind a time you never want to see again. Maybe it's an embarrassingly low bank account balance or a season where you hated your life because of your crappy job. Do you want to go back there? Of course not. Remember your LOW, and you'll take all the initiative to keep it from ever being the case again.

L stands for your *LUW* (*or the Life U Want*). When everything is said and done, this is your final destination. What does your life look like? What's an ideal day for you? How do you see yourself as happy? Let this vision give you the excitement you need to pedal to the metal.

Get clarity on your WILL so you can get where you're going.

march

8

You do not need to be free of fears to be courageous.
The courageous use their fears to take their power back.

Who do you think of when you picture fearlessness? Is it someone close to you? Is it someone you admire from a distance?

No matter their proximity, if you told them you appreciate their example of fearlessness, they'd likely scoff at the thought.

Why? Because we *all* have fears. We're all a little afraid of something (or many things). It could be as small as a spider or as big as a life-altering decision. Fears tend to show up with a vengeance whenever we're making big moves in our lives.

Truthfully, there's no such thing as fearlessness; there's only how you let your fears define you. Acknowledge your fears. Say them out loud. Ponder the absolute worst-case scenarios, and notice how vocalizing them begins to strip away their power. The only way to keep fears from paralyzing you is to be self-aware, recognize the truth, and decide how to keep pressing forward anyway.

To have courage means to be bold and brave. You can do neither of those things if there aren't at least a couple of ideas giving you contrasting colors of fear.

What's something you're afraid of? Bonus points if it seems so ridiculous you don't even want to say it out loud. Maybe it's a looming anxiety or assumption. Perhaps it's that one nagging thing that continues to pull you backward in life.

What you worry about, you manifest. If you're going to manifest something that isn't real, why not focus on the desirable instead?

march

9

Trust the process. Your timeline is your own.

Comparison is a game that just never seems to end. No matter where you are in your life, you likely catch yourself charting against milestones that supposedly matter. And for the sake of what?

It all starts before we can even grasp any sense of self. Parents compare what month their baby started crawling or rolling over. Maybe you met someone at school who skipped a grade. Or, you hear a news story about the youngest-ever prodigy who made some groundbreaking, never-before-thought-of achievement. It never stops.

Will we ever measure up? We ask ourselves this more frequently than we admit.

"Am I enough? Will I ever be enough?"

The answer? Yes, you are.

There's no direct alignment between newsworthiness and fulfillment. What you do during your time on this earth is about quality, not quantity. Everyone has their timeline, and yours is yours alone.

Trust the process. Live your journey. Leave your legacy.

march

10

You can relax if you want to.

Have you ever found yourself in a high-pressure moment where it felt like you were the only one who *really* understood the magnitude of the situation?

It's times like these that people around us try to be helpful but tend to choose words that, quite frankly, achieve the opposite.

"Just relax," they say (as if it were the easiest thing to do).

"Calm down," they whisper (like you hadn't already tried that—multiple times).

There's something so aggravating about these phrases. They can really put you over the edge in the least ideal moment. Can you relate?

Is their intention in the right place? Of course! If we took a step back and observed their willingness to help, we'd see that no one's trying to send us spiraling. When we do lash out, it's our own choice. However, we'd be wise to remember (for the mercy of the ones who love us and are trying to help) that relaxation isn't a snap decision.

To help get you in the right headspace, follow this 1-2-3 approach:

1. Recall the last time you felt at ease. What elements were at play? Were you alone or surrounded by loved ones? Were you in motion or embracing the task of doing nothing?

2. Remove the pressures preventing you from feeling that chill energy. Notice what triggers your stress throughout the day. Perhaps it's your phone (put it aside for an hour), your dirty house (go outside), or sitting still is just too much (go for a spin).

3. Combine 1 and 2 to create your ultimate calming zone.

The next time someone offers you the not-so-helpful wisdom to "just relax," respond gratefully and let it go. Step away from expectations and step into your sacred space.

march

11

Listen to your body to move your soul.

The stability of your health is your ultimate thermometer. It tells you everything you need to know—if you're willing to pay attention.

Have you ever powered through weeks of late nights and early mornings, only to suddenly wake up to a terrible cough and head cold? Or have you been so "on" all day that when bedtime comes, you can't shut your mind off?

Your unexpected cold and constant exhaustion aren't a coincidence. Those are not-so-subtle signs from your body warning you of something bigger. Your body is screaming for care. All the hustling overshadows your body's cues that let you know exactly what it needs. Every night you lie awake counting sheep and losing sleep, your body desperately reminds you of its need for balance.

You can't be all things all at once. You aren't invincible. You won't feel okay after losing too much sleep or swimming in stress day in and day out. We need to begin treating the body that houses our soul like it deserves better—because it does.

Tune in. What's your body telling you? More importantly, how are you responding?

march

(12)

You always have options ahead of you.
Allow your heart to lead you out of your head.

Even when you feel backed against a wall, there's never just one option ahead of you. You have access to plenty more paths as long as you open yourself up to them.

We tend to panic when we feel trapped. Our brain goes into survival mode, and we jump to conclusions instead of finding the solutions we need. Every room has four sides for a reason, and the odds are that one of them has a door that may even be unlocked!

Be willing to look around, get outside of your head, and blaze a new trail. As you work up the courage to make your next move, think to yourself: "Why is staying here safe?" Call to mind what matters more to you at this moment: safety or opportunity. Your answer will vary depending on where you are, and that's okay.

The unknown is the ultimate distraction. When you find yourself there, remember you can shift fears to solutions. You just have to recognize when you're more in your head than your heart. Encourage them to work together.

march

13

Let them say what they will so you can get back to doing the work.

Hard work is never about them.

Not the man that's further along than you or the woman who always seems to beat you to every milestone. Not the family that appears closer together or the relative who emulates superiority. It's not about your neighbor who reverberates judgment, nor your dad who claims to be looking out for your best interest.

None of this is about them. So, it's certainly not *for* them either. What would it take for you to sincerely believe your hard work is *only* about and for you?

The opinions from the cheap seats aren't going anywhere. No matter what good you're doing, there will always be someone laying their unwelcome thoughts about it all over you. You may get stuck listening to them sometimes, but you're not responsible for giving them any power.

Rather than worrying about what they'll say, give them a reason to marvel at your steadfast focus. Nothing can throw you off your game unless you let it.

march

14

You are never defined by just one season of your life.

The past feels so faint and the future so elusive. But the here and now? It wakes you up every morning and reminds you how very real it is.

No matter what the present moment brings for you, it has a way of feeling especially definitive. You find yourself thinking: "Is this forever?"

We all unfairly restrict ourselves in this way, assuming that who we are right now is all we'll ever be. You may find yourself in a new job, stepping into parenthood, or moving to a different city. Suddenly that's all you are: your title, role, and location. You slap a label on yourself and keep it there. It feels all-consuming.

While labels may help describe this time in your life, they never define you entirely. There are so many moments, special occasions, emotions, tragedies, actions, milestones, labels, and achievements that shape the multi-layered miracle of who you truly are. Though you certainly are a masterpiece of all you've gone through, there's still so much more to you than just this human experience.

Remember to think beyond today when you define yourself. When we get caught up in the labels, we lose our whole selves. When we willingly accept all expectations, we lose the freedom to be present. Instead, experience this season as a moment to be grateful for as it passes.

march

—— 15 ——

*Spending isn't good or bad as long as you believe in
how money supports you.*

There aren't many guarantees in life, but there's at least one: Life is full of expenses. At times, that running expense list can feel like the only constant in our ever-changing circumstances.

The first step to identifying where your money flows is to pay careful attention. These days that can be hard to do. Here are a couple of ideas to set you in the right direction:

- Determine how much of your income you'll save every time you get paid. Set it aside immediately, if not automatically.

- Review your bank statements in a self-care ritual every month. Watch for sneaky fees or subscriptions that shouldn't have been renewed. Cut the fat when you find it.

- No matter how old (or young) you are, ensure you allocate income toward a retirement plan. Exponentially growing your money can only be done over time.

You build wealth when you're thoughtful about your money. Let that intention be your guarantee. Remind yourself that no matter how much or how little there is at the start, you have the power to bring what you need into existence.

march

16

---

*The only way to know if you can do it is to
show yourself you can do it.*

When it comes to mastering your morning, the tales you tell yourself matter.

"I'm not a morning person."

"It's just the way I am."

"What's the point of waking up earlier?"

When you say something enough, it starts to become true to you. Maybe you recite these stories all the time, so much so that they feel like facts. The minute you start believing these ideas, you write off all other potentials. You take away your chance to succeed by convincing yourself it's not even worth a shot.

No one is asking you to be different from your authentic self. No one is telling you that you need to be a morning person. What if there was a world of possibility available to you at a time of day that you've always ignored? Would you give it a try then?

If you're asking yourself "What if?" while you're used to thinking "Why bother?" then you may have just discovered an opportunity to show yourself what you're capable of.

The driving force lies in recognizing the potential benefits. Find the one thing that could make it worth challenging your previous narrative.

What would be worth getting up 20 minutes earlier for? How would you use your time if you were given an extra 60 minutes today? Starting the day on your terms might be the game-changer that connects you to a life filled with greater intention.

You don't have to be a morning person to make the choice to start your day with intention. Do it despite the momentary annoyance. That initial pushback will be short-lived in comparison to making your goals your reality.

march

17

You can't always control what you hear,
but you can choose what you absorb.

Would you ever tell someone else how they need to be? Of course not. You respect them and accept them for who they are and how they live.

It's a basic rule of human interaction: Everyone has the right to be who they are as long as we can do the same.

At least until their choice of how to be impacts *your* life. Until the sound of them living their life interrupts your state of flow. Maybe you're annoyed with the family who brought a baby on your flight because you're trying to sleep. Or you think someone needs to change the way they give criticism because it's hurting your feelings.

The sounds around us are inevitable. We can complain about the ones we think have to change, or we could build our resilience to tune out what doesn't work for us. Boundaries are one thing, but impossible expectations are entirely an area where we cannot play.

Instead of being in charge of how you believe everyone else should be, make sure you've first studied the one person you can actually control.

march

18

> *If you want to build the biggest building in town,*
> *you don't need to tear down anyone else's.*

This is your reminder that the world is *abundant.*

As long as you're open to the possibilities, you can go after the life that you want.

But we often forget that. We trick ourselves into thinking that because we see opportunity rising for others, the only way we can get some of that for ourselves is to pull it from their supply.

Building yourself up doesn't require that you bring anyone else down. Someone else's success is completely and utterly unrelated to your own. In fact, it's likely their ability to stay focused on what's right in front of them has allowed them to see such good fortune. Allow that example to teach you rather than disappoint you.

Pour all your motivating energy into laying the foundation for your own incredible successes. Giving away the attention you urgently need for your own journey will only slow it down.

Decide to only build up. Construct what will be your life's work with your words, your actions, and your ambition.

march

19

Choosing happiness means choosing carefully.

Choices surround us every day, so much so that we can easily slip into autopilot just to preserve our sanity. We rattle off our yeses and nos more haphazardly than carefully.

Whenever you have a gut reaction, don't gloss over that intuition. Acknowledge it and give it the attention it deserves.

Will saying yes bring you comfort? Will you feel a sense of ease? Will saying no foster regret? Will you feel deep disappointment?

When faced with a choice, our minds quickly turn to everyone else's perspectives. We're persuaded to consider everyone else's happiness in our decisions before our own. When you tune out the noise and feel the truth in your gut, you'll be more likely to make a decision that brings you happiness in the end.

Acknowledge the longevity of your choice as well. If it's not going to matter weeks from now, that's all the more reason to practice choosing what's right for you. It's the small wins that help us appreciate the power we have to make a decision.

What do you wish you were saying no to?

What have you not said yes to only because of the opinions of others?

Follow your gut and go after the life you want.

march

20

Take action at your best. Let go of the rest.

If life is an ocean, you're going to need to learn how to ride the waves. If there's one thing you can count on, there will be plenty of them.

The trick is to anticipate the challenges the best you can. The mistake most people make is assuming that you need to take on every single one that comes along. Sometimes you just need to sit in the current and let it ride.

When you find yourself stuck or uncertain, let the wave crash down on you. Feel it, be with it, and let it go.

We can't control everything that happens to us, and our reactions are usually a tell of whether or not we realize this. An overreaction is an attempt to take control where we actually never had it in the first place.

What would it look like if the next time you found yourself going through something, you just greeted it without an immediate plan to course correct? What would it be like to simply feel those moments?

Can you let the wave crash and trust yourself to keep swimming? Redefine riding the wave by letting yourself process through it.

march

— ㉑ —

The secret to a healthy life is hidden in your daily routine.

Your actions are *exponential*. Every day, with consistency, they add up for better or for worse.

There will be days when you wake up late, forget to fill up your water bottle, and couldn't care less about squeezing in some time for exercise because, well, that's life.

The question is: Are those days your exception or your rule?

What you do every day matters much more than what you do once in a while. If your daily life is filled with habits that hurt you rather than help you, the one day you tried to get your act together won't move the needle very much.

On the flip side, if your day is intentionally focused on your health (not perfectly, but thoughtfully), your off day is exactly that—an off day.

Momentum always leads to more, but it can and will go in either direction. Multiple positive actions motivate the next. Multiple negative actions also motivate the next.

Find the areas of your daily routine that could be switched to healthier actions. Level up little by little. Do one small step at a time, many times, until it is, in fact, habitual.

Your health is not only worth it. It's the biggest non-negotiable.

march

22

Finding your passion is mindful.
Following your passion is masterful.

Do you dream about doing what you love?

Do you know what you love doing?

Do you let yourself believe in what you love becoming a reality in your life?

You may think only the lucky ones get to do what they love, but it's not luck at all. The ones pursuing and living their dreams didn't just hit the jackpot. They didn't enter the lottery, cross their fingers, and hope for the best. They showed up. They took action.

It doesn't take luck to listen to yourself. It takes mindfulness. It also doesn't take luck to begin your journey. It takes consistency and devotion to be a student of the process.

Listen to your soul and what it tells you about your passion. Then, once you've grasped it, lean into it. When you show up for your highest self, you can become a master in anything your heart desires.

Don't just dream about what you love. Do it. You are capable.

march

23

Your success in the pursuit of happiness is directly associated with how you view your pitstops along the way.

The slowdown isn't always about slowing you down—it might just be a moment to catch you up.

We have to pause throughout our journey, so we don't let the whole thing fly by. Instead of fearing a change in momentum, use it as an opportunity to stop and smell the roses.

Look how far you've come. Appreciate the little things you're so grateful for that didn't exist before.

Even unexpected stops are opportunities to learn. You can opt to stay in the space of fear and make excuses. Or you can recognize that every unknown that pops up is testing your will to keep traveling to your destination.

The time you spend worrying about these moments is wasted. They'll never be as big as you exacerbate them in your mind. And, even when they astound you, you get only what you're capable of handling. Then—and only then—will be the time for you to navigate that process.

Life comes with challenges, but each is surmountable with the right outlook.

The only question is: Do you plan to keep going?

march

(24)

Respecting your time is respecting yourself.

Someone you know has a question for you. "Can you come to Caroline's birthday party this weekend?"

You rifle through your brain to remember who Caroline even is, but you aren't too worried. At the same time, you remember the very important project you've been working on during your limited weekend time while balancing a boatload of other work during the week. You think to yourself, "I really should stick with my plan, but I hate to turn down a nice invitation." Without any more details, you accept the invite with a wishy-washy answer and attend the party.

Now, imagine that same person asked you something different: "Can you give me $1000?"

Woah. Very different question, right? No wishy-washy feelings here. Thoughts race through your mind immediately. "How does someone just ask that like it's no big deal?" You fire off some qualifying questions to politely consider their ask while being secretly mindblown and having no intention of making it happen.

In the first scenario, you're giving away time. In the second, you're giving away money. The two are only as different as the weight you give them.

The time you have can *never* be replaced. The money you have—whether you decide to give it away, spend it, save it, or anything else—can *always* be replaced.

Be as diligent with how you spend your time as you are with how you spend your precious resources.

march

25

When we focus on building connection, we create a network.

The term "networking" has been tossed around so much that it's lost its meaning. It carries a false notion of "quantity over quality" and reminds us of painstaking conversations with self-serving people.

Creating a *real* network of people you can rely on is a critical step in all success.

These people support you, invest in you, and help you do the things you just can't do on your own.

When you reshape the narrative, you hold the secret to meaningful, needle-moving relationship-building. By connecting yourself to others (and those already in your circle to each other), you're creating a web of shared experience and knowledge. It's an incredible way to feel and be valued.

If you're still unsure of where to begin, ask yourself:

- "Which people in my circle have the potential to mutually benefit each other if I were to introduce them?"

- "Whose purpose is aligned with my own? How can we get together?"

- "If I could craft my ideal dinner party, who would be sitting at that table?"

Take those answers and let them excite you as you think about how amazing those relationships could be. Become the connector that's open, generous, and always looking for ways to lift up others.

march

26

The only one we're waiting for is you.

There's a fine line between looking forward to something and living in wait. The former is motivating, while the latter keeps you at a halt.

Are you looking ahead, or are you sitting in expectancy?

Why must we wait for the things that bring us joy if the purpose of the good life is to always *seek out* our joy? If you simply wait for the next thing that *could* bring happiness, are you ever really in control of your bliss? No one else can look out for your happiness because no one can know you the way *you* know you.

For goodness sake, acknowledge the powerful human you are and the soul within you that wants more!

Don't wait for the next great thing to just happen. Explore more joyous moments, and they'll occur more closely together. You just may find yourself looking forward to more than you thought you could ever deserve.

march

27

*The record player of the mind will advance as soon as you skip the track.
If the wrong message is on repeat, make a change.*

The limiting beliefs we unintentionally adopt are loud and debilitating. We feel broken, unsuccessful, or sad because we can't imagine what spurred those feelings not to be true.

Power of the imagination aside, the only way to find out what's true or not is to unleash the greatest vice of every negative thought: a *challenge.*

We challenge our minds by asking compelling questions. We find truth through questions that help us problem-solve, questions that help us discover ourselves, and questions that disprove nonsense.

Challenge your limiting beliefs to turn them upside down. Ask a question—or many questions—that help you discredit what cannot possibly be true because it cannot possibly be known. You'll soon get a realistic understanding of how things actually are.

Change the thought. Change the question. Change the outcome.

march

28

Be very particular about who you aspire to become.

Do you know where you're headed? Or, rather, where do you want to see yourself end up? After all, you really don't need a map if you don't know where you're going.

Deciding who to become and where to spend our time in this human experience is a *lot* to take on! It can feel daunting looking ahead on this journey. What if we can't figure it out? What if we're wrong? What will we do then?

Take the pressure off by putting your decision-making cap on.

Instead of looking at this as a looming deadline, remember it's an exciting adventure. This is your *life*! Act like it! You're going to encounter a ton of twists and turns, and, yes, you're even going to change your mind. And that's okay.

Your worries are driven by outside sources. What people will think. How you'll appear. If you'll mess things up.

If you knew you couldn't fail in anyone's eyes—especially your own—what would you do? Be very clear about the life you're choosing for yourself because it paints a picture of what you hope to attract.

Your higher power and the Universe are waiting for you to let them know what's next.

march

29

Having gratitude is not about doing the right thing.
Having gratitude is about creating a better state of mind.

There are times when gratitude feels like a breeze. It's all comin' up roses, and everywhere we look is a shower of blessings! These moments are deeply appreciated but usually fleeting.

We quickly forget gratitude when we need it the most. It's the presence we need when we're in our greatest struggle. It's the calling card that'll remind us of a way out of our self-destructive thinking. To only be grateful when things are going well means wasting every other moment of life's journey.

Making time to observe what you're grateful for isn't about doing the right thing or completing a homework assignment. It's the inner work that must be done over and over (as often as possible) to shift your attitude toward all that's possible, both now and in the future.

"I'm grateful for the age my children are right now because the moments will go by so quickly."

"I'm grateful for this job and the purpose it serves in delivering me experience for my future."

"I'm grateful for the roof above my head that protects me now while I build upon the next one."

We know we're *supposed* to be grateful for the simple things in life, but what does that look like in real practice?

It means that no matter the circumstance, you can always find something.

march

30

Only you determine your worth.

One of the many downsides to not being comfortable discussing finances is the great possibility of undervaluing yourself. We need to know what we bring to the table. We need some context around where the demand exists for that particular contribution.

Through this process, you must remember something absolutely vital to your livelihood: Only you determine your worth.

Yes, we need some external information to assess the going rates and median salaries. Yes, this will give us a bit more confidence in our ask. It can't, however, be the entire story. So you must not let it. The market matters, but only to an extent.

You are so much more than what you do. You are so much more than what your title says. You are so much more than your credentials. Allow yourself to get educated, and use the data as just the beginning of what you have to offer.

Your value is your performance at the highest level. It'll be much easier to communicate the value you have to offer when you've done your research and already set your standard.

Raise your standards. Raise your price. Increase your worth.

march

31

The biggest obstacles ahead are simply tests of your conviction.
Anticipate them and prove your commitment.

Every day we encounter bumps in the road. Some are big. Others are less significant. We might wish they weren't tripping us up at all, but the ones that bring the most challenges suggest something more.

The obstacles you encounter are the surest sign that you're making progress.

If you know where you want to be, then you're starting to go after it. This is the first indication you give to the Universe that you're ready and willing to take on the journey, whatever it brings.

Remember these stories of those who achieved greatness and the tough times they pushed through:

- At 15, Jim Carrey was already beginning his journey in comedy and performing standup. He'd dropped out of high school to work as a janitor and support his family.

- Stephen King had written four novels before he wrote *Carrie*, which was rejected 30 times before Doubleday finally agreed to publish it.

- By his sophomore year of high school, Michael Jordan was rejected by the varsity basketball team and placed with the junior varsity lineup. His coaches thought he needed more development (and they preferred a taller player).

- During a disappointing 7-year stint of peddling fax machines through door-to-door sales, Sara Blakely wished she was promoting something self-made and exciting. One day, she discovered a super-slimming hack with a pair of cut-up pantyhose, and her company Spanx was born.

Nothing worth having comes easy. Take on the challenges and fight your way to victory.

april

april

Procrastination is merely the assumption of time given to you.
The only time you have is now.

Everyone deals with procrastination. Whether we're not feeling up to the task or we're paralyzed by performance anxiety—it's a universal struggle.

If you dig deep enough, you'll find that avoidance comes from a combination of a scarcity mindset and imposter syndrome.

You're not afraid to work on that presentation. It might be a bit boring, but that isn't what's stopping you. You're avoiding it because you fear your work won't be worthy of a high grade once it's all said and done.

You're not truly afraid of calling someone on the phone. You're debilitated by the idea of opening yourself up to potential rejection.

You're not scared to become a massive success in your career. Actually, that would be amazing! You're secretly worried you'll never be able to reach that level (despite your consistent baby steps that say otherwise).

We don't procrastinate because we're lazy. We procrastinate because we've lost (or never had) the belief we desperately need in ourselves.

Why are you actually procrastinating right now?

Get to the root of your answer, then remind yourself there's *no better time* than now—because now is all you really have.

april

2

Do one thing today to help your health.

Every day has the potential to be *your* day.

What does it take for you to be mentally, emotionally, and physically at your peak?

We know our ideal scenarios for the day like the back of our hands. Fueling your body with wholesome foods and movement. Setting aside time for a bit of morning meditation. Waking up on the right side of the bed. Of course, life doesn't always go that way.

Tackling the trifecta of your health in one day—mental, emotional, and physical— may be too grand of a feat. Instead, pick one area to focus your attention on.

What can you do to make a small (but impactful) contribution to your health today?

Some ideas to start with:

- Commit to a 15-minute walk around your neighborhood as a building block for the 5K you want to run someday.

- Reevaluate your dietary health by picking up a book at the library that feels like an inviting first step.

- Do a web search for a therapist who can help you process the thoughts that are bothering you.

You don't have to tackle everything all at once. Pick just one thing to start with. Healthy habits build upon themselves. The more often you do them, the more you'll *want* to do them, and the quicker they'll become a habit.

What will be your one thing today?

april

3

When you aim to be perfect, you aim to fail.
Choose progress and enjoy the success.

Pressure holds enough weight on its own, but our minds have a way of *doubling* that heaviness.

You know how it feels. You didn't do something exactly right. Something didn't go the way you wanted it to. You ruminate and kick yourself as if you actually committed a crime. Though whatever happened certainly wasn't *that* bad, the feelings persist.

It's hard to forgive ourselves when we don't deliver on our expectations—especially when we meant to help someone else. And yet, while you stress about the past, those you fear you let down are likely already focusing on the future.

What will you do to be better? What do you wish you'd have known before you began? How can you demonstrate what you've learned from this misstep?

Share your imperfect self. Let others see your work-in-progress because—spoiler alert—no one *actually* expects you to be perfect.

Others may hope for their own perfection just like you do. However, they can't possibly have the same expectations of you because they're impossible expectations from the start.

There's only one failure when things don't go quite right, and it's the refusal to reflect on what went wrong. When you welcome honest contemplation, you'll see more clearly how to succeed in the future.

april

4

The secret to building wealth is a combination of action, resourcefulness, and a commitment to making a better life.

One of the great misunderstandings of our society is the role money plays in our lives. Many call money the root of all evil. Some assume it's not something that could ever be abundant for them, and others believe there's just never going to be enough.

What limiting views do you hold when it comes to money?

Whatever they are, reset your outlook with one very important, clarifying fact: Money is a *resource*.

Take away all the stories and feelings about it. Just look at it for what it is. When you do, it's much easier to move forward productively in a financial conversation.

Wealth-building isn't restricted to a certain group of people. However, it may feel that way because of the great number of systemic issues that hold many individuals back. Yet, when we see money as a resource, we can learn to increase our net worth by treating it as the simple math problem it is.

Start constructing a life with more financial resources by realizing this fundamental truth: Building wealth doesn't require making more money. Building wealth requires *leveraging your money wisely* to achieve your life vision.

Everyone has a different interpretation of what they need to enjoy their life and feel taken care of. The financial resources you need completely depend on your vision. When you know your vision specifically and clearly, you'll be motivated to do everything in your power to make it happen.

All you truly need to shed money limitations and create an abundant life is to be resourceful, take consistent action, and demonstrate commitment to your vision.

april

5

Can you have it all? Maybe.
Will it make you happy? No one knows.

Long ago, it was somehow determined that "having it all" was the ultimate status in life. But, despite the fact that everyone around you is reaching for that pedestal, it doesn't have to be *your* highest goal. It doesn't even have to continue to be the standard.

Society placed this unattainable expectation in your mind, and it's time to reassess your motivation to reach for it. You get to set whatever bar you want.

Just for today, resist thinking in terms of five and ten-year plans. Just for today, focus on thinking about the here and now.

How did you really feel all those times you tried to balance "having it all"? Were you actually present? Did you enjoy what "all" felt like, or did the strained attempt to do too much only lead to empty achievement?

Rather than stretching yourself in all directions, point yourself toward one focus—a present desire—and let go of the rest.

april

6

The only shortcut in life is the long road of building upon who you know.

Life is all about people.

Connection is the core of what we're here to do. It's what motivates us, fills our cups, keeps us sane, and guides us in our personal and professional lives. Yet, we tend to feel icky about the word "networking" when it crosses our minds.

There are two common misconceptions when it comes to networking:

1. It's all about using who you know to get ahead.
2. Quantity matters over quality.

Let's shut those assumptions down right here and now. Knowing people who may connect you to opportunities doesn't need to feel out of character. No one on this planet has gotten anywhere without knowing good and helpful people along the way.

As President John F. Kennedy once said, "Ask not what your country can do for you, but what you can do for your country." We're here to contribute to the greater good, and when we do that, people remember us.

Stay curious about the people you meet. You may not always have the answers to someone else's struggles, but you can make a difference by connecting them to someone who does. If you wish for others to help you, use that energy to first find ways to support others.

We need each other to lean into the life we want. The more people you know throughout your life, the more opportunity-filled your life will be.

Today, make it about someone else. What will you do for *them*?

april

If you want to fly, give up the things that weigh you down.

Having doubts about yourself doesn't make you unique. Unfortunately, self-doubt is a burden we all deal with. The choice to see beyond your doubts and uncertainties, however, is what *will* make you stand out.

Our minds get caught up in old thought cycles, especially those that don't serve our best interests. We spend decades affirming our shortcomings, which only solidifies their place in our story. When it comes to being our own greatest critic, we win the title every time.

It doesn't have to stay that way. What's more, it doesn't *get* to stay that way.

You get to decide the perspective you lead from. You have the final say in whether those old, limiting narratives continue into your present and future. You get to skip to the next track if you want to, or you can keep playing the same broken (and inaccurate) records on repeat.

Even if you made some mistakes in past relationships, does that make you unworthy of being in a healthy one now? Maybe you lacked career drive historically but are newly ignited and ready to move forward. Does your old pattern dictate how much you apply yourself?

Past mantras don't have to be present realities. Let go of them and allow yourself to fly.

april

8

Your time for sleep is the ultimate escape. Release the day.
Take the break. Wake up refreshed.

As much as we'd all like it to be, relaxation isn't automatic. You have to put in the work in order to get the reward. Fortunately for you, that work is some well-deserved rest.

Sounds simple enough, right? It's more difficult in practice, but it's worth it every time. How do you feel after you've achieved the sleep you need? It may have been hard to make the time for it, but you're always going to feel pleased when it's said and done.

Getting enough rest is foundational. It dramatically impacts every other area of your life. The next time you achieve a solid night's rest (heck, *every* time you do), track it. How do you feel? How did you get there? How did it impact your day? Why is it worth making it a habit?

Keep assessing. Keep taking inventory of how your mind and body feel. Embrace the good when it arrives and generate more by reverse-engineering it.

april

9

Talk about your blessings more than you talk about your problems.

They say misery loves company for a reason: Complaints are more contagious than compliments.

Whether we admit it or not, we're all guilty of getting sucked into the gossip mill. On some level, we feel comfortable living in a problematic place. It's easier to talk about, and it fills a space that can feel distressingly empty.

Slipping into the storytelling of excuses or mediocrity doesn't make you a bad person. It makes you human.

Talking about possibilities and ideas may sound all well and good, but in practice, it can feel awkward and unrelatable. It might feel unnatural to speak highly about ourselves, especially when we fear how others will perceive us. We wouldn't want them to think we're bragging about having *gasp* *happiness* in our lives, would we?!

The same rule applies to your wealth. We tend to focus on what we don't have, what we're not getting paid, and how we're being overworked, overlooked, and undervalued. What we don't realize is that staying in that space is the same as shutting out abundance. It's letting the Universe know you're not open to the idea and should move along to someone else.

Rather than filling conversations with what you don't have, change the dialogue. Pay attention to what's working in your favor. Decide that something better is coming for you all of the time. What you think, you attract. What you say is what will be.

The truth you want is the truth you could have. Let it be known. Don't just hear good things today—be the person saying them.

april

10

Defying your obstacles starts with knowing exactly what you're dealing with. Not worse than it is. Just what it is.

When you were young, a good morning might have just been the relief that the monster in your closet was no longer coming to get you.

Maybe you were convinced that monster really existed, or you simply feared the darkness. Maybe it was the school day scaries, curiously creeping in over what the next day would bring. Whatever it was, you outgrew it. You overcame it. And just like then, you can find that relief again.

It sounds so silly when you think about the monsters we're dealing with today. Especially since they live in a much scarier place than your closet—they've taken up residence in your mind! They're quite comfortable there, knowing they can talk you into fear all day long. No wonder our obstacles feel so scary all the time.

The solution may not be as soothing as a night light, but it's just as simple. You defy your obstacles by first defining what they actually are and the power they *actually* have.

Recognize the issues you're fighting. Not what they *could* be in the future. Not what they became in someone else's experience. Instead of assuming the situation is already growing into something much bigger, assess it as it is right now.

The sooner you come to terms with what's really scaring you, the sooner you'll realize your power to overcome it.

april

11

There is only you and the success you wish to achieve.
Take a moment to think about what that really looks like for you.

You *will* have an impact.

In fact, you've already had one. Your influence has extended throughout more lives than you know, and it'll continue to do so beyond your years.

Take a moment to reflect on your personal vision. How will you impact the lives around you? What will the success of your mission look like? When you clarify the details, your impact becomes more than just conceptual—it becomes attainable.

Believe that your prosperity is inevitable. Get caught up in the whirlwind of your own possible future rather than trying to keep up with how others define their success. This isn't just about the power of positive thinking. It's about the power of knowing and having *certainty*.

Imagine that success-filled future today. Fall in love with the *future* you who already resides *inside* of you. Take every step with extra intention as you inch closer to that reality.

Act in pursuit today, knowing your impact has already started. The wheels are in motion, and the momentum is there. Just keep going.

april

12

Make no choice for what is out of your control.
Make careful choice for what is.

Before you step into the world today, remember this: *Not everything is about you.*

First, this isn't a personal attack. This isn't an obvious callout. It's a mentality that'll genuinely help you create more perspective and positive energy in your life.

We're faced with thousands of decisions all day, every day. Something new is always happening. When it crosses your path, you might mistake it for something that's just been dumped on your plate.

But not everything is about you. Something isn't your responsibility just because it exists. Something isn't your responsibility just because it distracted you. Something isn't your responsibility just because it entered your universe.

Decisions are hard enough. We need to save our energy for the moments when it really matters. Not only will you make decisions today, but you'll also have to decide whether or not it's even on *you* to make that decision in the first place.

Start from the mental space that it's not about you. Don't let your ego make you think that something is your task just because it's in front of you. Then, when it is indeed something that must be handled by only your authority, choose carefully.

april

Don't live up to their expectations. Surpass them.

The standards you have of yourself matter.

They're the North Star for everything you'll become. They matter more than any other pressure you feel, and they'll continue to matter more than any curveball that comes your way.

Knowing this doesn't change the fact that you'll feel outside pressure. It's inevitable. People will always want to see you do, be, and achieve what they find acceptable. There's no getting around it. Just like you can't be controlled by another person, you can't stop someone from sending their opinion your way. At the same time, you don't need to give them a megaphone. Their expectations don't always deserve the spotlight they demand.

Instead of letting outside voices make more noise, let your steadfast focus drown out the irrelevant. This powerful dedication to your vision will result in something quite serendipitous.

Not only will you make your dreams a reality, but you'll find your own standards eclipse the expectations others try to put on you. True devotion and unwavering passion have a way of silencing even the harshest critics.

Let yourself lean into your inner wants. Meet those expectations. Outperform every outside projection.

april

14

Perfect conditions are fleeting. Flawed circumstances have staying power. Embrace what you have in this moment and power through.

Perfection is never the goal.

When you find yourself paralyzed by the idea of making everything perfect, remind yourself of your secret weapon: *resilience.*

Remember all the times you've felt worn down, lost, or even hopeless. What happened next? You got through it. You *went* through it. And, on the other side, you were stronger for it.

You stayed then. You stayed for the *you* standing in front of the mirror now, and this version of you is undoubtedly grateful for the grit you gained.

It's easy to forget this because we'd prefer to have everything go according to our plans. We'd rather not assume the same adversity will find us again. But, when you reflect on the resilience you've acquired, you remember that you're capable of outlasting the moments that initially seem impossible to get through.

Leverage the power of hindsight to prepare yourself for what's ahead.

april

15

You don't have to be an accounting expert.
You just need to hear the right advice on a regular basis.

It's true—you don't need to be an expert. Your desire to succeed is far more instrumental in your long-term success than your status is. Drive counts for a lot more than we recognize.

Even if you feel completely lost about the steps to take in your financial life, here's some good news: It can only go up from here! You can only find *more* clarity from this point on.

Commitment will propel you forward. Dedication will develop more for you than your resume or any degree. What looks good on paper doesn't matter half as much as what drives you on the inside. Once you have the drive, you'll get further than most. Filling in the gaps in your knowledge will be easy after your ambition is in place.

Rather than thinking about all that you don't know right now, figure out who *does* know. Then, ask them. People are your greatest resource. Ask for help. Be eager to learn.

No one expects you to know it all.

Seek out what you need to know to get you where you want to be.

april

Learn to let go of what no longer serves you.

It doesn't matter who you are: There's something you're holding onto that's holding you back.

It could be your friend who's been around since kindergarten that tends to pull you into childish behavior. It could be a thought pattern you developed that sends you into a downward spiral of overthinking. It could be the job you outgrew long ago but kept because you can't imagine disappointing your boss.

How does it feel after you've been around that friend? Does that thought pattern ever lead somewhere helpful or just to the same negative space you've visited a thousand times before? What could happen if you welcomed your growth, left your job, and pursued something new?

The daily choices we make add up exponentially. Who we spend time with, where we let our minds wander, and the work we do shape everything about how we show up in this life. Ultimately, they either propel you forward or drag you backward.

Let go of what no longer works for you. Fill that newfound space with the possibilities of what you could grab onto instead.

april

Offer credit where credit is due so that your own well-deserved recognition can come back to you.

As the saying goes, "A rising tide lifts all ships." With that in mind, it's well within your power at any moment to be the force that lifts others up.

When you spot excellence in action, *always* shine a light on it. When someone goes the extra mile, give them a nod of recognition. Make it your mission to never miss an opportunity to acknowledge someone.

Paying it forward will benefit you, too, though our ego tries to convince us otherwise. Our ego tells us that another's success is a sign of our own not-enoughness. It tells us to only focus on ourselves if we want to reach acclaim. It tells us that someone else's gain must be our loss.

Our ego is *wrong*. That tunnel vision keeps us from reaching our full potential by refusing to acknowledge the greatness around us.

Start today by quieting your ego. Compliment someone you might ordinarily overlook. Recognize a chance to highlight someone else's work instead of seeking credit for yourself.

Most of all, remember that another's success isn't your failure. Our fear keeps us from seeing good in those around us because we're tempted to believe it'll detract from our value. It doesn't.

Emulate an abundance mindset. There's more than enough to go around. For you. For us. For them. For all.

april

18

Let today's small wins shine like a beacon of hope,
welcoming your massive upcoming victory.

Even with the clearest of goals in mind, it's easy to get overwhelmed by the steps it'll take to reach them.

Time always seems to be speeding up and running out. Life feels like a race against the clock. We wonder if our daily efforts are moving the needle at all—if they'll ever amount to any tangible milestone or noticeable progress.

That feeling—however strong—doesn't have to be a life sentence.

Achievements are nothing without the journey it took to reach them. Life's too short to wake up every day hustling, only to end the day defeated because you haven't hit your target yet.

Your small wins along the way can feel just as satisfying as the ultimate triumph. Your biggest victory consists of *every* step working in tandem to make your dreams a living reality.

Acknowledge the small wins and celebrate them for what they are: an essential stepping stone to your success. It'll be great practice for the massive victories you deserve.

april

19

Your value lies in the solutions you provide.

The ability to anticipate obstacles is a great skill—especially when it leads to avoiding a catastrophe or a potential failure. Unfortunately, not everyone sees it that way in the moment.

Pointing out problems to the people around you is only as valuable as the speed with which you share them. People want these things said fast, like ripping off a band-aid. Plus, what you say next will make or break your potential to shine in this scenario.

Fair warning: It's unwise and unproductive to treat this situation like you're the anchor on the evening news, alerting the town of the dreadful things that are happening. You also want to avoid being the person who gawks at the issue in disbelief like, "Geez. How are we going to survive this one?"

Solutions are all anyone really wants to hear. If you absolutely must be the bearer of bad news, be sure to also be the bearer of gifts soon after as the provider of resolution. Be the person who suggests appropriate action instead of just watching this fire burn. Come to the table with practical ideas, even if they aren't chosen in the end. It's not about being the hero. It's about lifting everyone else in the midst of this event.

To take it a step further, finding improvements *before* there's a problem is a golden opportunity. Do more than solve problems when they come up. Solve them before they become a problem.

Spend more time looking for solutions than observing problems.

april

20

A life led by curiosity and discovery is a life filled with great excitement.

When was the last time you learned something new?

Even if you're not a big fan of school, knowledge fuels passion. The more you know, the more you want to know. Remaining genuinely curious is an opportunity to continually fill your cup.

Your passion in life matters, but many people lead their entire lives without ever finding it. Others lose it altogether. If you're lucky enough to grasp what passion feels like, it means you remained open enough to discover it in the first place. This is the sign of a lifelong learner, and now you must do everything in your power to hold onto it.

In order to stay curious, stay in the moment. When you think you already know—listen instead. Don't be afraid to say, "I don't know."

Your measure of success is never about how much you know. It has everything to do with what you *do* about it.

Activate your inner student to kick your passion into overdrive. Let your desire for more energize you.

april

Decide to be happy. It's good for your health.

Can you remember the last time you smiled?

Go ahead and try right now! *Smile.* You can do it!

Your smile fights stress. Put simply, your brain emits tiny molecules to fight off those worrisome feelings every time you let a grin spread across your face. When you're happy, the endorphins, dopamine, and serotonin flowing through you will elevate your mood and help your brain thrive.

It sounds too easy, right? "Just choose to be happy." This advice may even seem laughable when you can point to the hundreds of reasons why a smile doesn't quite fit the vibe at this moment.

It's the simple things that help us realize how much is actually within our power.

Sure, we're distracted by that looming work deadline. Our kid's teacher continues to point out where our pride and joy isn't excelling. Our parents' health continues to decline, reminding us that they're indeed mortal. The reasons to stop smiling feel endless.

If your mood is at the whim of every changing circumstance, you'll be taken for a ride that doesn't stop. Put that energy into turning your frown upside down.

There will always be worries waiting to consume your joy, but circumstances don't have to determine your attitude. Fortunately, you get to choose. That's certainly something worth smiling about.

april

22

Worrying about what you don't have is a symptom
of vision loss for abundance around you.

Leaning into abundance is more than a life-long task—it's a moment-to-moment commitment.

So much of what we encounter throughout the day hardwires us to believe there *isn't* enough. Not enough time, sleep, energy, patience, money…the list goes on.

Scarcity mindset says that the goodness around us won't stick around forever. It causes urgency and fear as we desperately work to make this amazing feeling last. But, despite how real it may seem, a scarcity mindset is a reflex that doesn't have to be your reality.

In the act of self-preservation, we default to negative possibilities. We think we're protecting ourselves by assuming the worst-case scenario in the hopes that nothing will surprise us. But we're actually projecting more than protecting.

How often have you started something new only to assume it'll be taken away? Maybe you entered into a new relationship just to immediately think of all the ways it could go wrong. Or you walked into your first day on the job already on edge about not living up to expectations.

If the good things that happen in your life are immediately paired with skepticism and doubt, you're not alone in your struggle.

Change your perspective to one of idealism. It starts by looking at everything around you (and the wonderful things in your life that are naked to the eye) and seeing them as evidence to the contrary. Abundance is *already* here.

If it weren't possible to envision more, how did what you've achieved so far ever come to be?

april

23

When you make a routine out of connecting with people,
you routinely connect to new opportunities.

People will take you places.

Connection is much more than a two-way street. It's a complex web that'll link you to many different ways of going after the life you want. And it starts by building *one* meaningful connection at a time.

You never know who might be the *right* person to know. It may not seem evident on their resume or in their title, but everyone has something to offer. Stop searching for them, and let them find you as you remain open to connecting with many personalities along the way.

Every relationship will develop you, whether it offers you exactly what you were hoping for or something even better. People bring opportunity, insight, and support. Even the unsuspecting connections you've made throughout your life serve a purpose. Remember to think beyond the business card and resume appeal.

The more you connect, the more seemingly "out of the blue" opportunities will find their way to you. Read between the lines and embrace the web of connection in your life.

april

24

Those who make an honest assessment of their time can reverse engineer the way to achieving their goals.

Did you wake up this morning only to dread your overloaded task list?

The curation of a to-do list comes from the best of intentions. You're just trying to keep track of it all and don't want any balls to get dropped. But now, you've given yourself the mother of all lists with an utterly unreasonable weight of responsibility.

Because you want to—what? Do it *all*? Not only do you not have to do it all, but you can also do *so much better.*

Keep your lists. There's no reason to throw them out completely. You just need to know what to do with them. Just because they exist doesn't mean they're your solely your marching orders. How will you prioritize what needs to be done so you actually have the time to focus?

Reduce your assignments to that which only you can (and should) be doing. Find the tasks that are extraordinary to you and your skillset. This is where a productive process begins.

Take a reasonable list of your top priorities and compare it to the actual time available to you. It's not about what you have to get done anymore. That's a forgone conclusion. It's about *when* they're going to happen.

Those who schedule real time on the calendar to produce results are the ones who experience real progress toward their goals. The more realistic you are about what's possible for you in a given period of time, the more your dreams can start to become a reality.

If it must be done, find—then define—the time.

april

25

A moment of success is just patience dropping in to say, "told ya so".

Congratulations, you've arrived!

After all that work—the planning, the executing, the persevering—you've made it to the top. Now that you're here, take time to celebrate. Acknowledge what got you here in the first place and pat yourself on the back for it.

Each moment of success is valuable, no matter the size.

Some monumental milestones are etched in gold, while some smaller benchmarks are penciled in along the way. They're each stepping stones toward your ultimate success, and they each deserve to be acknowledged. The work matters as much as the outcome—oftentimes, even more.

Any true, lasting success takes intentional time to build. If you're looking for instant, trendy success that'll disappear as fast as it arrived—you can get that now. Or, you can pursue the success that comes with staying power.

The key is time. Putting your hours in. Showing up not just once but again and again. Even when you're the only one there.

The next time you have a big win land in your lap, remember how it was more than worth the wait. Know that this was exactly the right time for it to show up because, by some divine happenstance, you were only prepared to receive it *in this moment.*

Take a deep breath. Be fully present in this moment of success. You deserve it.

april

26

If you can dream big, you can create something even bigger.

It all begins before.

Before you profit from your great invention.

Before you start a foundation that contributes to the cause you care about.

Before you build the perfect home for your family.

It all begins *before*, and it all begins with a dream.

You determine the value placed on your dreams. You've always been the one putting the price tag on your worth. If the amount feels low, you know who you need to take it up with.

The resources you need, the money it'll take, and the profits you'll gain *all* come in time—but none of it can happen without a dream big enough to carry it all.

You're worthy of everything you want. Have the same tenacity with your imagination as you do with the opportunities that come your way, and you'll see more of them popping up in precisely the places you hoped for them to.

Start recognizing the value of your dreams. See your worth before you begin pursuing those dreams.

april

27

Choose a soundtrack for your life that reminds you of what you can do.

For every "can" that crosses our minds, there are about a hundred "can'ts".

Our brains have a funny way of multiplying the negatives to feel bigger, heavier, and somehow much more believable than the positives.

Limiting beliefs only appear factual when you let them become the dominant soundtrack in your mind. If you want the clamor of can'ts to win, it will.

It's easy to forget that our thoughts aren't always reality because the feelings attached to them seem infallible. Feelings are valid, but they aren't facts.

How do you want to feel? What will you decide to hear more of?

If you want to *feel* like you can, find the thoughts that remind you that it's possible.

april

28

Your reaction doesn't add or take away from any given situation.
It adds or takes away from you.

It happens to us constantly, and yet it still catches us off guard.

We're just going about our day when suddenly something inconvenient, unexpected, or downright hurtful happens. "This wasn't in my plan," we think. Impatience and frustration immediately show up, more than eager to fight this battle for us.

We may not be able to pick and choose the situations we find ourselves in, but we certainly can decide how much control the situations have over us. Rarely can we ever control our circumstances. We can, however, always control our reactions to them.

Think of this whenever you find yourself at your wit's end. Step back for a moment and acknowledge the options ahead of you. How do you want to be remembered at this moment? More importantly, how do you want to feel once the moment passes?

Do something that future you would be proud of. And don't be surprised if that something turns out to be nothing. Action or inaction, either way, your future self will be grateful you made a thoughtful choice.

april

No one will believe you until you believe yourself.

We spend a great deal of our lives persuading.

You persuade an employer to see your credibility so they might give you a job or raise. You demonstrate your problem-solving skills to a potential client, so they decide to hire you. You show how you're a trusted and devoted friend to create a lasting connection with someone.

Whether you realize it or not, you're consistently selling yourself to others.

When you're trying to persuade someone, there's no room for hesitation. There's no time for questioning yourself. You never buy into a sales pitch when it's clear the seller has *no idea* what they're talking about. Or worse, when they have no passion behind the words they're saying.

Instilling belief in others begins when you've internalized that belief yourself. The same goes for how you carry yourself. If you don't embrace self-awareness, know what's true to you, and present yourself with confidence—there's no way you're going to get someone else on board with you.

Something incredible happens when you start to believe in your own potential. Your words feel stronger. Your choices mean something. Suddenly, you're not just hoping for who you might be *someday*, but you're presenting yourself as that person *right now*.

Today, own who you are and what you share with unwavering resolve. Soon enough, others will catch on.

april

30

You've already found your passion. You just haven't given it the acknowledgment that it's worthy of your attention.

How often have you said to yourself: "If I could only discover my passion, I'd know exactly what to do with my life"?

On some level, we all believe if we could just find our passion like everybody says, *everything else* would fall into place. We assume that magical "aha!" moment is the ticket to a life of free-flowing motivation and ease. We all want more out of every day. We want to feel excited and wistful. We hope to be enthusiastic and full of ambition.

Our world is full of evidence that people can find their passion and create a really amazing, unique path for themselves in that realm. At first, that realization is inspiring! But then, reality sets in. All those who have "figured it out" also bring on extra pressure that suddenly it's about so much more than knowing what you love.

We seek out those examples and instantly place all the responsibility for a financially lucrative life in line with that passion. We think, "These people love what they do, and they make money doing it?! OMG, can I please have that?!" Thus the confusion on what it means to discover your passion.

By placing undue stress on how your passion is supposed to perform for you, you ignore the things that actually bring you joy. They haven't earned your respect because they haven't ticked the box of becoming your career or wealth journey.

Pay closer attention to the moments you look forward to. What puts a pep in your step? Simply give acknowledgment to what you love when you find it. You don't need any more answers about it now. Just focus on feeling good.

Discovery comes to those who show up occasionally.
Success comes to those who show up consistently.

Our wildest dreams are often very different from the here and now. To achieve a new reality, most of us believe we need an extreme change of circumstance.

Nothing could be further from the truth.

If extreme changes were the only way to succeed, abundance wouldn't be as accessible as it actually is.

All that's required of you is patient persistence. This is how you'll see the possibilities of your imagination come to life.

Give it a try. Discover the path you want to follow and then commit to it to see what happens. Rather than looking for immediate results, look for the consistency of how you show up. That alone will tell you everything you need to know about the success you desire.

To live your dream life, you can't just pop in occasionally. It takes action, on repeat, until one day you look around and realize you're living your greatest dream. It takes action even when you don't feel like it. It takes action, unwaveringly, even when you start to wonder if your small efforts are contributing at all.

Think about what an average day of showing up regularly would look like for you:

- What's something you'll have to do every single day?
- What mindset will you need to remain diligent all day long?
- What obstacles can you look for so they don't catch you by surprise?

Being occasional shows you're open to an easy way out. Being consistent shows you have your eye on the prize.

How will you persist and go after the life you want?

May

To be and feel your best, you don't need to go it alone.

You're the expert on yourself. Especially when it comes to your body, you're more in tune than anyone else.

Your awareness of hunger, fatigue, and energy can't be determined by someone outside your skin. Your body's subtle (and not so subtle) cues are yours to observe— but just because you *notice* them doesn't mean you naturally know how to respond.

This is where you get to tag in the experts. The world is filled with brilliant people who have devoted their lives to finding solutions for health and wellness, often because they themselves have struggled in a way that you might be as well. To learn from their experience is a great luxury not to be taken for granted. Their insights are yours for the taking.

You have *one* body for the entirety of this human experience. What signals have you noticed from it lately? What's it need in order to live at an optimal level? Is it possible that you need to call in for some help?

Perhaps you wake up exhausted every morning, or you can't shake the afternoon lull that takes over your body. Maybe you struggle to fall asleep, or your ongoing need to move your body is exhausting in itself. Whatever it is, someone else has been there and can help by sharing their expertise.

It's never a weakness to ask for help. It's an incredibly brave second step toward living a better, healthier life. The first step? Acknowledging what your body is telling you in the first place.

Listen carefully and proceed accordingly.

*If you can't imagine your desired success,
you've already made up your mind.*

Can you picture yourself cashing the check? Hiring the team? Building the house? Autographing the book?

If it all feels too far-fetched, it's time to revamp your perspective. Your imagination is a powerful tool and an even more compelling destination.

Too often, we stop ourselves from *truly* going there in our minds. We have a hard time letting our imaginations run wild because of how attached we've become to the rules of the ego. We become restricted by the familiar limits around us and the circumstances that greet us daily.

Why not immerse yourself in endless possibilities instead?

All it takes is the intention to consistently remind yourself of those possibilities. Their ability to become real starts within you. Your ability to stay focused on them comes from nurturing a relationship with your deepest desires. Without a purposeful focus on the inner work, you'll keep interacting with the much more visible reminders from the limited world around you.

Fantasize about the happiness you want, the success you seek, and the future you deserve. Immerse yourself. Where are you? Who's by your side? Most importantly, how does it *feel*?

To take action, you have to believe that what you're going after is possible. Envision it today so you can live it tomorrow.

The first step is mindset. Always.

The thoughts of others are none of your business.
Release yourself from the responsibility.

Caring for other people *while* caring for ourselves is a delicate balance.

The moment we prioritize others' thoughts and opinions over our own, we sway too far off-center. As a result, we lose our balance—and our sense of self.

Human connection and care for others are major factors for our happiness. It's natural to want to know what someone else thinks or how they feel, whether we want to ensure they're comfortable in a situation or we're seeking a touch of validation.

Recognizing when those insights are valuable and when they aren't is a critical skill. This skill matters even more when we're gathering opinions about the decisions we're making for our lives.

When you're doing the work to improve yourself (especially in the beginning), you need to be able to identify the times when outside judgment isn't necessary. In fact, unless someone has either been in your place before or is the type of person you align with, their opinions are likely to be totally irrelevant to your growth.

Save yourself the work of having to be in the know of everyone's thoughts all the time. You'll find you have the clarity in your own mind to stay laser-focused on what's most important to you.

May

5

Those who are busy with everything choose to master nothing.

You take action with the best of intentions.

Action makes you feel powerful. It gives you direction. It makes you feel worthy. So, you keep moving and inevitably get stuff done along the way.

But equating a constantly flooded task list to a real, intentional purpose is a crucial mistake. We get caught up in doing a million things, thinking our ability to check box after box brings us closer to fulfillment.

Busy is a choice—and an easy one at that. The more meaningful option is mastery. Mastery of your passion. Mastery of your dreams. Mastery of the life you truly want for yourself.

To master is to command the attention of both yourself and the challenge at hand. It's to gain expert knowledge not just for a label but for the feelings you get when you engage. Feelings of real happiness.

We blur the line between mastery and task-checking because all action feels like it must count for something. The truth is that taking on one irrelevant to-do after another will never be anything but a distraction. The only way to achieve mastery is to narrow your focus and stay true to only that which moves your heart in the right direction.

Do you want to become fluent in a new language? Take up sculpting? Write a bestselling novel? Be the best parent ever? Become a world-class baker? You can do it all, just not all at the same time.

If you want it to mean more than just another box to check, you must focus your attention right now on becoming a master at your craft. This is the action that'll bring you peace.

How can you choose mastery over busyness today?

May
6

You won't wish the day away when you decide to make it yours.

Every one of us has had a day where we'd just rather…not.

We'd rather not get out of bed. We'd rather not talk to people. And we'd rather not do all the things we know the day is going to require of us.

Those not-so-lovely days will come around now and then, but they're meant to be the exception—not the rule.

Fortunately for you, you have a great deal of influence on how often they come around.

If the first moments of your morning contribute to a day that feels out of whack, how can anything else get better from there? This is all about how you decide to take ownership of your life. This is your first moment of the day to show who's boss.

The Universe knows you have big plans for your life, and they start with small, intentional actions in the morning. Actions you've chosen. Actions that are right for you and the season of life you're in right now.

Take the pressure off your day by taking ownership of how it all begins.

This is your time.

may

Rather than giving anxiety a name, find the truth in its source.

Worry. Frenzy. Distress.

When these feelings arise, they seem unavoidable. Uneasiness and concern infiltrate our minds, causing whatever's been stewing inside to bubble up. Challenging that anxiety is a real feat of strength.

Practice overcoming the unexpected by not settling for a stress takeover. Don't let the fear win. Hold onto your power instead of giving in and chalking it up to a loss for that moment, that day, or worse—even longer.

"Why am I uneasy? What triggered this panicked moment? What's at the root of my feelings? Why can't I just get it together?"

Worrying is nothing more than the manifestation of the worst-case scenario. Let's be real—no one wants to see the worst-case scenario happen. Ever.

The Greek Stoic philosopher Epictetus said, "When I see an anxious person, I ask myself, what do they want? For if a person wasn't wanting something outside of their own control, why would they be stricken by anxiety?"

When anxiety strikes, take a moment to pinpoint the desire that's causing it. If you notice you're pining after something that's out of your control, focus on how you want to *feel* instead of what you want to have.

may
8

Take ownership of what you do to grow every day rather than focusing on the "should dos" you see around you.

When was the last time you looked around to see someone else doing something worthy of applause and immediately faulted yourself for not doing it first?

You likely don't have to go far to retrieve that memory since we often do this to ourselves multiple times a day.

Have you ever looked at what you *yourself* are regularly doing that not many others are? Whether or not they wish they'd thought to do it first is irrelevant. All that matters is who you are when no one's watching. That's the authentic *you* becoming the person you're meant to be.

Look at your strengths through this new lens. Make a list:

- "What's something that comes naturally to me that might be scary to others?"
- "What have I finished that other people can't imagine starting?"
- "When have I leaned in where others would avoid a situation entirely?"

Sit with these answers. Recall how you feel when you execute them. Store them away as proof for the times when others' actions feel like a sign that you're not enough. All of these unique facets of you are cues pointing toward your highest self.

Give yourself credit. It might be exactly what you need today.

You're never too late. Age has nothing to do with potential.

Each birthday is an incredible gift. Another year of wisdom, more life experience, and the possibility for better.

Yet, instead of being liberated by this annual milestone, aging tends to come with the opposite feeling. We see it as a sign of what's not yet been done or measure our lives against the benchmarks of others.

Keeping score is a lose/lose battle every time, especially when we do it with arbitrary metrics. Why do we bring ourselves down year after year instead of celebrating the occasion of our growth? Why do we get caught in an endless cycle of age comparison?

Here's a dose of perspective for you:

- Vera Wang didn't launch her company until she was age 40.
- Maya Angelou became an author at age 41.
- Henry Ford was age 45 by the time he created the revolutionary Model T.
- Julia Child wrote her first cookbook at age 50.
- Arianna Huffington founded The Huffington Post at age 55.
- Iris Apfel continues to build her fashion empire at age 100.

If you want to observe the ages of accomplished people, use that data to feel empowered instead of discouraged. We need to let go of our need to feel impressive for our age and have gratitude for any age we get to become.

May

There's no such thing as coincidence.
Especially when it comes to wealth.

Isn't it great when something good happens at *just* the right moment? That money you found in your old jacket pocket. The check that came in the mail unexpectedly. The second you discover money that's been unaccounted for, you feel a bit of relief and a pep in your step.

When you're feeling gratitude for this moment, remember that the money that suddenly appeared did so when you were ready for it. It's not a result of happenstance—quite the opposite.

Every penny you meet is a result of the manifestation of your desires. It's a culmination of all the moments that your mindset was in a beautiful, abundant state.

For more moments of magic like these, lead the way with this wealth-building mantra:

"I am a money magnet."

Have gratitude for the money that comes when you call, but don't attribute it to luck.

Your efforts in nurturing an abundance mindset deserve to be rewarded. Recognize and appreciate them. Then, give yourself credit.

You are a money magnet.

You do enough. You have enough. You are enough.

Slow down.

Just for a moment, hit pause. Let all the thoughts in your mind stop racing. Give yourself permission to slow down.

You *do* enough.

It may not feel like it, but you do more than enough. While you probably have a list of things that "should" be happening and you "should" be focused on, you're already doing more than you credit yourself. Know that no matter what you do from this point forward, you already do *more* than enough.

You *have* enough.

This is another belief that feels challenging to accept. Resources might seem short, and the things you want to have may feel far away. You know what you want, and you're going to go and get it, but first, know that you already have *more* than enough.

Life will continue to remind you what else is out there and how much more you could have. If you don't appreciate your current reality, none of it'll matter. The current reality is very simple.

You *are* enough.

There's nothing else that needs to be done. There's no one else you need to be. You're already worthy, and this is your time to enjoy it. Be sure to choose your time wisely so you can do just that.

May

12

The measure of true care for others begins with the measure of care for yourself.

You're a good friend. You check in on the people who matter to you. You notice what they need and love to offer help when you see a chance.

It's not just admirable. It's a sign of the real care you have for people. The question is: Do you let that love spread to yourself as well?

You deserve to be cared for just as much as you care for others. The standard you hold yourself to as a friend must be the same as how you show up for yourself.

Take inspiration from the safety advice you hear on a plane before takeoff to secure your mask before assisting others. We cannot continue to be the best version of ourselves for others if we haven't first ensured we can be that for ourselves.

When we personify what we want to put out into the world, we can finally begin to feel the way we deserve.

Connect the dots between what you do to how you feel.
What are you doing with the best intention in your heart?

As you go through the motions each day, it's easy to lose track of your big-picture goals and intentions.

Maybe you started following some of your daily habits with the right state of mind, but things took a turn, and now you're just not feeling it.

Do you dread going to your job? Is your task list mocking you? Have you put off the commitments you should never have said yes to in the first place?

The more we're not energetically on board with our days, the more they take a toll on our bodies. Your mind sets the tone, and the whole vessel gets affected when it's told it's in a state of suffering.

What are you doing when your intentions are in the right place (not just because it's the right thing to do, but because you still feel a high vibe when you take on the task)?

If you were to go through the list of things you do today and take note of how you feel about each item as you do it, what percentage of your day feels great? What percentage is full of anxiety? What percentage feels like you're in a state of flow?

Keep track of your feelings. Determine if your intention is still aligned with how you spend your time. Care for the body that takes you through the whole experience by checking in and adapting accordingly.

May

14

If your perception keeps you from feeling how you want to feel, change your mind.

We often look at those around us to get a gauge of whether or not we've been granted permission to feel the way we want to. However, this only prevents you from getting closer to the state of mind you're aiming for.

You can feel the way you want to feel. No permission necessary.

Do you wish to feel supported? Choose to feel that way.

Do you wish to feel focused? Choose to feel that way.

Do you wish to feel respected? Choose to feel that way.

You can feel the way you want to feel. No permission necessary.

If you instead go around pointing fingers and placing blame on other people for not lifting you up in the way you need to be, you've not only given *away* your power, but you probably didn't even know you had it in the first place.

Life can be fully wasted if it's spent shifting the blame off ourselves and living in a state of victimhood. Rather than assuming everything is happening *to* you, decide what's happening *for* you.

Use this as an opportunity to remove distractions and show how you tactfully take charge.

Do you wish you heard compliments from others about your work? Pat yourself on the back instead and share with them how proud you are of the progress you've made.

You get to choose how you feel. No matter what.

may

15

The more you flex the muscle of progress toward a goal,
the better trained you will be at achieving goals throughout your life.

Do you feel a lack of connection with success?

It might feel like something that never really happens in your life, always just out of reach or specially reserved for everyone else.

Every day, we go through the motions trying to do the things that are best for us. Small wins happen all the time, but when we measure them on the wrong scale, they go unnoticed.

When you think of how you got your job, do you think of it as a surprising success or an inevitable result? When you think of how you completed a project, is it an achievement or something that just needed to be checked off the list?

While you feel like the wins of your life aren't quite measuring up to where they should be, you're not seeing the gains of your actions: *practice toward greatness.*

Most people think that the only way to do something big in life is to do something big every day. This is far from the truth, not to mention so deceiving that it might be the #1 reason people feel disappointed and unworthy. It results in the perfect chain of events to make someone give up and keep them from building their dream.

To become amazing at achieving goals means becoming consistent with making strides forward. Every big result came from the culmination of small movements in the right direction. Consistently.

Look at all you've done so far! Every little flex you've made is progress toward something big. Give yourself the credit you deserve. None of those moments were meant to be times to stop and be comfortable, and none of the future ones will be either. Each win is a victory for the person you have the potential to become.

May

16

An abundance mindset results in a desire for wealth.
A scarce mindset results in feelings of greed. The two don't intersect.

When you're born, you have no feelings one way or the other about money. Your financial opinions develop as you observe the world around you.

If you're surrounded by those who believe there will never be enough, you notice that they rarely let go of what they have and fixate on their belongings. They hold on tightly to the things they've accumulated.

If you're surrounded by those who believe there will always be enough, you notice that they often let go of what they have and see beyond what they own. They respect what they've achieved for themselves, and they treat those things well. Still, their quality of life isn't altered by its loss, should it occur.

Greedy feelings stem from the same scarcity mindset as a fear of *lack*. If you believe greedy people and money are bad, you're overcategorizing two very different things. A person with an abundant approach can't be greedy because they recognize money as energy and see it as the renewable resource that it is.

Be abundant in your thinking by asking yourself: "Can I still go after the life I want without the things I have?"

The answer might surprise you.

Everyone you meet has the power to impact your life.
Connect and grow.

You need them. They need you. We need each other. We all get to where we want to be by leaning on one another.

Take a moment and think of a handful of people that have influenced your life. How have they helped get you to where you are now?

It may not always be a significant relationship. It could be someone who made a brief appearance and left an impact on their way out. Or maybe it's someone who shows up for you daily without expectation of something in return.

Recall those who may have only appeared in your life for a season. They might have shown you where you could be one day or guided you to where you are now.

Think about those who have stayed by your side more times than you can count (and, in doing so, amplified the trust you now carry into new relationships). Think of the ones who poured into you so you could do the same when you were ready.

Today, look back at who shaped you *then* for the opportunities unfolding before you *now*. What patterns stand out? What energy are you attracted to that you could seek more of?

The people you connect with matter. And you matter to them. Remember the power they bring, as well as what you offer in return.

Start the day with quiet so you can hear more of who you are.

How you start the day is how you live your life.

It doesn't matter if you're a morning person or not. This is the moment you when you decide how you want to operate in life. Fortunately for you, it's a decision you get to make every single morning.

If you decide to wait until the very last minute to get out of bed so you're ultimately rushing to beat the clock, it'll catch up to you. If you decide you absolutely *need* to know what the rest of the world did while you slept and reach for your phone first thing, that rabbit hole will never end.

Why start the day with hurrying, stress, and the fear of missing out if it's not required of your lifestyle?

If you wish for clarity, start with quiet. If you wish for creativity, start with quiet. If you wish for happiness, start with quiet.

A day that starts with quiet is one where you're okay with being with your thoughts first. It's being unafraid to connect to your higher self before you have to connect with the outside world.

Don't mistake quiet for perfection. A quiet morning doesn't mean your significant other won't speak (they might), nor does it mean your children won't need you (they will).

We can only control what we can control. All we have to do is decide to take that control when we have it. Be unafraid to be with yourself to start the day.

Everyone else can wait.

May
19

*The answer to your question can be seen in the vision you have
for your life 10 years from now.*

When you face a new decision, every yes you say is a no to something else. As much as we're reminded of this advice, we often don't know when we're saying the right yeses and nos.

The truth is that you won't know until you make a choice. You might say yes to yourself and contribute your time to something you value. You might say yes to someone else and give energy to something that isn't as important to you (but will matter to someone you care about).

When you're stuck in indecision and wishing for a crystal ball to give you the magic word, remember this question: "If I say yes to this now, how will I feel in 10 years? In a year? In a week?"

You can even turn that question around: "If I say no to this, will I regret it?"

Your gut is likely already telling you what you know the answer is. Picture the needs of your higher self after time passes, and all is said and done. Acknowledging the outcome for your future self helps you navigate the now.

How you spend your time and where you allocate your energy matters significantly to the life you lead. It starts with a clear vision of where you're going and who you want to be when you arrive.

May

A good day is as simple as knowing how much you like yourself.

Today's assignment is to embrace the person you see in the mirror. Embrace them exactly as they are, with no hesitation. For once, check your judgment and criticism before looking at your reflection. Instead of defaulting to disappointment, offer grace and care.

Do the necessary things to clear the sleep from your face and the stale breath from your teeth, then look that person in the eyes and say: "Good morning! Good life! You are loved. You matter. I'm proud of you."

You deserve kindness no matter how you feel about what you've done or not done—just like how every other stranger you come across deserves the same courtesy. The same benefit of the doubt. The same unearned, unwavering kindness.

There's no additional qualification needed. No fine print. Just the permission you desire offered on a silver platter with nothing but a steadfast belief that it's going to be a good day.

What would it feel like to embrace yourself like this every morning?

We rarely offer ourselves the same kindness we freely give to others. We spend so much time criticizing, doubting, and noting room for improvement, yet we'd never dream of treating our best friends with the same level of scrutiny.

Life is too short to not to be your own advocate. Today and *every* day, offer yourself the same energy you give to everyone else.

may

Move.

To keep yourself sharp, you have to be—and stay—devoted.

You know the first law of motion: An object in motion stays in motion, and an object at rest stays at rest—unless acted upon by another force. You are that force. You need to intentionally decide to keep moving (in every sense of the word) in order to tackle what life may throw your way.

Mentally, you've hit that wall before. Work feels redundant, your job no longer excites you, and you feel stuck.

Emotionally, you've caught yourself questioning your match. You look at your partner and feel indifferent instead of swept off your feet.

Physically, you've found yourself worn down. You can't find the workout that keeps you moving, so you think of quitting altogether.

Every scenario stems from a lack of engagement. Work may have become boring, but you played a role in that. You and your partner may be misaligned at the moment, but that's not on them alone. You're tired physically because you...stopped...*moving.*

Be the force that keeps yourself in motion. This doesn't mean slowing down won't make sense at times. But if you're asking yourself why things feel stalled, check your own movement to see how you've been complicit in these conditions. Then, make a change.

22

Another person's surplus does not equate to your deficit.

Life is a challenge.

When you find yourself in an overwhelming moment, it's easy to mistake up from down, happy from sad, and even good from bad. We lose perspective quickly when we're frustrated.

It's no surprise that as we race through our own obstacle course, we feel defeated when we see someone else having a much easier time with their own. Your immediate judgment might be that there isn't enough to go around. If there are positive results in someone else's lane, then they must have come out of a supply that's no longer available.

This is exactly where things go wrong, and our results turn mediocre. Jealousy restricts positive energy and clouds your thoughts with limiting beliefs.

Break the cycle by recognizing what you're actively manifesting in your life instead of fixating on someone else's. Leverage jealous moments as opportunities to refocus on what matters to you. Remove the emotional clutter and become laser-focused on what you manifest for *you*.

The moment you feel a pinch of jealousy, scarcity, or sadness for someone else's victory, repeat your new mantra:

"Thank you for showing me that my dreams are possible. This is the sign I needed."

Say it, then keep going.

Lower your expectations so that you can raise your standards.

You can wake up and start the day on your own terms. You can build good habits that'll enrich your life. You can maintain your staying power when others would have already surrendered. You hold the power. You set the standard.

Sometimes, in a moment of weakness, you will falter. You will lose your patience. You will feel disappointed, especially when someone else isn't being the person you think they should be. That letdown can cause you to waver.

Having expectations of others is a one-way ticket to the land of disappointment. Expectations are a detailed manual for how we think other people *should* conduct themselves (except nobody got the copy you wrote for them). It may seem reasonable to expect things from certain people, especially if the expectations have been clearly set for the role they play in your life. However, that means we simply built in an excuse that allows us to forget their most important role of all: being a human.

Standards are different. These are intentional guidelines that have been designed for you, by you. To hold yourself to a high standard means having a clear vision for how you can be the greatest version of yourself to the best of your ability. Will you be able to follow it perfectly all the time? Of course not. Because once again, we're all human.

Know the difference between elevating your standards and raising your expectations. One will set you up for success. The other will set you up for disappointment every time.

May 24

Who you choose to be is your decision.
Listen to the conclusions you've drawn.

We can be very quick to lead with the words "I'm not".

We think this proclamation protects us because it puts realistic guardrails on a situation. In actuality, it holds us back.

"I'm not a morning person."
"I'm not outgoing."
"I'm not an athlete."
"I'm not an optimist."

Before you make any declaration, remember this: Are you defining what you're not before you really know who you *are*?

When you say what you're not, you're informing everyone of limitations that may or may not really exist. Meanwhile, the most important of those listening are yourself and the Universe.

This is a great thing when you're focused on the circumstances you wish to attract in your life, but how many "I'm nots" have you proclaimed aren't a true indication of what you hope for yourself?

If there's something on your list of limitations that you wish were different, remember that your mind is powerful. How would you change your affirmations to align with the results you want to come into your life?

Before you list what you're not, lead with who you *absolutely are*. Then, let that person take you somewhere new.

May
25

Failure can only hurt you when you're unable to learn from your mistakes.

Failure isn't fatal.

It feels like a complete gut punch at the moment, but it isn't what takes you out of the game. Do you know what does? It's the inability to learn from your missteps that led to that failure in the first place.

Facing defeat hurts. It hurts your ego, your confidence, and sometimes even your belief that you're on the right path. If you're not careful, that doubt will stunt your growth. The people who go on to succeed (and yes, fail many more times) are the ones who stop to look at what *actually* happened.

While every failure brings frustration, it can also bring growth. We're all going to fail. If we're lucky, we'll fail a lot! Failing is only a sign that we're in motion. It shows that you're taking action. You're trying. You're doing the work.

Find a new ritual for your moments of failure. Instead of wallowing and worrying that you're not cut out for this, ask: "What has this failure helped me discover for a fact?"

Stop the storytelling. Don't try to rationalize. Keep your worries about outside perceptions at bay. Simply lay down the truth of the matter—objectively—so you know which lesson you don't have to learn again.

When you get beyond the momentary pain, you recognize the other side of failure: *progress*.

may
26

Don't be afraid to start over.

Your life doesn't come with a guarantee to follow a straight line. It won't always have the perfect storybook arc or follow any kind of formula.

Your timeline will look more like a child's haphazard scribble, thanks to the thousands of beginnings, endings, and middle moments. You can't be afraid to start over because the truth is you *already have* so many times.

Rather than fearing the unanticipated twists and turns, realize all of the wisdom your past life experience offers you.

Every new job is a chance to redefine the skills you want to acquire and how you want to be seen. Every new friendship is a chance to show up with more empathy. Every new move is a chance to begin with a fresh slate.

Each and every tangle has brought clarity along the way. You get more than one chance. You get all the new starts you actively seek out. Each reset is an opportunity to make the impression you want.

What will be your next first?

If you want to be motivated, go out and do something about it.

If there's one massive misconception about motivation, it's that it comes *before* you do the work.

Motivation is an intrinsic part of who we are, but it won't always be there right when you need it.

Motivation follows effort. It follows action. If you don't believe this, try it out the next time you need a little kick in the butt. Put on all your workout clothes and commit to five minutes of movement. Chances are, you'll end up feeling much more compelled to go another 25 minutes.

Don't wait for motivation to show up. Go out and get it. Motivation isn't something you have—it's something you *do*.

Motivation shows itself when you've found your calling and pursued it. It appears when you do the challenging work of taking those first unnatural steps.

The moment you feel the *least* motivated is the exact moment you must act with full force. Give it all you've got (despite your inclination not to), and you'll find that you can create the very motivation you're seeking.

Try it today and see what happens.

May

28

The people who will love you will find you as soon as you're ready to share yourself.

Looking fabulous from a distance doesn't change anything up close.

We try to curate our lives (especially on social media) to convey a particular "reality." But once all the edits are said and done, is any of it real at all?

"Keeping up with the Joneses" (or these days better known as comparison culture) is a burden we all know intimately. And it's quite the slippery slope. The lines between who you are and who you want to be seen as begin to blur so much so that when you're given the chance to show your true self, you may find yourself stumped.

Surface-level affirmation is instantaneous and fleeting. It gives us a rush, then quickly disappears, leaving us craving—needing—more. In turn, you stop connecting with yourself in order to feel a "connection" with the masses through likes and comments.

When you're ready to share yourself online, consider what your caption might say if it just held the truth. What picture would you post if your goal was connection rather than validation?

Who you really are is already more than enough. *You* are enough. No filter needed.

29

Your convictions are powerful, whether they help you or not.

There's an old saying that there are three sides to every story: your side, their side, and the truth.

The essence of it is simple: Your perspective isn't the *only* one—and sometimes not the most accurate one—out there. Ultimately, it's a reminder that we can find the truth if we remember not to merely take our own storytelling as fact. Too often, we refuse to stray from our own viewpoint, so much so that it limits our ability to see reality.

Discover this new word today: confabulation. It means that you replace gaps in your memory with (fabulous) falsifications that *you believe* to be true. When you confabulate, you don't even realize when you're lying to yourself because it's your conviction that you remember it correctly. Your convictions are powerful, so you have to challenge them when they're keeping you from the facts. Some things you remember are feelings rather than events.

Start your fact-finding mission from scratch with this essential question: "What do I know for sure?"

Shift your convictions by becoming more open to a new—potentially more accurate—reality.

Giving good advice is easy. Following good advice is hard.

Seeking advice is productive. Those who open themselves up to being vulnerable show immense strength.

With this in mind, be cautious of where you turn to for guidance. Welcoming an advisor into your life for direction means trusting them with your life. You may find that someone is more than happy to accept the role, but many people who seem to have all the answers don't automatically qualify to offer you direction. Before listening to their cues, assess if they appear to be taking the same advice that they have no problem doling out.

No one is perfect, and everyone goes through different seasons. Still, always listen to your gut. Would you take money advice from someone in great financial struggle? Would you take health tips from someone who only seems to stunt their own growth?

It's okay to hear what others have to say, but check your source before you put too much weight on whether you need to change your ways. Even those with your best interest at heart may not be the expert on the matter.

may
31

Be clear when speaking about what you do.
Drop the labels and share how you help people.

When you first step into the workforce, your toolkit looks something like this: Resume? Check. Elevator pitch? Check. Fancy industry jargon? Check! Outfit to fit the part? Bonus!

You start your journey and, along the way, inevitably get the question: "So, what do you do?" The words printed on your business card or LinkedIn profile might feel like the easiest shortcut to sharing your expertise, but they lack serious substance.

Rather than rattling off your title in response, think about what could pique someone's interest in a new way. Keep in mind that if they've already met someone with your identical position, they may decide what they already believe about you based on their experience. This introduction is your opportunity to stand out and make an impression.

Show how you're unique. Explain how you help people. You could say you're a coach, or you could say something like: "I help new mothers embrace their role and trust their maternal instincts without losing their identity."

You could say you're a consultant, or you could say: "I help young entrepreneurs get ahead and skip common mistakes by connecting them with empowering mentors."

You could say you're a marketer, or rather say something like: "I help creatives expand their reach by amplifying their work."

Notice the difference? These descriptions tease a mental picture that activates curiosity in a person.

A title means nothing. What you do to *serve* means everything.

june

june

1

Your current location isn't your permanent destination.

Comfort zones. Why is everyone so mad at them?

We've all heard advice aplenty that nothing great in life ever comes from staying in your comfort zone. We all know it's best to zip on out of there so we can discover who we were truly meant to be.

And yet, not everything in life is so black and white. It's time to stop giving your comfort zone such a bad rep.

Have you considered that it actually serves a great purpose?

It's a place for you to enjoy yourself without stress or expectation. It's a space for you to take it easy and a retreat for you to recharge your batteries.

It's true, not very much will *happen* there, but that's not what it's meant for in the first place, is it? Just like everywhere else, it's not a permanent destination. It serves a distinct purpose and can be used accordingly.

The dark and quiet places are only advantageous to us when balanced with trips outside in the light.

Respect your comfort zone for what it is: It's a place you can always return to when you need it, rather than a space you live in entirely. The more you embrace this, the better equipped you'll feel to experience all that life offers you.

To have more impact, be more specific.

Our society is captivated by influence. With the touch of a button, you can connect with hundreds, thousands, and potentially millions of people. You can find your tribe. You can discover people who think like you. You can become the leader of a pack.

For some, it's instantaneous—which sets the expectation that it'll be that way for all. When you start trying to build a community of like-minded individuals, you might get frustrated when it doesn't come as quickly as you assumed.

Those who do it well make it look easy, but the behind the scenes are rarely as polished. Look at where they started. They began by focusing on one person. They built everything by beginning with only the perfect fit in mind.

When you try to be all things to all people, you'll fail every time. Start with the one core individual you hope to impact. Let them know you see them. You hear them. Get to know them. Connect meaningfully, and you'll learn to attract the right fit for the value you have to offer.

Instead of thinking you need to be an expert covering all bases in parenting, be a resource dedicated specifically to offering homes with toddlers advice for handling tantrums. Instead of trying to cover all things nutrition, exercise, and sleep, be the go-to advisor on your favorite form of movement and how your audience can easily integrate it into their lives.

You don't need millions of people to buy into what you're selling—you just need the core group that can't get enough. It all begins with solving problems for your one perfect person.

june

3

Success is measured by your level of commitment.

Humans are captivated by achievements and metrics.

When we witness someone else's success, we instinctively assume their yardstick should be ours. For ambitious goal-setters, this is disheartening.

Arbitrary benchmarks are just a distraction. You compare yourself to someone else and think, "I don't have the experience they do." You think you're too old, too young, too pressed for time, too far behind.

Imagine running your first marathon. To cross that finish line, you have to do several things first. You have to pay the registration fee, buy the right shoes, figure out your training schedule, and—of course—tell your loved ones to be there for you on the big day.

None of those things matter more to your 26.2-mile run than your commitment to doing the work. Fail or succeed, we discover more about how to be better when we see our promises through to the end.

Whether you've been doing this your whole life or you're just trying to find out if you can finish something, this is *your* race and your race alone.

The only metric for success that matters is your ability to show up.

june

4

How you sleep is how you live.

"I'll sleep when I'm dead!"

We've all heard someone say this, or maybe even said it ourselves. That phrase really gets you pumped up, doesn't it? Like you're ready to conquer the world and there's no time like the present!

Or...not. Isn't it actually an exhausting reminder of how we're all burning and churning through life? Not exactly the best mantra to live by.

When you lose sight of your body's needs, you lose momentum.

We all get *one* vessel in this human experience. This one body carries your highest self through all of the incredible adventures of life. It only has a few requirements to keep you living optimally, one of the most important being *rest*.

All the day's challenges are heavy on both your mind and body. Leaving time to recover is essential.

The next time you feel tempted to put resting on the back burner, refuse to push through at your own expense. Decide to recharge rather than reduce yourself further.

june

5

*Don't avoid what's been unsaid just because
you haven't heard anyone say it.*

"Let's talk money!" ...said no one ever.

We're conditioned to avoid talking about finances at all costs. It's a tragic taboo in our society. We seal our lips anytime the subject of money comes up, and, as a result, we've chipped away at our worth.

When you avoid the conversation or pretend like you have nothing to learn, you're only doing yourself a disservice. Some questions are personal—no doubt—but being bold doesn't equal being intrusive.

Just because you want to level up your financial worth doesn't mean you're money-hungry or rude. It does mean you have high standards. You believe in the abundance of life. You know your time and effort are *worth* something!

There's still so much room for improvement in education about financial wellness. You must be your own advocate for your worth, communicate your value, and pave the way to the wealth you've earned.

Know what you want, and don't settle for a penny less.

june

The only person you have something to prove to is you.

You have the power to do so much more. To surpass expectations. To throw away the rulebook and hit the ground running.

The power is not only in you—it's generated *entirely* by you. When we forget this core truth, we hold ourselves back from taking the leaps to get us where we want. Every time we doubt our power, we take a step in the wrong direction.

The thing about permission is even when we *do* receive it, we often still hesitate to act. Because we're still afraid. The truth is that permission isn't actually what you need. You need confidence in your own abilities. You need to trust your skillset. You need to value your own opinion as much as you value everyone else's.

So, refuse to wait. Refuse to wait for someone else to acknowledge your power or grant you permission to go forth and act. Trust your gut—it holds the key to your next big move.

Until you do this, permission doesn't make a difference. It never did.

june

*Decorate the walls of your mind with art that
you've chosen yourself and absolutely adore.*

In your home, you curate a space you love. You buy furniture to comfort. You roll out rugs that welcome. You hang pieces that inspire.

Your mind is like another home. In fact, it's a home you can never be away from. Why not treat its walls with the same care you'd give the physical walls around you?

Have you ever thought about how much time we spend talking to ourselves all day, every day? Each new thought is like a piece of work hanging on the walls of your mind. No matter how the thoughts come to be, it's a collection fully curated by you. How carefully are you choosing what gets to take up your space?

Wayne Dyer emphasizes this in his book, *Excuses Begone*:

> You can readjust your willingness meter to avow that you're open to seeing an alternative vision by affirming: 'I am worthy of attracting unlimited abundance and prosperity into my life, regardless of what life experiences have gone before me. I only reinforce and contemplate images that are in harmony with this vision.' After all, it's your inner screen and yours alone. No one from your past has exclusive rights to what plays on your screen—you can display whatever you deem appropriate and can delete anything you choose.

Never forget: Your mind is a palace that's yours to decorate. Choose your pieces wisely.

june

8

Building connections is a combination of keeping relationships fresh and finding new ones to build on.

When it comes to the connections you get to make in your lifetime, there's no short supply of people to meet.

You have the privilege of growing the relationships you have while pursuing what you still need. Having a wide range of relationships will make you a richer, more cultured person and an incredible friend now and in the future.

How do you view all the connections in your life? Do you keep your heart closed to a few or open to many?

As terrifying as it is to put yourself out there, view your relationships from a place of abundance. Someone else out there is looking for a friend, a colleague, or a mentor just like you—but they can only find you if you show up. Remain open and honest about who you are with everyone you connect with, and enjoy the depth that authenticity brings.

No need to count up all the people in your life, but don't forget to ask yourself: "Can they count on me?"

The more you show up for those you associate with (while also remaining true to yourself), the more your connections will grow and multiply.

9

Take in the quiet and notice what you hear.

Let there be silence.

Close your eyes and sit with it. Give it a second. Allow the quiet to create space.

Space for you to think.

Space to let your mind wander with original ideas.

Space to be curious.

Space to *breathe*.

Silence can be uncomfortable, especially if you've avoided making space for yourself lately. However, it can also be *powerful*.

Instead of fearing what it's like to be alone with yourself, imagine what you could do if you leaned into the here and now without limits. What do you hear when you listen very carefully to your own thoughts?

In our quietest moments, we experience the gift of true honesty. We're able to think freely. Feel openly. Make calm, confident decisions.

Let yourself sit in that space. You may discover something you wish you already knew about yourself.

june

10

You can do hard things. It's called self-care.

The older and wiser you get, the more you realize that self-care is *so* much more than a bubble bath and some vino. While those are things you can delight in (and rightfully so!), they aren't what makes life feel like a breeze. They're the cherry on top.

When you roll up your sleeves and take care of the hard stuff, you're taking care of yourself on a whole other level. Try this new approach to self-care: doing the things you know are right for you because they help you take care of your *future* self.

- Take a 45 min walk without your phone.
- Review your credit card statement.
- Say no when you don't want to do something.
- Talk to someone about what you're currently struggling with.
- Cancel a monthly membership or subscription that you aren't using.
- Read ten pages of a self-improvement book.
- Pay your bills on time.
- Stop. When you've forgotten how to slow down.
- Act. When you've forgotten how to show up.

We're all dealing with something different from what the person next to us is going through. Don't let someone else's idea of self-care distract you from finding yours.

june

11

The past is a crutch that slows you down when you could be looking up at the light guiding you toward your future.

You're worthy of the now. You're worthy of the future. You're worthy of enjoying what's happening in your life without reservation.

How much of your life do you spend looking backward?

Does every first date pull you back into the doubts of past relationships? You find yourself overanalyzing what went wrong instead of wondering what could go right.

Maybe you start a new job and spend your first day comparing the new role to your last position, limiting your ability to be fully present.

The past has already served its purpose in your life. Yet, it's possible to strike a balance between leaving it behind entirely and clinging to it with a childlike grip. Whatever lies in the past doesn't predict your future unless you want it to. Instead, look at what's unfolding in the here and now. You'll see that the future depends on you and what you're doing *now*.

The past is out of your reach, so leave it there. Give yourself the gift of the present moment and create your incredible future.

june

12

Don't abandon your journey for greatness on detours of outside approval.

Boom. Direct hit. Your ego has been bruised, and you're feeling it.

Someone took a good look at you and made their opinion known. Whether they saw what you were doing, wearing, working on, or how you were conducting yourself—they came to their very own personal judgment call.

And then, they delivered it: a nice big, juicy dose of unsolicited advice.

You've probably found yourself in a moment like this when someone offers you critique. Blindsided, you forget how to exit your ego from the situation, and instead, you absorb it.

Pause. Why is it your job to handle this advice at all?

Of course, this is a loaded question. There are so many reasons why! It may be because it comes from someone who loves us and has our best interest at heart. Maybe the advice comes from someone who's inspired us to be the best version of ourselves.

The truth is that caring counts for something. We feel that if we can find a way to stay true to ourselves while also getting the approval of others, we'll feel better about ourselves.

But that's just never the case.

You can't be your fully expressed self and *also* be what anyone else wants you to be.

It's more than okay to hear people out for what they think, especially those you love. At the same time, it's a non-negotiable for you to follow the truth that's right for you. When the two don't align, always choose the latter.

june

13

Your credibility is directly associated with your authenticity.

Someone's *always* trying to sell us something.

There are pop-up ads everywhere and commercial breaks constantly. You know you've felt seen when you're served an advertisement of precisely what you were *just* thinking about.

Think of all the ads that distract your thoughts daily, from the billboards you drive by to that annoying jingle you can't get out of your head.

Out of all the noise, which ones do you actually buy into? Even though you see sales slang and hype for what it is, you still feel connected to something that speaks to you.

The same goes for how you present yourself. In a way, you're a living ad yourself, asking everyone to buy into what you have to offer. Don't be the surface-level persona. Go deeper. Let the credentials and titles and technical skills take a backseat for this ride. Start from a place of authenticity. You're a human being, and so is everyone else around you. We're hardwired for connection.

Relate to who you're talking to. Find common ground. Keep it simple. Be honest. That's what truly gets attention—the rest is fluff.

If you want to speed up, factor in the slowdown.

When it comes to going after the lives we want, we're ready to hit the ground running full speed ahead. The energy is so thrilling that the absolute *last* thing we want to do is slow down. To truly reach our potential, however, we must care for our humanity along the way.

Imagine you're taking a road trip. You've planned for the next long stretch ahead of you, but you also notice your diminishing energy. Each rest stop you drive past reminds you how badly you need a break. Every time you ignore those signs, you disregard the self-care that'll take you further in the long run. Before you know it, you can't keep your eyes open, the car is out of gas, and you've detoured away from the destination you initially set out for.

The more often you ignore the symptoms that try to tell you how to better care for yourself, the more inevitable burnout becomes.

How often do you ignore your warning signs?

You'll go further (and faster!) when you respect the time you need to slow down. Instead of letting yourself reach a breaking point, factor in time for self-care. It'll *always* be worth it.

june

15

*The journey of investing in yourself begins the day
you decide to reach for better.*

It's easy to forget just how much authority we have in our own lives.

Many of us wake up believing that the day has already been determined and we're just rolling with the punches. We take our agency to choose for granted and end up letting life decide for us. What you're entitled to is completely up to you and the work you put in. You can decide that you deserve better. You can decide right now.

It all begins with the consistency of your decision-making.

Maybe you've kicked things off by focusing on creating wealth in your life instead of living paycheck to paycheck. Or perhaps you've chosen to pay off the debt you desperately want to be rid of.

That initial decision to act is a critical *first* step, but it's not the only step. Recognizing your realistic limitations matters just as much. Stay fixed on your goal but malleable in your follow-through. Understanding what you can control is vital to your ability to stick with your plan.

Your path may need to change, and that's okay! That only means you're willing to do whatever it takes to make your dream happen.

Acknowledge what you want. Decide that you're powerful enough to go out and get it. Trust that you'll do it.

june
16

Remember Rule Number 6.

We spend a lot of time trying to figure out how to deal with the people in our lives. Ironically, our greatest obstacle doesn't lie outside ourselves but rather *within*. It's time to look in the mirror and face the greatest ego of all: your own.

In their book *The Art of Possibility*, Rosamund and Benjamin Zander illustrate how our ego gets in our own way:

> Two prime ministers are sitting in a room discussing affairs of state. Suddenly a man bursts in, apoplectic with fury, shouting and stamping and banging his fist on the desk. The resident prime minister admonishes him: "Peter," he says, "kindly remember Rule Number 6," whereupon Peter is instantly restored to complete calm, apologizes, and withdraws.
>
> The politicians return to their conversation, only to be interrupted yet again twenty minutes later by a hysterical woman gesticulating wildly, her hair flying. Again the intruder is greeted with the words: "Marie, please remember Rule Number 6." Complete calm descends once more, and she too withdraws with a bow and an apology.
>
> When the scene is repeated for a third time, the visiting prime minister addresses his colleague: "My dear friend, I've seen many things in my life, but never anything as remarkable as this. Would you be willing to share with me the secret of Rule Number 6?" "Very simple," replies the resident prime minister. "Rule Number 6 is 'Don't take yourself so goddamn seriously.'" "Ah," says his visitor, "that is a fine rule." After a moment of pondering, he inquires, "And what, may I ask, are the other rules?"
>
> "There aren't any."

Whenever you feel overcome with emotion, worried about your appearance, conflicted about a situation, or just can't understand—remember Rule Number 6.

june

Your time is finite. Make the most of it, one moment at a time.

What does it actually mean to live every day to the fullest?

We say we want to embrace each moment, but it's difficult to fully understand the gravity of such a statement. Since it's both easy to say and challenging to grasp, let's start with what it *doesn't* mean:

It doesn't mean adopting everyone else's bucket list.

It doesn't mean every day has to be filled with the extraordinary.

It doesn't even mean you have to have a good day every day.

We only have so much time, so why waste any of it trying to do what you think you *should* do? If you truly want to make the most of this life, there are no guilty pleasures or wasted moments. There's no such thing as frivolous time spent in self-discovery.

Be driven to discover what brings you connection and purpose. Let what feels good feel good and seek out *more* of it. Outside perspectives and unnecessary expectations will always try to trip you up along the way.

The more clarity you have about who you are and what fulfills you, the more opportunities you'll have to live your life on purpose.

june
18

Own your actions. Own your life.

As much as we may act otherwise, there's not much we can control in life. With most things outside of our rule, all that remains under our authority are our actions and responses. From them come your thoughts and words, and from there, your sense of purpose, daily disposition, guiding values—the list goes on.

It's easy to forget just how much control we *do* have. We may know that how we act is entirely up to us...until something we don't have control over happens, and we spiral.

Taking ownership of our choices—no matter the circumstance—is the only way we can be the leader of our own lives.

Doing this is, of course, easier said than done. Responsibility is a hard habit to maintain, especially when it's so much more natural to justify, explain, or blame a situation. But, when you do, you give up the precious power that comes with holding yourself accountable.

Reframe the conversation with yourself. When setting a nutrition goal, instead of saying: "I am going to try and be healthy," say, "I am healthy". When you find yourself dealing with a challenging person, assume they're doing their best and put yourself in their shoes.

Creating the life you want happens in the small moments when you own your actions instead of letting outcomes happen to you.

june

19

*To have a vision is to know how you'll leave the world
better than you found it.*

Your existence in this time and place—this moment—is no coincidence. In the same way, the dreams and ideas bubbling up within you are yours for a reason.

You aren't just the one for the job—you're the *only* one. No one can do it the way that you can. Your specific perspective, upbringing, curiosity, and talents all culminate in a vision that can only be created by *you*. Whether or not it'll be achieved depends on whether you accept the mission.

How can you transform your own corner of the world to be better for everyone?

You might start in the simple places. At your workplace, in your neighborhood, or at home. The real destinations that'll be forever changed are the ones you'll find inside the people you affect along the way.

When all is said and done, how will the lives you touch be better off from the impact you leave behind?

20

You can do more. You can also do less with more intention.

One of the greatest fallacies of productivity is equating it to how busy someone is.

Taking on tasks in bulk. Constantly in the pursuit of checking the next box. Rushing from commitment to commitment. This isn't productivity, yet the more we try to do it all, the more we perpetuate this misconception.

When we don't feel like we've done enough, we try to *do* more.

When we don't feel like we have enough, we try to *get* more.

When we don't feel like we are enough, we try to *be* more.

We fill up on *more* in the hopes that we'll eventually experience what the seemingly unattainable "enough" feels like. Every time we finally reach the benchmark we thought would bring us fulfillment, a new one appears ten steps in front of us.

How do we get off this ride of striving for more (while never thriving along the way)? Instead of pouring all your energy into *more*, identify what few things are really worth it. Hone in on them.

The more awareness you have of what brings you joy, the easier it'll be to decide what deserves your effort.

june

21

If the advice is unsolicited, so is its meaning.

Opinions. We all have them.

Along with our litany of opinions, we carry assumptions. We assume we have the right to share our opinions anytime, anywhere. Though we don't hesitate to vocalize our own opinions, we roll our eyes when we're on the receiving end.

Opinions will never stop coming your way. That's a guarantee. You can ignore this and allow others' opinions to continue to surprise you, or you can prepare yourself for them and minimize their impact when they pop up. You may not get to choose what you receive, but you get to decide how you *respond.*

You're the gatekeeper. You hold the veto power. Others' words only carry as much meaning as you allow them.

Start by taking back the power. Is this opinion coming from someone whose approach you value? Do they have authority in the area they're commentating on? If you were an employer checking the resume of a potential hire, would you hire this person to advise you?

Keep this as your guide: If they don't pass your test, deny them access. Embrace this mentality with the energetic boundary you've set to protect yourself. Your life cannot be stripped down to their passing thoughts of you. They don't have all the facts and feelings earned by living in your shoes each and every day.

When someone's uninvited opinion arrives, let them feel heard, smile, and stay true to what's right for you.

Check in with you. Mental you. Emotional you. Physical you.
Notice what feels right for you.

If you want to take care of you, you have to take care of *all* of you. Your health is multifaceted, and you'll start to feel the lack if you don't treat it as such.

When it comes to your health, your intuition deserves more credit than you might think. You may not be able to tell the whole story on your own, and that's okay. (We have experts for that. Use them!) But when you're tuned in enough to acknowledge what you feel and know what you need on a regular basis, you're doing the work to truly take care of yourself.

Are you feeling tired but emotionally content? Do you have a lot of energy and consequently a great deal of focus?

Everything is connected. While it's impossible to stay in an ideal state of mind, body, and soul at all times, you can make strides by addressing the little things every day.

Give yourself a quick evaluation:

- How am I feeling mentally? What kinds of thoughts am I entertaining today?
- How am I feeling emotionally? Is a feeling lingering that I still have yet to properly address or process?
- How am I feeling physically? What do I specifically need to carry myself through this day?

Make a habit of acting on the answers you receive. After all, you *are* hearing them from the most important person in your life. You.

june

23

*Know the place where you feel the most in your element
and visit it often.*

Flow.

When was the last time you felt it?

It's that treasured state of being where your mind is simultaneously unaware of anything around you and unbelievably tuned in to whatever you're doing. You feel *present.* You feel *mindful.* You feel *activated.* It's the ideal state of consciousness.

We get so wrapped up in our daily demands that we forget to let our higher selves live in this space. Then, when it's been long enough, we forget where to find flow state or what it even feels like at all.

Remind yourself of the source of your greatness by sending yourself there. Reap the benefits of feeling *exactly* where you're supposed to be, doing *exactly* what you're supposed to do.

While it's impossible to remain in this state forever, every minute you spend there is the epitome of living your best life. Deliberately devote time to this state by making it happen like it's your top priority.

june

Visualize an incredible life so often that it feels more like a memory than a dream.

No one—not even you—will be able to predict the incredible heights of the life you'll live.

We look around, straining to see something real and inspiring around us. We look outside ourselves to wrap our minds around our potential, but we should be doing the opposite.

Life is abundant, but our surroundings often reflect more limitations than possibilities. If you want to know what you're truly capable of, you have to *decide* to be open to anything. Once you've agreed to this, there's nothing holding you back.

Connect your imagination to your beliefs. Let them work together to bring a new reality to your life. Make statements about your life that are already exactly as you want.

"I make more money than I know what to do with."

"I have the deepest friendships with people who love me for me."

"I have full-time freedom to pursue anything each day I get to live."

Wealth begins with an abundance mindset. Amazing relationships begin with an abundance mindset. Pursuing your destiny begins with an abundance mindset.

Visualize a specific number in your bank account. See yourself checking the balance and feeling the relief. Visualize laughter over an amazing dinner spread with the people that make you feel the most like yourself. Visualize waking up every day with a smile on your face and excitement for what you're ready to go out and do.

If you want it, see it. Envision it. Become it.

june

25

When you "should" all over yourself, you stay stuck.

At its core, "should" is nothing more than a code word. It appears the moment you recognize an external expectation that you're not genuinely driven toward. The word "should" implies some level of desire, but it doesn't originate from any real internal motivation.

Do you remember the last time you said you should do something? "I should start waking up early." "I should get my annual checkup." "I should be better at answering my texts."

Should you really? If you sincerely felt that thing was something worth doing, wouldn't you be *doing* it already? You would've taken action before the word "should" ever left your mouth.

What if we felt empowered to talk about what *we* have decided for ourselves rather than what *others* have decided for us? The former could be the single most powerful mindset move to change your life, while the latter leads to unstoppable feelings of not-enoughness.

There must be alignment between what you "should" do and what you intend to do.

The big picture comes together with the lens you look through.

Picture the ocean. You're standing on the beach, looking out at the vastness of the water. Captivated. If you could, you you'd take it all in, but there's no way to capture its immensity all at once.

Its size is unimaginable. Its mystery, even more so. How can you possibly embrace the whole thing at once? Simply the experience of dipping your toe in and feeling every wave could be all you need to navigate your way through.

Imagine what it would feel like to stand in the water and ride every wave. As you wade further out, you let yourself notice each new crash of water, smell the salt, and feel the full extent of the experience. Instead of trying to know all of it, you embrace it one wave at a time. You take on what you can when you can. And hopefully, you enjoy the process.

What do you want most at this moment? Say it out loud. Acknowledge it. Resist the urge to cling to it and instead experience it as it comes to you, one step at a time.

june

If you want a relationship to pick up where it left off, pick it up.

Life happens. We grow up. Circumstances change. Relationships drift away. We move on. We change.

Maybe nothing bad happened necessarily, but the thought of picking up the phone to call that old friend seems too ridiculous to even dial a single number. You worry the call will be filled with guilt or awkwardness rather than excitement.

Great relationships are amazing. Though you may not always see them, they're always there.

Flex your reconnection muscle and open up your long list of text messages. You'll notice your closest friends and family at the top, where you're used to chatting with them daily. For today, scroll to the very bottom. All the way back to your oldest text messages that technology has been saving just for this moment.

Pick a name that makes you the most curious. Maybe a name that sparks happy memories. Or maybe one that stirs up unfinished business you'd like to smooth over. Let go of why you lost touch and fire off the few keystrokes it takes to say a long overdue hello.

You might include something funny that happened recently that reminded you of them or simply mention that you were thinking of them. Whatever you need to say to wrap your mind around reaching out.

No matter how your message is received, you've proven to yourself that it's possible to let people know you care about them, even when it's not easy. You showed yourself you're not afraid to fail if their reception isn't all sunshine and rainbows.

Whose energy could you welcome back into your life?

june

28

It's time to rise. Will you?

We've all been there. We've had to drag ourselves out of a very comfortable slumber to face a less-than-exhilarating day. We've pulled ourselves up, gotten ready, and taken on a day that leaves us wanting more. We find ourselves doing this on repeat, exhausted, but still pushing ourselves forward in the hopes that the next day will bring enthusiasm.

We all want to have something to blame when we sleep through making our dreams a reality. But those annoying alarm chimes will neither be the reason you leap out of bed nor the reason you oversleep.

This doesn't have to be your story. You deserve a day worth jumping out of bed for.

What have you committed to doing that you'd cancel if you could? What would be the most exciting way to spend your day every day? What have you been saying yes to that's stolen time from a heck yes?

Be honest with how your days have escaped you. When you unpack these answers, you may rediscover the power you need to make a necessary change.

june

29

Things are only as good or as bad as you decide.

We see what we seek.

This means our minds have a great deal of power over any given situation.

When you fear your partner's response to a challenging conversation or look at the cars on the road as barriers to being on time—your default perception is negative.

You're stuck on what will go wrong, and therefore, that's the energy you attract. What will unfold before you is very likely to resemble exactly what your mind proposed. Why shouldn't it? You're already looking for evidence that supports that outcome.

Do you wish things were turning out better than they've been lately? It may feel impossible to just *decide* to look for the good, but start small. What if you didn't bring preconceived notions with you into every new scenario? What if you chose an open mind instead of a skeptical one?

Deciding whether something is good or bad is a judgment. Let the situation show you what it is before you label it.

The less you attach unnecessary meaning to the day-to-day in your life, the less of a rollercoaster you'll find yourself on.

june

30

Don't just read success stories. Create them.

You know you've read a good memoir when you're totally enraptured with the narrator's story. After you put the book down, you feel compelled to continue the journey. You want to learn from their mistakes and leverage their advice in your own life.

Who doesn't love a success story? We all enjoy rooting for a positive outcome. Cheering on a journey is inspiring in itself. And it sparks a kind of quick-fix motivation that can jumpstart a vision we may have for our own lives.

There's one catch. Be careful with your newfound knowledge. Before you start down the road of comparison, tell yourself the only thing you need to know to move forward:

"I've just seen what is possible. I can emulate this result."

Take what you've discovered and begin writing your own game-changing tale. Your process won't look the same as what you've seen before, but if you stay flexible in your approach, you've opened yourself up to a story worth telling someday.

Imitation may be the highest form of flattery, but at some point, the allure fades. Get inspired by their story, but always remember the irreplicable power of your own.

july

july

1

Greatness comes from the audacity to be focused.

Have you ever been described as a "jack of all trades"? At first, being seen as someone who can truly do it all feels like the highest compliment. A badge of honor. The ultimate people-pleasing achievement.

But, when we slow down to understand the label, is it really that much of a compliment? Do you really *want* to satisfy everything for everyone...*all* of the time? Is it actually a powerful pursuit, or is it more of a burden that you can't seem to let go of?

When we set out to do it all, we sacrifice depth in favor of breadth. While it may be possible to do many things, it's impossible to do them all well. What if, instead, you were thoroughly excellent at *one* thing? The best in your industry. The go-to person. The thought leader.

If you're feeling scattered, identify the one thing you'd gladly dedicate all your focus to and ditch the rest. Once you've named it aloud, go all in. Invest your time. Focus your energy.

Be a master of one instead of a master of none.

Find what moves you.

The best thing you can do for your body is to give it the gift of movement. The *second* best thing you can do is acknowledge that your ideal formula for movement won't look like everyone else's.

There's no one-size-fits-all answer. You'll always be able to find people boasting about the latest and greatest workout regimen. You'll catch yourself comparing and asking if you're doing enough, but simply because the new trendy workout routine doesn't connect for you doesn't mean you should throw in the towel.

Maybe it's never been your thing, or maybe you just haven't found your outlet. Opt out of the pressure by acknowledging this: Movement doesn't have to mean fitness or exercise. Movement, at its core, is what elevates your energy.

Find what simultaneously brings you joy *and* energizes you. When you do, it'll feel less like a chore and more like a gift. It's not about being the best; it's about taking care of yourself at your best.

july

3

Make deliberate decisions so you can stand by them
without standing trial.

What you've done (and even what you haven't) will always be an argument someone can use against you. If you anticipate that before it catches you off guard, you can refrain from taking things personally.

There's no reason to react negatively to others' opinions about your decisions. Instead of entertaining self-doubt, stand strong and allow the spectators to take ownership of their own reactions. That's on them, not you.

If you're doing the best you can with what you have, you're already in the clear. You're making the right call for you—and that's all that matters.

When we live like we're always being put to the test, we put ourselves on the defense. However, the offensive approach leads us on a more proactive journey.

At the end of the day, how someone perceives you doesn't really matter. What matters most is if you can stand behind your actions. If you confidently trust that you did what was right for you, there's no reason to wait for a jury's verdict.

When it comes to your life and your choices, you've *already* earned the last word.

The pursuit of your freedom is about more than independence. It's about the confidence to contest the status quo and be truly, unapologetically you.

There's so much to learn about life.

While much of what we're taught comes with great intentions, we have to be careful with what we absorb. Some lessons trick us into believing we're expanding our minds when we're actually learning new ways of limiting ourselves.

Our teachers don't know the perimeters they've placed on us. They're simply doing their best to share their experiences so we can grow from their knowledge.

The most powerful lesson of all is rarely taught, though it'd pair perfectly with the rest: The answers we know now are *only* the beginning. We can't know for sure that what's right always will be so (and the same goes for what's wrong).

We crave direction, so we're quick to accept all information that comes our way. We use it to get more comfortable but then refrain from stepping out of the box to discover something new. We unknowingly submit ourselves to being *stuck*. This is the way things are, and so we must only do what works within these confines.

How can you ever be fully expressed without exploring beyond what the rules say? If you seek freedom from that box, you can't wait for the confidence you need to break out of it. You must claim it now and agree to take on the consequences of your journey.

Go after your freedom. Create your confidence. Do it by not accepting the status quo as fact.

july

5

Believe in the moves you make for yourself.

Billy Idol sang it best in "Dancing With Myself."...We really are all out here just dancing with ourselves.

We may not wish that to be the case because everything appears to be better when you have a partner to share it with, but you have to own your moves before you can create more of them with someone else. Until you strengthen your own self-belief, you'll always be following someone else's lead.

The moves you make *matter*. The actions you choose *matter*. How much you believe in yourself *matters*. You must stay true to your intuition so you can consistently move forward. In turn, you'll attract the right people to join you along the way.

What would tomorrow look like if you confidently stepped into each decision with courage? What might you discover about yourself?

Cue the music.

july

The feeling of judgment always comes from within.

It's enough to make your heart race—the moment you hear petty words from another person or a conversation doesn't go quite as you expected. You wish you could turn back time immediately and avoid their looming judgment.

At first, you're of sound mind. Then, that familiar instinct bubbles up, and you feel the need to defend yourself. The stress of someone not seeing eye-to-eye with you is so upsetting you might even end the conversation in conflict. All because you opened up.

Are you truly owning your decisions if you can't help but explain yourself to anyone who questions you? Part of being your own person—and the beauty of free will—is that we all have the right to our own opinions.

That doesn't mean our opinions carry more weight over someone else than their own. It goes both ways. What someone says *about* you or *to* you doesn't automatically become the end all be all. How you decide to feel about it does.

Whenever you feel judged, pause before you react. Turn your attention away from the outside source that triggered you and observe the feeling coming from inside. Why are you letting their words hold power over you? Is the judgment truly coming from them, or have you created it with a combination of their words and your own negative thoughts?

When you uncover how you habitually let judgment provoke you, you learn how to live with the disappointment of others. In turn, you can carry on creating a life of your own design.

*How you begin your day is an opportunity to show yourself
what you're willing to do when no one is watching.*

There's a common misconception that the morning routine is some sort of secret weapon. It seems like every massively successful person has cracked the code and that to achieve anything in life, you must follow their lead to the letter.

This is only partially true.

The magic of the morning is in how you demonstrate to the #1 person in your life—*you*—that you're looking out for their best interest. The rest of the day will bring plenty of external expectations and unsolicited opinions. The sooner you remind yourself that you're focused on what's important to you *before* anything else, the sooner you start demonstrating real progress.

What's important to you? What's something small you can do about it right now? What incremental step taken *every single day* could create incredible leverage that gets you ahead?

This is why we love the idea of habits and self-development. We see that they could give us an extraordinary life, so we immerse ourselves with the information to make it happen.

Yet the needle doesn't move until we do. When you execute, you prove to yourself that you're in it to win it. You demonstrate that you'll go out and collect that confidence instead of waiting for it to show up at the perfect time.

This morning, tell yourself that you not only believe in what's possible but that you'll get started on it right away. Set the tone and follow through.

july

8

To start each day on your terms, close each day with that same intention.

It's no secret that the start of your day today actually began last night. There's never just one beginning or endpoint to living out an intentional day.

Your pursuit of a good life is only as good as your ability to be all in, morning and night. Each good morning can inspire *you*, but you must first inspire *it*.

At the end of each day, make space for what you truly need to ensure tomorrow has the best chance of being everything you want it to be. If you need a little extra rest for a prosperous day, take it at your soonest opportunity. The way you wind down, the time you take to reflect, and the amount of sleep you get might seem like silly chores until you feel their exponential impact the following morning.

Take small steps of intention that give you real power, and you'll experience what it feels like to truly thrive.

july
9

You will see your intentions materialize when your beliefs match.

You can have a life filled with happiness and wealth.

This is true whether you were born into money or not. You deserve it, whether you feel like you know what you're doing or not. You are capable, whether you grew up surrounded by abundant thinking or not.

When it comes to money, we all have limiting beliefs. They're a result of our childhoods, our workplace experiences, and our reactions to current events beyond our control. These beliefs become a big part of us. Ultimately, they determine what leaps we take and what risks we avoid.

They're called *limiting* for a reason. Consciously or not, they hold us back.

You're worthy of living without limitations. You're worthy of the happiness you seek. It's not a bad thing to want to have enough. It's not a bad thing to want *more* than enough, either. It's not the sign of selfishness that everyone likes to preach. You should have the freedom that comes with financial security. You shouldn't have to stress about the number in your bank account every day.

There's nothing you need to prove and no hoop you have to jump through. All you need to do is allow yourself to have beliefs that match up with those intentions.

When you uncover your limits, you make space for your intentions to take the lead.

july
10

Discipline is the mystery behind every superpower.

Self-control. Good habits. Grit. Discipline.

These are the attributes we wish for (admittedly, to the point of jealousy at times). They're the traits we tell ourselves would solve all our problems *if only we had them.*

But what if these weren't what you needed to achieve your goals? What if you could get where you wanted without them?

High performers are often mistaken for magical beings who have it all figured out. If they want a fit body, they make it happen. If they want more money in the bank, they go out and get it. If they want to create their empire, then—BOOM—there it is. They seem to know exactly how to ignore distractions so they can get their results the fastest.

Newsflash! Their "effortless" results occur for a multitude of reasons, and magic isn't one of them.

If you come across someone who created something amazing in their life, listen to their story. Observe it. These people aren't immune to challenges and distractions. They simply anticipate their weaknesses and combat them early.

Instead of comparing, share in their commitment to self-observe, adapt, and create a path fueled by discipline.

Your value to others begins with genuine curiosity.

What you do matters just as much as *who* you do it for.

Value starts within. It starts with a sense of direction and a core purpose.

We all want to put our best foot forward. We want to do more, be more, and act more often. But, before you act, you must first understand what you're going after.

Create an amazing life by looking around to see what's happening outside of yourself. Acknowledge the worlds of those around you. It's as simple as recognizing the needs that already exist in the community and the faces you see every day.

Express genuine interest in what someone's going through and take the opportunity to help *before* they have the chance to ask for it. The habit of offering small, thoughtful gestures builds a strong sense of service over time.

The good fortune that comes to you happens when you offer service to others.

july
12

There's nothing holding you back from who you choose to be.

When you imagine a day in your ideal life, you probably see a lot of things. Things you don't have yet. Things you haven't done yet. Things that seem impossible.

If only they were true and you had the opportunity to do all those things now. Then you'd be the person you've always dreamed of, living the life you've always wanted.

If only.

But you've got it backwards (at no fault of your own). Society leads us to believe that superficial achievements must come first, though nothing could be further from the truth.

The path isn't Have → Do → Be. If that were the case, you'd forever be waiting for external circumstances to grant you permission to live a life of your own design.

Follow this path instead: Be → Do → Have.

Be someone who lives like the person in your imagination—the person who's already immersed in that mindset and lifestyle. Be in gratitude for all the wonderful things that you have now. Then, and only then, set out to achieve the things you don't *yet* have.

When you stop blaming the lack in your life and become a person who doesn't observe that lack at all, you welcome all possibilities.

Today and every day, don't worry about doing or having. Just be.

Something better is on its way to you right now.

Good things are coming. Always. Whether you believe it or not. However, if you do believe it, that truth will grow. Faster. Bigger. Stronger.

Our world encourages us to forget this, so we'll constantly pay attention to whatever unfortunate situation plops in front of us. The dramatic. The challenging. The awful. You're tricked into thinking you must be in the know about *all* the negativity so you can look out for yourself.

It *is* important to look out for yourself. Look out for the things so grand and beautiful that you'll be filled with an excess of gratitude and self-awareness—so much so that they cushion the blow when less-than-ideal situations come your way.

Change your approach to a mindset of inevitable abundance. Know for sure that what's to come will be exactly what you want or something even better. Something better is always on its way to you.

Uncertainty is persistent, so reassess how you view the unknown. Believing in the good that's coming is far more exciting than holding your breath and waiting for the other shoe to drop.

So, decide to breathe and believe. It's far more enjoyable.

You can be the person who is too busy for what's important, or you can be too busy doing what's important to realize how busy you are.

You say it. They say it. Everyone says it. A curious acquaintance asks the classic question: "So, how are you?" Without hesitation, we respond. "Oh, you know... busy busy!"

What else is there to say?

Our task lists loom. Calendar appointments consume. House chores rear their ugly heads. We continue to lean on the word "busy" as the only possible way to summarize all we have going on.

But the more you explain how busy you are—both to yourself and to others—the more ordinary tasks will keep you from the important work you *could* be doing. Every time we settle for busyness, we settle for less.

When you catch yourself about to proclaim how busy you are, ask yourself what you're avoiding. Are you avoiding the critical steps toward a more intentional, better life? Are you avoiding making real progress by instead checking endless boxes? Are you avoiding a more honest conversation about what's really on your mind?

Quit being "busy." See it as the copout that it is. When you do, it'll be much easier to assess what needs to stay on your plate and what can wait. Take the necessary steps toward a life you want, and enjoy the process too much to realize how busy you are going after it.

july

15

When in doubt, ask for help.

Not knowing is never a sign of weakness. Quite the opposite, really—it's a sign of intelligence.

When you know what you *don't* know, you can determine what you're going to do about it. No matter the subject, all you have to do next is find someone who has the experience to offer. You get to learn from others, skip their mistakes, and find a more efficient route to where you want to be.

Let go of the assumption that you need to be a financial expert in order to build wealth. No one ever said you had to have a degree in finance to make a living. All you need is a willingness to know and grow. Luckily, you've already got both, so no biggie if you aren't the money master just yet.

We're all just trying our best to wrap our minds around income, investments, expenses, and everything else that comes with them. The smartest people with money don't pretend to know it all. Instead, they seek out the help they need to better themselves.

When the moment strikes where you aren't following along with the conversation, say those magic words: "I don't know". Use them as an opportunity to ask someone to elaborate on what might be a critical piece of missing information for you.

When it comes to your money, it doesn't pay to play pretend.

july

16

Only you will know the difference between refueling and procrastinating. Know your intention and take the break you need.

The line between a healthy pause and *unhealthy* procrastination is blurry, especially in this day and age where we see everyone around us hustling nonstop.

We all need to take a pause. Some find the power of the pause in short moments that pop up throughout the day, while others notice they need longer stretches to reset fully.

Before you give yourself a hard time for the breaks you know you need, remember that every time you pause, you protect yourself against what could instead be a much bigger spell of burnout.

In times like that, you really *do* need to take a break and fuel up. Other times, you're ignoring the task in front of you in favor of another shiny task. The only way to know what you're doing is to be in touch with your own intention.

Only you'll know if you're on a social media scroll because it's more interesting than your to-do list or if you've decided it's your treat for a job well done. Only you'll know how many hours of sleep will equip you to be the best version of yourself tomorrow (or if those extra hours were truly unnecessary).

Be honest with yourself.

Gently call yourself out when you need it, the same way you'd kindly hold a friend accountable. Rest when you need. Get back to life when it's time to. The judgment call is completely up to you.

July
17

You may not be able to control change, but that doesn't mean change gets to control you.

The secret to success is *clarity*.

Clarity over what you can and can't control. Clarity over what's on your mind and what's controlling your mind. No matter what situation you find yourself in, you retain the ability to respond thoughtfully.

Change is the one constant in life. Yes, it might still surprise you in how it shows up, but if you acknowledge that it's life's single guarantee, you can move on much more easily. Temper your emotions. Monitor your reactions. Become clear instead of living in fear.

How will you greet the change that comes your way?

The more you practice the noble pursuit of controlling only what you can control, the better prepared you'll be to face the uncontrollable. When unwelcome change does come your way, you'll be able to respond calmly rather than react out of frustration.

Control what you can. Forget the rest. Repeat.

july

18

There's no such thing as experience without commitment.

How do you usually evaluate someone else's credibility?

Is it how many times they failed and tried again? Is it the sacrifices they made to build their success? Is it the passion they have for their work?

Typically…it's none of the above. We (unfortunately) tend to look more at the credentials on someone's resume and the titles they've held rather than the person they are.

Success is more than experience. We get hung up on our track record because we've been told our entire lives to focus on getting to the next thing. It's a go, go, go trajectory that leaves little room for contemplation.

The constant work you've poured into your career holds value. Every sacrifice you've made, the hours of dedication, the pivots and turns—they all count for something. But, at the same time, you are more than the bullets outlined on your resume.

You tell yourself that you can or can't do something based on metrics that only measure a single facet of success. No resume can ever accurately convey the most important driving force: your *commitment*.

What would happen if you let commitment be your focus?

Apply for that job. Put yourself up for the promotion. Challenge yourself to see your potential beyond what the words on the page tell you. You're more than benchmarks and milestones. Find freedom by loosening your grip on them.

If you want to prove you're listening, then simply listen.

You're having a conversation with someone you love, so of course, you want to show them how much you care. You chime in with the occasional "yeah" and "uh-huh" every now and then and even pipe in a similar story to show that you're following.

But you're so concerned about ensuring they see you paying attention that you forget to just listen.

Suddenly, when you think you're shining like a star in this conversation and ask one more question for clarity, they respond: "Can you just let me finish?" Ouch.

"I am listening!" you think to yourself as your frustration grows. Your intention is there, but it's not quite landing.

We put so much pressure on ourselves to let the ones we love know we're hearing all they want to share that we end up doing the opposite. We can't shut up with our own thoughts, and we end up missing the assignment completely.

But you're only human, and your heart is in the right place. The last thing you want someone to feel is that you're not acknowledging them, but unfortunately, that's all they can hear from your moving lips.

The next time you want to prove to someone that you can listen, do that and *only* that. Put your phone away. Stop multitasking. Look them in the eye and receive their message without offering commentary, comparison, or questions.

Your time to share will be invited before you know it.

The motivation that fails you is that which is out of reach.
The motivation that fuels you is in your possession already.

Are you ambitious? Yes.

Are you inspired? Absolutely.

Does that mean you'll be motivated all the time? *Of course not.*

It's 100% normal not to feel the drive you'd like to every second of the day. It doesn't make you any less worthy of having your dreams come true. In fact, you're in great company.

What you make happen *in spite* of not feeling motivated is what differentiates you from the rest of the pack. The achievers of the world are familiar with the consistent ebb and flow of inspiration. It's nice when it's around, but those flighty feelings are too unreliable to wait for. Instead, they stay clear on the one thing they need to push through no matter what: their why.

Why are you on this path? Why is it going to benefit you in the end? Why is it beneficial to you now? Why are you showing up every day to do the things that most people wouldn't do every day?

You can Google the best motivational videos. You can read an incredibly motivational book. You can listen to wonderful motivational speakers. But, just like the caffeine in a cup of coffee, it eventually wears off.

Call upon your own instincts, desires, and, yes, *motivations* to remind you every morning why you'll do the hard things even when you don't feel like it.

The feeling of motivation you're craving doesn't come when you're at a standstill— it comes when you take the initiative to make a move.

july

21

Celebrate. Every. Single. Win.

Remember being a kid and feeling that rush of excitement when you found a penny on the sidewalk? A little unexpected triumph, just waiting for you to claim it. You thought, "It must be my lucky day!"

Back then, our lives were measured in smaller victories. The wins were simpler, and the losses were far less devastating. Fast forward to the present, and you're all grown up! With time, you now have the greatest triumph of all: knowledge. You know that the size of the win doesn't matter. You understand that every win counts.

When you acknowledge every bit of goodness that comes your way, you invite more goodness to join the party. A penny here, a forgotten $20 bill in your pocket there. They'll always add up. The wins, when received openly and graciously, turn into wealth.

This isn't just the kind of wealth that comes from an overflowing bank account, but the kind that creates an abundance mindset. It's the kind that comes with the feeling of *having* enough.

The little wins. The big wins. They're all trying to tell you that the Universe has your back, and there will always be enough for you…if you're ready and willing to accept *all* of it.

The amount is never really the focus—your attitude is. Be a person living from an abundance mindset. Own that it's never about the size of the win. It's about the perspective you receive it with.

july
22

Those who consume themselves with what they'll say they'll do aren't focused on what they know they can do.

They say actions speak louder than words for a reason.

Wayne Dyer shares the power of announcing your intentions in his book *Manifest Your Destiny*:

> The moment a thought is presented to another it is weakened. Maintain privacy concerning your own unique, possibly mysterious to others, powers to attract to you what you desire.

It seems counterintuitive to keep what you want to manifest to yourself, but it's also a reminder that it all starts with you. Whatever you tell the Universe you want to see more of in your life must radiate authentically from within you. You need to believe so deeply that the actions you take every day will lead you closer to the reality you want.

Stop nourishing your ego with exterior validation. It's fleeting and momentary. It won't drive you forward or encourage your higher self. Take back the power you give their words. Your focal point needs to be the conditions you set, not their judgment.

What you intend to do and what you *actually* do are very different things. The former is a story that may not come true. The latter is a demonstration of the focus you keep in your mind.

You've been given the grace of self-awareness. Use it.

At this stage of the game, you know yourself pretty well (maybe even to the point where you can predict how you'll react in a given situation). You might have even been caught saying: "That's just how I am."

It's beautiful to discover new things about yourself—especially when you feel compelled to accept yourself as you are. But are you truly using this self-awareness to the greatest of your abilities?

We've all heard the cliché that history repeats itself. This is true in so many ways, most certainly regarding your personal experiences. Have you noticed any events that pop up and knock you off your mark? Moments that rattle you out of your focus for fulfilling your life's vision? Yes, you could say, "That's just how I am when these things happen." Or, you could try something new with this knowledge.

Remember the continued frustrations that arise at work, recurring tensions in friendships, or patterns in your relationships. With similar scenarios, it's important to look at the common denominator. Even when that focus is on you.

Go deeper with the traits you learn about yourself. The real transformation happens when you decide that you deserve better—and, therefore, must do some self-improvement.

It's up to you whether you keep reading the same history book over and over again or if you write a new one.

july

24

*Take care of your skin, and you'll start
entering a room like you already own it.*

When we're getting ready to be in the spotlight, we spend so much time on mental preparation that we can easily forget the rest.

We've been given this one body to live our full human experience, so it's vital we have our body's back. Like any relationship, it'll show up for us the best when we nurture it.

Your presence is directly tied to how you take care of yourself. When you show your body and mind the love they need, it becomes obvious to everyone else. It shows in how you speak, how you move, and how you make yourself heard. There's an unshakeable confidence that comes from being comfortable in your own skin.

The little things we do every day to take care of our bodies add up to the contribution we need for our mind and our soul. Make a point today to do those little things that'll add up tomorrow. Grab a few more winks by getting into bed early. Invest in a great moisturizer tailored specifically for your skin type. Schedule (and actually attend) your workout. Whatever these steps look like for you, embrace them.

Ask your body what it needs today, then respond accordingly.

july

25

"Someday" is not a day of the week.

Today is the day.

Today is your moment.

Today is all you have.

Someday will never be today. Not if you don't make it so. When you say "someday," you're saying something you know in your heart may never come true. When you say "someday," you shift the responsibility of possibility entirely onto the Universe—thus ignoring your role in this story. If you want to deliver marching orders to the Universe, you must remember to lead the charge with a display of actions in the right direction.

Never leave your greatest potential to someday. Find it in yourself today.

It's either a "Hell yes!" or a "No." Everything else is just pretending.

On the many occasions we've been asked to do something or be somewhere undesirable, we've learned to deflect in the form of a wide range of filler words.

"Ummmmm..."
"I'm not sure..."
"Maybe..."

We don't say these words because we don't know the right answer. We say them because we know exactly what the answer is, but we want to appear nice and avoid saying it. At least for now.

Here comes your friend, boss, significant other, parent, or anyone else with their request. Rather than responding with what's on your mind, you hear the words come out of your mouth: "I don't know. I guess I could?"

You have *strong* gut instincts. Past negative experiences may have fooled you into doubting them, but you already know what's best for you when you pay close attention.

What if, instead of beating around the bush, you led with your gut and delivered a strong, intentional no? The no that you wish you'd said instead of offering a halfhearted commitment?

Why is it a no? Well, that's simple. We wouldn't be having this conversation if it were a hell yes.

You are more than enough. You have more than enough.
You do more than enough. You will always be more than enough.

Why is it that as we grow up we're taught that there isn't enough to go around?

Too often, we hear about how hard life will be instead of about the abundance of possibilities.

If we believe that we only need to make *just* enough money or have *just* enough in our savings, then that'll be all we ever amount to. Take the preconceived notions and stories that don't serve you and let them go. We're not here to live a restricted life.

We can only avoid the baggage of worry in the pursuit of greatness with an expanded mind and desire for more. Put simply: You need a plentiful mindset to proceed. So, how do we shift?

If you want to build a life of incredible bounty, you have no other choice than to let *more than enough* be your aura.

Start by believing you're already more than enough. Who you are right here and now is exactly who you need to be. When you internalize that belief, you can strive to achieve more than enough in every area of your life.

july
28

*Instead of reaching for someone else's expectations,
blow your own expectations away.*

Outside expectations loom over every move we make. We first learn them from our parents or guardians. Then teachers, friends, acquaintances, and pretty much everyone else we meet let us know what they expect of us.

In the beginning, expectations can feel like a safety net. We may not necessarily *like* them, but we appreciate them to some extent. They act as a kind of grounding reminder that others care. The question becomes: When does that safety net start to hold us back?

If we don't start to question the expectations that dictate our steps, we never really move on from being the kid looking for approval. Not every decision we make can come with instructions or feedback. There comes a point when we must venture beyond external acceptance and recognize the importance of our *own* expectations.

If finding the right answer for you is a challenge, it might be because you're basing your decision on what everyone else will think. Others' opinions aren't controllable. Try as you might, they can never be known for sure (and therefore shouldn't be given too much weight).

Instead of being consumed by what the rest of the world will think, live up to your own incredible standards and blow every expectation out of the water.

july
29

Discover what self-care means to you.

They say that beauty is in the eye of the beholder, meaning that what one person finds beautiful may not strike the same chord in another. The same rule applies to relaxation: What works for someone else may not resonate the same way for you.

One person might find their calm enjoying some time at the spa, while another finds it on a jog through the park. You may only be able to relax after immersing yourself in a good book, while your partner can only settle in a bubble bath. How you do it doesn't matter. What matters is how *often* you find yourself there.

So, what gets you to that state? Where do you need to be to find your peace? Your calm doesn't need to make sense to anyone else—it only needs to restore *you*.

Let go of everything that doesn't check your box of tranquility. Let go of the criticism that prevents you from resting. You're not really relaxing if you feel guilty, so you must...let...it....go.

Find your slowdown and make the time to go there. Then, when you're in that moment, be fully present.

july

Those who live fully expressed rise, while those who worry about how they'll be perceived shrink.

Have you ever avoided an opportunity because of how it might look to those around you? How about avoiding saying something that felt unsaid but might not make for easy conversation?

We want to show love for those we care about, but it can be tiring to constantly worry about how you'll come off. We're so consumed with how we appear to people that we forget we should be focused on how we're supporting our true selves.

When we think about taking a chance on a new career, moving to a new city, changing our diet, or trying a new workout, we first entertain what friends and family will think instead of honoring what we want.

There will be moments when people think you're weird. There will be times when your family tells you they don't approve of the moves you're making. Someone may make a comment or poke fun, which is much more comfortable for *them* because they feel awkward not understanding you at that moment.

Every decision you make can affect others. However, it's your ego that's making you think that everything you do will put you on shaky ground.

You are alive. You are breathing. You are okay. You are loved. You are living a life that only you get to live—and only you can take that away from you.

Show me your calendar, and I'll show you your priorities.

The old saying goes, "When you fail to plan, you plan to fail." Nothing could be more true, especially regarding the time you've been gifted.

Time is elusive. It tricks you into believing there'll always be more, despite the fact that you know that's not true.

So, what do you do? What does it really look like to respect your own time?

Use. It. Up.

Every moment you're given is a space you control. You may think that's not the case because of your growing list of arbitrary tasks, expectations, and obligations. But these are simply external occurrences that make it easy to relinquish your duty to the time you've been granted.

You say you don't have time, but you do. It's just already been given away by you to something else. For every moment you're not dedicating your focus to your greatest ambitions, you must ask yourself: "What else could be so important?"

Those who are diligent about knowing where they spend their time are the ones executing a plan for life. Those who have no plan for tomorrow are letting life slip through their fingers.

Either way, it's your decision to make.

august

august 1

You already have everything you need to achieve your dreams.

When we set out to create a life of our own design, many of us defer to a formula: go to school, find the right internship, connect with the ideal mentor, build a credible network, get the perfect promotion, and so on.

It's good to know what you want, and having clearly outlined goals is a brilliant place to start. However, that list will soon feel like an endless assignment rather than a motivational pursuit.

If your list looks daunting, remember this: Whatever the items are, they're *all* within your power to obtain. That said, the list itself will never reflect your whole story. Milestones matter, but they're a drop in the bucket compared to all you'll gain in between them. If you're doing it right, your list is a *means* to an end—not the end in and of itself. There's so much more to success than the credits under your name.

Create a list that reminds you of what you already have working for you:

- Your why
- Your skills and distinct talents
- Your instinct
- Your ability to lean in
- Your unique life experience
- Your resourcefulness
- Your genuine curiosity

This list contains the most valuable assets you could ever have in your corner as you go after the life you want. When the chips are down, the degree hanging on your wall isn't going to be your golden ticket—the grit, dedication, and passion you poured into receiving it, however, *will* be.

august

2

*If you want to build a life of abundance, avoid taking advice
from those who teach from a place of limitation.*

Voices surround us on a daily basis. Some encourage us to break the mold, while others try to convince us that their way is the only way. A few influence our lives for the better; others try to hold us back. Many will claim they have your best interest at heart, even if their words don't seem to match that statement.

While it's admirable for someone to feel compelled to protect you from failing or getting hurt, it's not always beneficial to you. Learn to recognize when *their* story is morphing into your own.

Someone might be projecting unrealized worries or regurgitated fiction that'll only derail you. When you're steps away from achieving the greatness they missed out on, you might start to wonder if they were right after all. When this happens, *keep going*! You're almost at a breakthrough.

Regulate the voices you give space to in your mind. Are they building you up and productively challenging you? If not, what do they bring to the table besides worry, fear, or doubt?

The voices bringing you down reflect more on the person speaking than they do on you. Accept people for who they are and the stories they have, but don't absorb what doesn't serve you. You may not always get a say in what gets said *to* you, but you do get the final say in what sticks.

Seek out thoughts and ideas that deeply support you. Welcome them in with open arms.

august

3

Starting the day on your terms is just the beginning.
Carry that power and pour it into the rest of your day.

Morning routines get a bad rep, thanks to the endless misconceptions and misguided advice in the world. Let's set the record straight about what it takes to have a morning that energizes you.

A good morning is *not* about:

- Waking up before the sun
- Following every trendy habit on social media
- Being a "morning person"

A good morning is *really* about:

- Asking yourself what *moves* you
- Identifying that big, soul-defining purpose that you know has been divinely assigned to you
- Getting out of bed to live your life by fulfilling that purpose

When you start the day on your terms, you demonstrate your power.

The more you practice it, the stronger you'll be. And guess what? That power will translate to *every other area* of your life. When you start the day by reminding yourself of your inalienable influence on the environment around you, you can't help but carry that energy with you through the rest of your day.

It's not about the time on the alarm clock. It's about having agency over your decisions. You have the ability to choose anything right now, so choose to live on your terms.

august

4

It's not what you do. It's why you do it.

What are you doing all of this for? No, really. Why are you getting out of bed every day?

This isn't a trick question. There's no right answer—there's only the answer that's right for *you*. That answer is the key to propelling you forward.

Before we really immerse ourselves in the answer, we consider what it'll sound like to others. Whether it's convincing enough. Whether it'll gain their approval. We look outside ourselves at what seems to work for others and try to adopt a similar path.

No matter how many people you attempt to map your life off of, eventually, you discover the truth: Even if you follow their lead to the letter, your results will never be the same. You simply can't copy and paste someone else's why onto your life.

The root of why we do what we do is perhaps even *more* important than the actions we take. Actions are immensely valuable—but only when you know why you're taking them. A why without a how can be easily remedied with a little research and support. A how without a why? That'll get you nowhere.

Knowing the truth of your intention is essential. If you don't do that inner work with yourself, no one else will.

august

5

Connect people to each other and then celebrate
their success as if it were your own.

Connections are everything.

Every connection we make is part of a much larger, more powerful network. We *need* each other. We *depend on* each other. We *go further* together.

When was the last time you openly celebrated someone else's success? When did you last introduce two people you knew would mesh well?

These are the moments that people remember you for, and they're the reason people will look to you as a generous facilitator of connection.

Be the one who cheers on everyone else. Be the one who takes the time to have a real, thoughtful conversation. Be the person who never shies away from a warm introduction.

So many of us operate our network with scarcity in the passenger seat. We end up hoarding all the good eggs to ourselves or fretting over whether we're giving a good opportunity away if we spread the wealth.

Think bigger than that. A victory you helped facilitate could be just as valuable as one that impacts you directly.

That's the beauty of real connection: Success for one is success for *all*.

To move forward, we must take care of our mindset first.

Health starts in your mind before it moves to your body.

Have you ever heard the phrase "it's all mental"? It comes up in the worst moments when the absolute *last* thing you want to hear is that your mindset is the reason you're in a certain situation. Major eye roll.

It's easy to get defensive when someone implies the problem is simply in your head. But that's not their intent.

Call to mind the things you think you can't do because you're out of shape or the emotions that make you feel like there isn't a way out. Maybe you haven't started a new workout routine because the domino of negative thoughts is debilitating. Maybe you avoid improving your daily habits because staying stuck feels safer than facing change.

Instead of giving in to the overwhelm, *lean into it*. Create clarity about your next steps by getting a better understanding of your present fears. We don't need to ignore our problems or pretend they don't exist—quite the opposite. We need to assess them for exactly what they are so we can recognize fact from fiction.

It won't be easy, but it *is* possible.

Once you get in your head that your mind is a vital ally to your health, the positive impact will influence your whole body.

august

Release your old stories to make space for new ones.

Humans are incredible storytellers. We can make meaning out of just about anything if given a chance:

"I messed up that interview so badly. It must be a sign this job isn't meant for me. I knew that would happen. I never was good at _____ anyway..."

"Nah, I can't train for the half-marathon with you. I couldn't even run the mile in middle school. Running has never been my thing."

"I can't help that I _____. It's just the way I've always been, ever since I was little."

What stories have you been holding onto for a long time? We all have them. Did you ever stop to consider where yours came from?

At a young age, we're desperate to feel secure. We cling to stories—good or bad—in the hopes of feeling like we belong. It works in the short term, but at some point, we outgrow them. Yet, out of habit, we keep holding them tightly. They give us a safe expectation to meet, a defined box to fit. Stories, labels, or limiting beliefs (whatever you want to call them) become our security blankets.

The tired ol' tales you're clinging to today are only still true if you let them be. If it feels scary to finally shed them, imagine what could fill their space! While they may have served their purpose for a while, they were never meant to place a ceiling on who you could become.

Release what doesn't fit and embrace what feels right. You can always change it again down the road.

august

8

To live an abundant life, stop telling yourself a story of scarcity.

There never seems to be enough.

By the time we pay the bills, put away a little savings, and use whatever's left to feel like we didn't do all this work for nothing, it's difficult to imagine there's more where that came from.

But we must.

The only way to actually attain more is to believe there *is* more out there for the taking. Beyond that, we must also deeply believe that we're deserving of the abundance we wish for.

A scarcity mindset is used to running out. You may not know what it's like to have enough and feel worthy of it. Therefore, you continue to operate at a level you're used to without realizing how you can influence the story.

What would it feel like to have more than enough? What would you do differently? How would things change?

Start charging what you know your work is worth. Start asking for what you know you deserve to receive. Start showing up as a person that already believes they've earned a spot at the table.

Yes, it's scary to assert yourself in this new way. But a beautiful thing happens when you do: The rest of the world *pays attention*. They learn to respond accordingly.

To live an abundant life, you need to believe you're worthy of it. Not just worthy of achieving abundance once, but keeping it long-term.

An abundance mindset plays for keeps.

august

9

The challenges on the road to success are plenty and inevitable.
Anticipate them and own the process.

Success is only yours if you take ownership of the path you took to get there.

Own all the late nights you put in to get your hustle off the ground. Own every ounce of effort you put in to get that vision in your head out into the world. Own every time you fell and got back up. Own all the small victories that got you to the finish line.

But…if we're talking about *real* ownership, we have to acknowledge *every* aspect of the journey.

Own that you chose to hit snooze for a week straight. Own that you procrastinated. Own that you chose to binge that show again instead of reading the book sitting on your nightstand.

This is far from self-deprecating—it's empowering. You'll find that owning up to your mistakes as confidently as you own up to your victories *adds* to your efficacy rather than diminishing it.

There's no such thing as a perfect streak when you're seeking success. Let the process be what it will be. Own all of it and keep going.

august

10

Make the good happen for you.

You are the co-creator of your life. You get to help attract the good things. You get to put yourself in a position to receive the goodness coming your way.

So, what are you waiting for? While you're sitting and waiting for something to happen to you, you could be working toward *making* it happen for you.

True goodness begins when you make the decision to start.

It begins when you make the conscious choice to stop waiting and wishing. You can hold out for hope, but decisive action will get you a lot further (and much faster).

What have you been putting off that you could really be working toward? Are you waiting around for the stars to align perfectly, or are you so convicted by this dream that nothing can get in your way?

It's time to put your movements where your mind is. Pair your ambitious desires with an even more ambitious response. You are capable of *great* things. You *will* make great things happen today.

Look for the evidence. What have you been able to make happen so far? What if you stepped it up a notch and lasered your focus? What could you accomplish then?

Do it again tomorrow, and the next day, and the next.

Do it for you. Every single day.

august

11

Drown out self-doubt with what you know for sure.
Stay focused on results instead of reactions.

We have an incredible ability to doubt ourselves. It's the ultimate *anti*-superpower.

Self-doubt is like that unwanted houseguest who overstays their welcome, going about their day as if they truly belong there. They snuck their way into your mind and made themselves at home.

You're so used to seeing them around that you don't know how to begin evicting them. Worst of all, they keep taking up more and more space and getting more and more comfortable. Soon, there won't be room for anything else.

It's time to kick self-doubt out. The only reason you don't believe you know what's right for you is that you haven't had time away from the bad influence you're used to.

What self-doubt doesn't want you to know is that it has successfully distracted you with the "how". "How will I do it? How will I know it's right?"

How you'll accomplish something isn't the most important thing. It'll come in time. Your questions will be answered when you take action, but none of that'll matter until you focus on the results.

What's the vision for this journey? Do you believe it's possible for a person to achieve such a feat? If so, why not you?

Put your focus on knowing that it's possible and envision that it's already yours.

august

12

Do it for you.

Approval.

We're all guilty of seeking it. No one's immune to the need for validation—no one.

Just because it's something you find yourself hoping for doesn't mean you're flawed or weak. It just means that you're human and—even better—self-aware.

As you seek to balance your need for everyone else's appreciation with your desire for inner confidence, this is a friendly reminder that external approval never lasts.

Does it feel great for a moment? Absolutely! Maybe even longer than a moment. But it still fades, and then what?

At some point, you have to decide: Are you living for that quick fix of fleeting validation? Or are you living for your own sense of worth? Are you spending your life waiting for someone else's positive reinforcement? Or will you allow yourself to recognize a win, even when you're the only one who sees it?

Recognize *all* the positive acknowledgments (both internal and external) when they come your way, but remember that lasting fulfillment comes from within.

august

Activation is the main indication of real inspiration.

We love to believe that motivation is necessary for movement.

When we don't have motivation, we beat ourselves up, thinking it's the ultimate secret ingredient to make things happen in your life. The truth is, in most cases, you may just be uninspired.

When you're inspired, you feel a higher connection. You're literally *in spirit* with who you truly are and who you want to be. It makes sense that feeling uninspired creates a gaping disconnect. You become detached from the creator in you that was put here to do something great.

How will you spark that connection again? It's quite simple: through action.

Of course, the chicken and egg dilemma will hold you back. "Shouldn't I be inspired so I can take action?" Many people make the mistake of waiting for inspiration to strike, and no action is ever taken.

You simply can't know if you're connected to your higher self until you take the actions necessary that make you *feel* that connection. The flow, excitement, motivation, and wonderful feelings that come from finding your inspiration are what keep the object in a *consistent* state of motion.

Find your inspiration by trying new things. Get inspired by giving your ideas a chance. Feel the spirit within you by exploring somewhere or something new.

How will you activate yourself today?

august

Today's preparation is rehearsal for what's on its way to you.

Our days can easily slip into monotony.

Wake up, brush teeth, work, come home, repeat. Over and over again.

The routine of it all can leave us feeling defeated. If you're stuck on autopilot, remember this: How you do *anything* is how you do *everything*.

Every moment is a rehearsal. Even if your daily tasks are far from where you'd like to be, it's never been about the task anyway. It's about the effort.

How you handle that tedious project at work is how you'll have grit in the hustle of entrepreneurship. How you show up with enthusiasm to the mundane is how you'll lead a team with a smile on your face when times are tough. How you care for your friends and family on a daily basis is how you'll greet strangers with empathy, even when it's hard to.

If you're in the messy middle right now—stay there. Settle in. This is the place where the real work gets done. When no one is watching, you're steadily moving toward the success you've always dreamed of. Before they know it, you'll have surpassed every expectation and be blowing everyone out of the water.

That wow factor only comes with the ability to do the work despite all the reasons not to. And there will *always* be reasons not to.

Your next big break and game-changing opportunity could be lurking around the corner, just waiting for you to stumble upon it.

august

15

If you don't like the feeling, change the thought.

We're quick to believe every thought that enters our minds. We have thousands of them each day—who has the time (or the energy) to question every last one? Most of them immediately become unchallenged facts, much to our detriment. Whether time allows it or not, being the gatekeeper of your mind is crucial.

We let our negative thoughts roam freely like toddlers discovering their ability to run around and break things. They're just doing their own destructive thing, unaware of the consequences. You can decide to ignore them, teach them something new, or let them become the new head of the household.

Have you tried questioning the thoughts that cross your mind rather than blindly adopting them as truth?

Write those negative thoughts down. Look at them individually. Ask questions as though you're putting them on trial for their credibility.

"Do I really believe this?"

"What evidence can back this up?"

"What would the opposite belief be?"

"How can I reframe this within what I know to be true?"

It takes practice to really see yourself for all that you have to offer. It takes practice to flex the muscle that changes the conversation. Similar to how you wouldn't stand for someone bashing your friend, don't let random thoughts tear you down.

At the end of the day, you get to say which thoughts rule and which ones get vetoed.

august

16

When you ask the right questions,
you become the most interesting person in the room.

Is there anything more disheartening than being stuck in a one-sided conversation?

Sure, you greeted each other and exchanged polite how are yous—but from then on, it's their monologue, and you're the audience. You walk away socially exhausted and uninspired.

On the flip side, how amazing did it make you feel the last time someone tossed you a genuine question about what's going on in your life?

Tell me about your new position! What's been the most rewarding part so far?"

"How's your daughter doing? Is she still interested in the arts?"

"You're engaged?! Congratulations! How did you and your fiancè meet?"

An open invitation to share something you care about is invigorating. Plus, it's an unbelievably easy gift to give someone else. When you're included in a conversation, take the initiative for a deeper dialogue.

Decide to ask the questions that you know will make a person feel seen and heard. Doing this does more than build relationships; it gives you a real look into who they are behind all the formalities and small talk.

Be the most interesting person in the room by asking the questions that make someone else light up.

august

Take the pressure off. Because you can.

You are so many things.

You're a creator, or a problem-solver, or a caretaker (or even all of them at once... plus *more*!). Yes, you're undeniably many things to many people—one of them being your own worst critic.

Whether you've acknowledged this before or not, it's really not all that helpful to hear. It's just a reminder that you're not only dealing with heaps of outside expectations but also your *own* self-inflicted pressure.

Let's use this annoying reminder to advance our cause. Let it be a sign of the little white flag inside you asking you to surrender the pressure that just cripples your progress anyway. See that unnecessary pressure for what it is and *let it go.*

You have so much to offer. You will get it done. You will leave your mark. This task, project, or routine isn't going to make or break that fact.

If you could take some pressure off of yourself right now, where would you give yourself some grace? What have you been convincing yourself must be done *just right* that actually just needs to be...done?

What if you could use this internal power for self-assessment for good? How much further could you reach if you channeled it in the right places?

When you take the pressure off—even just a little—you pick up power you didn't have before. Hold onto it.

august

18

*Free your emotions from their socially acceptable boxes
and simply let them be.*

From the moment we become self-aware, we realize that some emotions seem preferable to others.

"Happy," "excited," and "calm" feel free and safe. "Frustrated," "angry," and "misunderstood" feel constricting and confusing. Unless we unlearn the belief that emotions are capable of being "good" and "bad," we'll spend too much time pointlessly labeling them rather than processing them.

And, what for? All the energy we pour into characterizing what we're feeling gets us nowhere. We spend hours trying to assign good or bad to what we're experiencing, only to turn around and judge ourselves for those experiences anyway.

Doing this creates more problems than it solves. Think of the last time you got frustrated with yourself for feeling sad because you couldn't determine *why* you felt sad. Or when you got annoyed by your anxiety rather than sitting with it to work it out.

Emotions exist for a reason. They don't need to be good or bad. They just *are*. And they can guide us if we listen to them. How different would it feel to welcome your emotions with open arms rather than shutting them out?

By taking on an attitude of observation, you're able to notice what your emotions are telling you rather than interrogating yourself over them.

Labels are for containers, and you, my friend, cannot be contained.

august
19

When you're generous with who you know,
the quality of your relationships expands and grows.

The more people you actively bring together, the more abundant your life will be.

With each person you welcome into your circle, you gain another perspective on life. Another plethora of new ideas. Another background distinct from your own. Not to mention, you've drawn yourself nearer to *their* circle of influence as well.

Your relationships are a reflection of you: your energy, your willingness to serve, your curiosity, and more. Simple math would say that the more you nurture the relationships you have, the more you multiply the effects they have on your life.

Imagine the possibility of merging two friend groups you love from different areas of your life. Think of two professionals you've come to know in your career and how their skill sets might benefit each other. When you invest in the relationships you have, you manifest prosperity for all.

Bring people together and create a greater collective. Because of you, everyone will grow from a feeling of togetherness. And, in a world of scarce thinkers, that's an actual superpower.

august

20

It's not the qualified who get called,
but the called who become qualified.

You've been waiting for someone to tell you what you should do with your talent. You've been waiting for someone to tell you that your knowledge is *worth* something. You've been waiting for a stamp of approval.

But—you'll always be waiting. Because when we decide how a package must be delivered to us, we miss other surprises along the way.

You have a genius to offer. Yes, *you*. And it's being communicated to you right now. All you have to do is open your mind to how it's being expressed to you.

Observe your support system, your community, and your friends. What signals are being shown that you're not seeing?

There's a golden thread running through the fabric of ways people come to you for help. You have no problem offering them assistance because their ask alone lights a fire of passion beneath you. You might not see the value in what you offer them yet because it's as natural to you as breathing, but it's making a difference.

You are making a *difference*.

This is why they come to you. This is why they need you. Refuse to devalue yourself just because you haven't received some arbitrary certification. Credibility comes with time, but you're already prepared for what you're meant to do. You just have to keep helping and continually learn from that practice.

Feeling qualified will matter less once you feel your calling.

august

When you keep promises made to yourself, you create confidence.

Once we experience the gusto and courage that comes with confidence, we can't help but crave *more of it*. But where do we get it? How do we maintain it?

There's a secret to confidence. You need to FLIP it on:

F stands for Focus. People who exude confidence demonstrate the direct result of where they focus their energy. To build confidence, you need to know what area of your life you want to enhance. Where do you want to be more confident? Focus on that.

L stands for Launch. If you want to feel more confident now, you must *start*. It's the only way to change the story you're telling yourself about how hard your area of focus is. It may be hard, but it's not impossible. Take a step. Make a move. Launch into the area you want to be known for and begin the process.

I stands for Inner Work. No, confidence doesn't just show up and stick around forever. It's something you have to constantly work at, and that work happens in your mindset. If you compare yourself to everyone else all the time, you'll quickly diminish your confidence. If you pay attention to what you need for your mentality, you nurture a confident vibe.

P stands for Practice. The focus needs to be there. You must start. Constantly check in and see how you feel or if you're in alignment. And then you do it over and over and over again. Every time you do, you pick up a little more confidence along the way.

If you want to feel more confident, practice, practice, *practice*.

august

22

> *You are a creator when you share yourself and*
> *your genuine care for others.*

What does it mean to create?

Whether you were that kid everyone believed would grow up to become an artist or creativity has always felt like something beautiful that's just out of your reach—you were born a creator. It's an inherent mindset, regardless of the means you go about it. And it requires your focus and thoughtfulness.

There are two simple barriers to entry to accomplish the work of a great creator:

1. Clarity of your individual strengths
2. Awareness of how your strengths can help other people

These are the basic necessities of all creators, plus a simple starting point that allows creativity to begin flowing naturally. The medium is yours to choose. The aesthetic is whatever you'd like. The style, tone, message, format—it's all up to you.

Creativity itself won't always come easily, but the natural growth of ideas that comes from letting your mind wander will. Simply think about how you'd like to leave an impact. Creativity will follow.

Whatever it is—it's your creation. Let it look like you. Make it sound like you. Craft it in a way so your community can feel something from your work. To do so successfully is to be a great creator.

august

23

You don't have to rip yourself into pieces to keep others whole.

Recognizing your own needs is a vital (and often overlooked) aspect of relationships. Moreover, you aren't required to impair yourself to be a resource to others.

Without honoring that responsibility to yourself, you'll never fully be able to support anyone else around you. No matter how you spin it, sacrificing yourself is never going to amount to someone else's happiness.

You deserve to feel whole.

Two people without their life vests on are both more likely to drown. One person *with* a life vest, however, will be able to help more than just themselves.

For today, try a new approach that keeps you thriving. Before contemplating what those around you need (you'll get to that, you always do), assess your mental, physical, and emotional health.

Which part of you is asking for attention? What area is seeking healing? Every side of you deserves to be cared for. Hear yourself out before taking on others' requests. You'll be better for it, and so will they.

Focus on healing yourself first so you can help others from a place of wholeness.

august

24

*It's a beautiful day when you would redo your
Done List all over again.*

Today, make a list of everything you did yesterday. Label it your "Done List".

What did you accomplish? How long did each task take? Rate each item for how you feel having now completed it.

Now, looking at that list, would you feel excited to do it all again? If today were Groundhog Day and you're Bill Murray reliving the same realm of possibilities as you did the day before, would you be thrilled to dive in or panicking to find a way out?

The most accurate way to measure whether or not you're creating a life of your own design is to look at your responsibilities, your calendar, and everything else that makes up your day-to-day life. Your time doesn't lie—it's the real proof that you're either doing *exactly* what you set out to do or that it's time to reevaluate.

Each morning is a chance to reflect and reset. From there, it's your chance to start changing what doesn't fit. Act accordingly.

august

25

If life were all about getting exactly what you want,
it wouldn't be that interesting.

There are endless types of goals.

Personal goals. Professional goals. Health goals. Relationship goals. The list goes on and on.

No matter the type, they all share a common need: *accountability*. With every goal, you must hold yourself accountable to achieve it, whether you're successful in the end or not.

The significance you place on the process matters *more* than the achievement itself. Are you striving to hit empty milestones, or are you following the why that drives you? If you're unsure, notice if you're energized by the process or quickly discouraged by not getting what you want. Your response holds the key to what will truly drive you forward.

Allow yourself the grace to set goals *and* to question them along the way. There's no rule that says your goal can never change. You may set out to do one thing and later find out there's much more to the story you could never have anticipated.

It's those who are open to that discovery and committed to staying power that succeed—not because their goals worked out perfectly as planned, but because they were flexible in how it all went down.

Who you *become* in the journey toward achievement is far more important than how you get there.

august

26

You are the one that can make this happen.

Today's all about *you*! You've got a lot to offer, and no one can do it the way you can.

You have a distinct set of skills and talents. You have a unique background and individual life experience. You have an eye for things that no one else would see.

You might be thinking, "Wow! Look at all I've got going for me!" And, you're right! But alternatively, you'll also be held accountable for making *use* of this special perspective of yours.

Now, if you're reading this and holding your breath because you think it's too much pressure, remember these individuals who were in the same boat:

- Arianna Huffington was rejected by 36 publishers. That's right, over three dozen major publishing houses said no to her second book. In the end, not only did she get published, but she went on to create *The Huffington Post*. You know, just that little digital news source that went on to get acquired by Yahoo.

- 22-year-old Oprah Winfrey was fired from the evening news at her local Baltimore station for being "unfit for TV". Yes, the same Oprah that went on to dominate television, reaching 15 million people *every day* on The Oprah Winfrey show. She now holds too many accolades to count as a powerhouse entrepreneur, producer, philanthropist, author, and celebrated cultural icon.

- The Editor-In-Chief of American VOGUE magazine, Anna Wintour, didn't have the glowing start one might expect. Wintour was fired after nine months as a Junior Fashion Editor at Harper's Bazaar for being too edgy. She's now one of the biggest names in the fashion industry today.

It doesn't matter what the world is telling you right now. *You* are the one who's going to make it happen.

What do you have to do to pave your own way?

Even when you think you know, embrace an "I don't know" mentality.

Do you ever notice your gut instinct to say the words "I know" when someone tells you something?

Of course, it makes sense when you actually *do* know what you're being told, and you want to confirm you're on the same page.

Saying "I know" feels harmless, but it's an effective way to kill the conversation. It shuts down the opportunity to learn. When we stop thinking of ourselves as perpetual students, we miss unexpected discoveries that can change our lives.

Try letting go of the ingrained assumptions that no longer serve you in your relationships. Open your head—and your heart—to the possibility of *unknowing*. This gives you so much freedom to absorb more than you would have ever expected.

Whenever you're having a conversation you think you can predict, lead with what you *don't* know. Genuine curiosity creates connection. You'll grow from it—guaranteed.

august

28

Inhale motivation. Exhale limiting beliefs.

Our minds can sometimes feel like endless mazes of self-doubt.

Maybe you're guilty—as we all are—of layering distractions into your day to avoid being left alone with your thoughts. Or you take on more than you can handle to keep your mind busy. Whatever your "solution" may be, the motivation is the same—to avoid yourself.

Avoidance is human, but it's also a one-way ticket to...nowhere. Literally. While it might be an easy ride when you're on it, eventually, it gets old.

Awareness gets you to a better place. The only way to conquer something is to work through the limiting beliefs that have spun up over time.

It's time to challenge the narrative in your head that keeps saying nothing is possible. Consider these scenarios:

- Reviewing a job opportunity over and over but not submitting your resume. While you've been consumed over the one bullet of criteria you *technically* don't meet, you could instead draft a cover letter that would prove you have what it takes to crush it in that position.

- Dodging a tough conversation because you're sure they won't listen anyway. Commit to finding common ground to give the conversation a fighting chance.

- Doubting an investment you're considering making. You're sure it's right for you, so now is the time to revisit your budget. Let your instinct drive you forward instead of fearing the uncontrollable.

Take a deep breath and let go of what's limiting you.

When you mentally declutter, you make room for possibility.

august

29

Be the vision you seek.

When we see someone achieve something we want, we tend to default to comparison. As the saying goes, "Comparison is the thief of all joy." At the moment, we're robbed of the opportunity both to lift up someone's success and to inspire ourselves.

Rather than fixating on what they have that you don't, use others' success as your own visionary launchpad. See it as a sign of what's possible. Let it push you further into action.

Now, you might find yourself asking: "What if everything I want always feels out of my reach?" It's a common question, and you aren't alone in wondering if it's true. It's hard to set aside our scarcity mindset to think more positively about the hopes we have for ourselves.

To attract what you want, you must first *emulate* the vision.

Constantly living in a mindset of being *without* causes stress and anxiety, but being *with* inspires gratitude and vision. Leveraging our desires without letting jealousy trip us up means walking through each day as someone who's *already seen* these luxuries take place. When we begin acting as the person we wish to become, we feel the gratitude that makes it possible to get there.

The person you aspire to be is well within your reach. See that person in the mirror right now.

august
30

Your choices are always within your power.

It's no secret—there's not a lot we can control in this life.

That said, there's quite a lot we control about how we go about *living* it—and that makes all the difference.

No, we can't control the weather, the traffic, our nit-picky coworker, or our car that keeps stalling. We can't craft a life immune to obstacles or even a single day free of inconvenience.

Externally, there's nearly nothing we can control. But internally, we get to *choose* everything—and that simple distinction can transform the way you exist in this world. The power to choose is yours no matter what situation you're in. Your reaction, perspective, words, and beliefs are all your choice.

When you tap into this strength, you'll realize that you don't need to control the circumstances around you after all. You already have what you need to create the life you want, right here and right now.

There's only one way to lose this power, and that's when we forget to use it entirely.

Focus on what *does* lie in your control. Be as picky as you'd like in that space. Harness that power so that no matter what comes up, you've got just what you need in your back pocket.

august

31

*Where you stand with your current relationships is
a perfect place to start.*

You may not be a celebrity, but that doesn't mean you can't have an entourage.

You have your people, and that's plenty to get started. The kicker? Those people can only support you as much as you *seek out* their support.

How often do you lean on them in your growth? Have you considered the ways they might be eager to offer advice or a helping hand? When was the last time you asked a family member for their thoughts on a problem? Or a time you reached out to a friend for their expertise in an area they love?

Now, of course, your friends and family don't solely exist to serve you. It's a give-and-take all the way.

We coexist for a reason. We can work in tandem, lifting each other up as we go. Let go of the idea that you don't know the right people. Look around you and see who's here, now. Those are the people to focus on. Those are the right people. Lean into those who have gotten to know you and are eager to show support.

Act with generosity of spirit and thoughtfulness. Show people why they should think of you when their friend needs to meet someone great.

september

september

1

Seeking perfection leads us to pressure, not purpose.

Overcoming perfectionism is a lifelong challenge.

Perfectionist tendencies come from years of limiting beliefs that we've accepted as gospel. We place immense pressure on ourselves to hide our flaws, exceed every expectation, and avoid failure at all costs.

The race to maintain a perfect appearance inevitably leaves us feeling defeated. But despite our exhaustion, we keep at it because *it's all we know.*

Reject the lie that everything will fall apart if you don't meet impossible standards. Remember this fundamental truth: You're *already* enough. There's no human on the face of this earth that's achieved perfection in all they do—you are no exception. If that's the case, why should you take on that burden?

In fact, many of the greatest leaders and most innovative individuals were the ones who accepted imperfection as part of the process rather than a threat to it.

No matter how little you've done, how much more you could do, or how different it feels from your norm—let go of the need to appear perfect. Replace it with complete and utter trust in yourself.

When you show up—flaws and all—you can stop existing to perform and simply exist to enjoy.

september

2

What surrounds you reflects how you use the power within you.

Logically, we know we can't control our circumstances. Emotionally? Well, that's a different story. The line between what we can and can't control gets blurry when we view it through an emotional lens.

If you're unhappy with your surroundings, first consider how many of them are predetermined and how many are truly your choice.

You keep a dead-end job because you think you need the paycheck. Instead, you could do a simple math equation and discover the thousands of other ways to get out of a toxic environment (*and* make the same cash).

You stay with an ill-fitting partner out of fear of being undesirable, assuming that being mistreated is still better than being alone. But falling in love could be right around the corner if you prioritize the most important person you'll ever know—yourself.

You're more influential than the disappointments in your life. You're more compelling than the stories that limit you. Look for evidence that you're capable of more, and then make that evidence the new narrative.

When you start to believe a better story, you paint a better picture of your life.

september

3

No one has all the answers,
but you can learn something from anyone.

It's easy to put successful people on a pedestal, especially when all we can see is what's missing in our own lives.

We assume those that are better off must have it all figured out. How else would they have reached such achievement?

The reality, of course, isn't so black and white. The only real difference between you and the next person is *experience*. Those who we assume know it all actually don't. They simply took a chance, tried something, and learned in the process—something you, too, are fully capable of doing.

We may not all have the same resources and privileges, but we can always borrow wisdom from the person next to us.

It's unrealistic to expect that one day you'll have all the answers. Even if you did, it wouldn't make for a very interesting life, would it?

Keep in mind that when you're willing to fail, your odds of success rise exponentially.

september

4

The life you want is within your reach.

All you have to do is reach (which—for some of us—can be a terrifying notion).

Reaching means leaving what you know for sure and entering territory you don't yet know. Reaching means stepping out of your comfort zone and walking into the light where you'll be clearly seen.

Instead of being unnerved by it, allow it to energize you. Gain momentum with small daily movements in the right direction.

Create those few extra moments for yourself to be alone. Wake up 20 minutes earlier for a morning walk before you're expected to support everyone else. Announce that 30 minutes after dinner is "family quiet time" so you can curl up with a book while the kids do homework.

Pursue your creative calling even though you can't replace your 9-to-5 income with it yet. Find the perfect freelance client and ask them for an opportunity to get some experience with a deal they cannot refuse. What's the worst that can happen? They *do* refuse? Move on to the next until you get the chance you need to build confidence in your work.

Discover a path to living in your dream locale in the mountains, even if it's hard to imagine leaving the life you've built. Start with long bi-annual trips to the place you might one day call home and play the role of a resident trying on their new city.

You're never stuck. You always have options. Accept the invitation to go after them for the sake of your future self.

september

5

Something big is on its way to you. Something better is coming.
What you attract will arrive.

Speak the words you need to hear.

Write the message you need to read.

Picture the vision you need to see.

The only way to truly believe that something better is possible for you is to make the mental shift yourself.

Our brains are wired to keep us safe, so naturally, our default state of mind trends to what's *not* possible. Our mind tries to rationalize and protect us from disappointment. But we feel something more in the depths of our souls. Dare we pay attention to it instead of making an excuse to let it go?

Go on.

Get your hopes up.

Dream big.

Good things don't come to those who wait. They come to those who *watch* their vision come to life.

september

6

*The difference between what you know and
what you become is what you practice.*

As you read this book, you're already doing the inner work.

As you make tough decisions toward real self-care, you're doing the inner work.

As you stick with your morning routine to begin the day on your terms, you're doing the inner work.

Don't lose sight of all that you're accomplishing. There will be a moment when someone comes along and challenges you. Their words may feel like a threat to your peace, but they're only a test.

They're in your way for a reason. Pay attention. Maintain perspective. How you respond is a reflection that your inner efforts are working.

Remember what you've been doing behind-the-scenes and remind yourself what you're capable of continuing to achieve. Perhaps you saw their criticism coming, or maybe you feel so sure of yourself that their words carry little impact.

Ultimately, none of that matters if the ego has decided to step in and run the show. And not just their ego—but yours as well.

Taking someone down a notch and letting them know why you're the bigger person is always a display of the opposite. Letting their disruption completely derail you is evidence that you've completely lost sight of the track.

What you practice is what you become. If you want to prove that you have inner peace, the only person you need to prove it to is yourself.

september

7

Don't let later become never. Do it now.

You want to be ready. You want every step to be defined before you begin. You want to know you'll be okay with whatever comes your way.

We all wish for certainty, but life doesn't operate that way. You simply can't *know*. You can't receive any guarantees. All you can control is the next step you take.

There's a reason that getting started is so hard. Beginning requires accountability and trust in yourself. Accountability is crucial to remind you when you're not doing what you said you would. Trusting yourself gives you a soft place to land when doubts show up along the way. Whatever you do, don't lose momentum.

When you say you'll get to something "later," you're telling yourself that it's not enough of a priority to warrant action now. When you get into the habit of saying "later" about the things that might fulfill you, you unintentionally invalidate your happiness.

You won't know anything until you start to do *something*. Any action is better than no action. This is your permission to stop putting off what you could have already started.

september

8

*You can work hard to get their approval,
or you can be yourself and achieve your own.*

Hands clapping. Faces smiling. Pride gleaming.

These are the reactions we remember from our early achievements. We quickly learned that if we do something well, we earn approval. And it feels *good*.

Then, somewhere along the way, life takes a hard turn. Suddenly, getting applause or a word of affirmation isn't such an easy feat. Expectations grow. Praise is scarce. Small wins feel far less satisfying than before. Validation doesn't go as far as it used to.

It's hard to let go of the need for outside approval when it's always been a dependable motivator. We were trained to strive for it, whether it was in the form of grades on our report cards or kind words from a superior. We must shift our expectations of achievement, so we're not waiting for others' encouragement to move us forward. We have to be able to propel ourselves.

The more power you give away to others, the less you keep for the person whose opinion really matters—you. Every single time you give more attention to what they think, you tell yourself that you trust them more than you trust *yourself*.

If you truly believe in what you're doing, you already have the only approval you'll ever need.

september

9

Will you sweat today?

The best thing to do when you need to change your mindset is to change your physical state. Get out of your mind and step into your body. Put all the energy of overthinking toward something that gets you unstuck.

Movement has a way of activating every part of ourselves beyond just the physical. It makes you feel better, think clearer, and unlock more energy. The mind and the body are deeply connected—the more you get them to work together, the better off you'll feel.

Not sure where to begin? Focus on anything that makes you feel better having done it. Think of the thing that leaves you with *more* energy than what you started with, and go do it for as long as it takes to achieve the mental clarity you need.

When you walk, feel your feet making concentrated contact with the ground rather than measuring an arbitrary distance. Take time to observe your surroundings. Dance until you make yourself laugh instead of worrying about hitting all the right moves. Go to a yoga class because it's the one time of day you notice yourself taking purposeful, deep breaths.

Everyone's best movement is different. No matter the scope of yours, remember to make the mind-muscle connection. Even the smallest shifts in our bodies make a tremendous difference in our health.

Seek out your movement today and feel the benefits that your body sends to you in deep gratitude.

september

10

If you must procrastinate, let it be for something better than worry.

Why are you waiting to begin?

There are millions of reasons we delay the start, and you can probably rattle off more than a few off the top of your head.

When you stare down your argument for procrastinating, how many of your worries are legitimate? How many are generated entirely by fear?

It's not easy to admit when we feel afraid, but we will cop to worrying instantly. Maybe it's because worry feels more justified as an act of protection from the unknown. Maybe it's because we want to feel confident on *some* level, even if it's in the creative way we dress up our doubts.

While you're procrastinating, you're making a giant assumption about time you're not guaranteed.

Much worse than the act of procrastination is engaging in it for the sake of worry. Worrying is an active manifestation of something bad happening. Not only are you wasting time, but you're fixating on a worst-case scenario that'll likely never come to pass. You have *much* better things to do than live a life consumed by worry.

Instead of leaning on procrastination, step up. Let the obstacle know you're ready and willing to find a solution—no matter what it takes.

september

11

You'll never know the true extent of your legacy,
but the lives you touch will.

You have what it takes to stand out.

The probability that you came to exist on this day, in this time, and in this unique way is unbelievably miraculous. The sooner you realize this fantastic truth, the sooner you can embrace the one life you've been given.

Each of us has a desire to leave our mark. The difference between those who stand out and everyone else around them is that they had the audacity to *do* something about it.

You can wake up daily and imagine the legacy you'll leave behind because recalling that vision will drive you. However, you must also actively pursue that vision right now and every day. You're blessed to be here. What you do and who you affect today will matter.

Be the person who speaks up in the meeting instead of holding in your ideas. Be the friend who makes the effort to show you care. Be the one who does everything in your power to elevate the person next to you.

You have one life with a million opportunities to reach further, impact more, and act with love. Each one is a chance to make your mark in the way only you can.

september

12

Small steps are a sign of big things to come.

Your mind is a playground for huge, game-changing ideas. It's your space to imagine, manifest, and envision anything you want.

So—*go big*! Don't hold back. Declare the greatness you know you're capable of. It all begins in that beautiful mind of yours.

This is especially the case in your financial life. Without the right mindset, your boldest ideas will seem way out of reach when you open your eyes and take a peek around.

Money is energy. If we energetically match ourselves to the outcome we want, we can attract it into our lives. Nothing is going to magically appear, but you make it possible by focusing on the end result rather than obsessing about getting there.

Keep your vision top of mind. This is how you appreciate each step you take toward a dream coming to fruition. Manifest first, and then always *act* on it.

See it in action:

Manifest: You dream of opening your own brick-and-mortar shop.
Act: Open a store online to begin building a startup fund.

Manifest: You want to invest to create abundant income for your family.
Act: Open an account and put a small amount from each paycheck away.

Manifest: You hope to build your own home.
Act: Connect with people who have experience in the home-building process.

Every big dream is a collection of small steps that could lead to your reality.

september

13

Trust your gut. Always.

Your greatest resource isn't something you can learn in school or find in the latest self-help craze. It's not available for purchase or on loan. The truth is, it's something you already possess at this moment. It might be hidden under a few layers of doubt and indecision, but it's there.

Intuition is an inherent part of the soul enveloped by your body. Whether we tune in or not, our gut knows what's good for us.

Think about the time you had a bad feeling about a so-called "friend" in school or the job you sensed was too good to be true from the interview. In those moments, your gut might have been the *only* one seeing a red flag. People might have thought you were crazy for turning down an opportunity or switching paths, but you knew the truth all along (even if subconsciously).

There's something both satisfying and disappointing when you realize later that your gut was on point about something you wish wasn't true. Even if you made the wrong call and went against your intuition, the relief of realizing you *knew* all along is powerful.

Take advantage of your insanely spot-on ability to know what's right for you. Say *thank you* to the cues you receive by giving them a bigger role in your decision-making.

september

14

Your willingness to help carries much more power than how you help.

When was the last time you heard yourself say: "How can I help?"

We think we need to qualify ourselves before we can lend a hand, but it's not what we do that stands out in these moments. It's the fact that we showed up.

You might believe you need to know more before you can contribute. This imposter syndrome keeps you from becoming a more fully expressed version of yourself. There are no requirements to being helpful aside from being *willing*.

Before you assume you won't be much help, simply ask what you can do and listen to the response. Provide for the need you see in front of you. It'll likely be much simpler than you anticipated—but you'll be offering true value to someone.

When everything begins to feel overly complicated or confusing, remind yourself that you're always capable of showing up. Regardless of the result, you'll prove that you're someone who will be there for others.

september

15

A good morning routine isn't about the routine at all.
It's about the support it offers you.

Something inside of us longs to see a string of checkboxes all neatly marked off, one by one. That satisfying feeling from all our small, consecutive wins sparks even more motivation. We find ourselves seeking out more chances to feel accomplished.

Routines offer the consistent success you're craving. The more routines you lean on, the more agency you have in designing the life you want.

But that's not the only magic of having a routine. Every time we rely on simple rituals that work for us, we save brain space from unnecessary decision-making. When we take the fulfilling (yet easy) steps to start the day, we build our confidence for all the greater feats coming our way.

You get to determine your routines. It doesn't matter if your morning routine is five minutes long with a few key steps or two hours of slow and steady prep work. Is it there? Does it exist? Most of all, are you present in those moments?

You'll know your routine works when it supports you in becoming the best version of yourself for the rest of the day.

september

16

Let your success be your noise.

We put in a great deal of work to improve our lives—from our morning routine to our daily habits to practicing self-discipline. After all of that effort, naturally, we'd like to be seen for our successes.

More often than not, what we believe to be our greatest attributes aren't always our greatest talking points. What might be intended as a life update or hot tip will often be received otherwise when it comes unprompted.

To share a beautiful and authentic version of you means letting your work speak for itself. Those who perform at the highest level know that true success is *illustrated* rather than announced.

Authenticity is attractive. When you walk into a room, fully confident, unapologetically yourself—you don't need any noisemakers or extra fanfare. You don't need a script or running list of accolades to roll off your tongue. Your presence emulates the product of your best life lived.

The best conversationalists are the ones who listen. Meanwhile, the results of their work naturally illuminate them.

september

17

*There's no greater obstacle in life than
the inability to make a decision.*

Analysis paralysis is a fickle friend.

You've met her from time to time. She's the one who shows up unannounced and makes your head spin when what you really need is determination. She keeps you in an unwanted cycle of inaction: questioning and wondering rather than *moving*.

You might think your careful consideration (also known as indecision in disguise…) helps you prevent mistakes and failure. And yet, you've already made mistakes and failed by procrastinating yet another decision.

The mistake you make with indecision is losing precious time. The failure you encounter with indecision is losing the chance to learn from real experience. When you take action, you take on the risk of making a mistake *and* the exponential benefit of learning from experience.

Decide today to take one simple step in the right direction.

september

18

You can always make more money. You can never create more time.

Have you been overspending your time lately?

Your time on this Earth can't be stocked away for later. Your minutes tick away one by one, whether or not you're doing something meaningful with them. The good news? While each passing moment slips away, you still have a say in where it goes.

We're constantly judging how our money gets spent, yet we rarely blink an eye when we let precious family time lose out to being on our phone or answering just a few more emails. How would the flow of our days change if we spent our time as carefully and thoughtfully as we spend our money?

There's nothing wrong with paying a little extra attention to where your money goes, as long as it comes from a place of purpose rather than a place of scarcity. Money comes and goes, but the time you've been given is the true finite resource on the table.

september

19

Honesty is the greatest antidote to imposter syndrome.

If you're lucky enough to be unfamiliar with the self-diagnosis of imposter syndrome, here's a brief summary:

"Imposter syndrome is a psychological pattern in which an individual doubts their accomplishments and has a persistent internalized fear of being exposed as a 'fraud.'"

Sound familiar?

While it may not require a diagnosis from your doctor, it does take a big toll on your mental health. The fear of someone calling you out for being unqualified in any given scenario causes you to walk on imaginary eggshells. The result? You're unable to reach your potential and build the confidence you need to keep the negative self-talk out of your mind.

When these feelings set in, remember that the opposite of an imposter is an *honest* person. You're not a liar. You're not a fraud. You're not a deceiver. You're an ambitious professional going after the life you want, and you're showing up every day to ensure the job gets done.

Don't take yourself out of the running before the race has even started. Resist the urge to look over your shoulder and worry about how they perceive you. Step outside of yourself and recognize that everyone else has their own self-hindrances they're trying to deal with as well.

Worry less about being an imposter and instead embrace the honest, driven individual you are.

Stay in *your* lane. Run *your* race. Own *your* path. Do it in the best way you know how: from an honest place.

september

20

*Think about what people will say about you after you're gone
rather than what they think about you right now.*

We're all human. And, as kindred spirits, we care about each other. Sadly, we often confuse our care for others with caring too much about what they think about us.

"Will they think I belong here?" "Do they think I have what it takes?" "What will they say when I leave?"

We spend so much time stewing on the small stuff when there's much more that matters in the big picture.

It may feel counterintuitive to disregard outside opinions in order to focus on how you'll be remembered after you're gone. However, that's because the former will keep you small, and the latter is what makes a real impact.

Trade instant gratification for a sense of greater significance. When you know what you're already worthy of, the way you live this human experience carries more magnitude.

Of course, the only way to get that knowledge is to have a conversation with your highest self to stay inspired. Checking in with your core identity keeps you on track and offers the right perspective—not just about the here and now but about your long-term impact as well.

Others can't offer you what you need right now—or ever. When all is said and done, only *you* can do that for yourself.

september

21

Today is another chance to be better.

Making (and keeping) healthy habits can feel like a "one step forward, two steps back" kind of game.

We have the best of intentions for our bodies and nutrition, but the uphill battle of implementing those changes can feel impossible. You may even feel like you've fallen victim to your vices.

Maybe you want to incorporate more movement into your day, but exercise feels like an obligation rather than something you enjoy. Seek a workout that excites you, no matter how unconventional or silly it might seem. It could be as simple as embracing your dancing feet when you get ready in the morning or while you clean up the kids' toys. Your idea of movement doesn't have to fit into someone else's box.

Perhaps you keep trying to update your diet but find yourself eating the same things a couple of hours in. Instead of overhauling your entire plate, recognize what feels safe about your old habits and address that first.

Even if you took a couple of steps backward yesterday, today is your chance to move forward again.

september

22

We have the time if we want it.

The sound of time scarcity plays on repeat in our minds. It's a catchy tune that's hard to get out of our heads...you might recognize a few lines:

"If I only had more time."
"I don't have time for that."
"There's not enough time in the day."

Despite how very real those thoughts are to you in the moment, you have the time for what you want if you *make* time. You may very well be overbooked, but the calendar isn't to blame. You're the keeper of your own time card.

It's a hard truth to hear. It means you need to make the right decision for yourself, which often doesn't align with others' agendas (not just sometimes, but many times throughout even one day). Still, the only way to get this song out of your head is to find a new one that represents the focus you have on what's most important to you.

Rather than playing the victim every time you catch yourself triple-booked or completely out of spare minutes in the day, ask the hard questions instead.

"What am I doing that doesn't matter?"
"What am I doing out of habit that doesn't need to be done by me at all?"
"What am I doing just because someone else expects me to?"

Take the lead on your time, and you'll find you already have enough.

september

23

Are you going through life with your fingers crossed?

Your life is unique and irreplaceable. It's full of possibility and potential. Depending on how you approach it, you could end up with a very wide range of results. Anything that precious (and that malleable) is worth a thoughtful strategy.

We start out doing what we think we're *supposed* to do. We subscribe to some fixed idea of how things *should* turn out—and we often stop there. In case you haven't figured it out yet, here's a spoiler: That approach is nothing more than a shortcut toward a disappointing existence.

Hope has its place, but it's no strategy. Sitting back and assuming things will eventually go your way is the opposite of an action plan.

Hope is best paired with a big ol' dose of momentum. Having a vision so clear that you can taste it is just the start. The real excitement comes from going after what you want.

Pursue what you desire most and savor the process along the way. In that space, you'll experience the essence of a truly lived life. You'll uncover your wisdom and get closer to really living your dream.

Keep hope alive, but don't just cross your fingers. Face your challenges head-on. You can absolutely handle it.

september

24

Surrender to rest. Let sleep bring out your best.

Anyone who once dabbled in the self-destructive hobbies of all-nighters or living by caffeine alone can testify that consistently losing sleep will only end up a nightmare.

There's *so* much life to live, and yet we can't do it all. We try. We stay up late. We burn the midnight oil. We rise early and exhausted. But there will never be enough hours in the day for us to do everything on our own.

There's no cheating the system to get enough rest. Every bit of lost sleep takes away from your overall health, your state of mind, and your ability to realize your dreams. Be willing to surrender so you can wake up not only refreshed but *ready* for what's next.

Get your best rest with these habits:

- Track your current sleep schedule. How many hours do you typically get?

- Assess how you feel in the morning. Do you feel groggy for hours after your alarm goes off, or do you leap out of bed before those bells chime?

- Take note of how long it takes you to fall asleep and why. What steps could you take to unwind further before getting into bed?

- Adjust the temperature of your environment for optimal comfort and consistent snoozing.

Observe what a good night's rest looks like for you. Once you define this, hold yourself accountable to make every night a good night. Then, dear friend, you'll literally be living the dream.

september

25

You can wait for permission. Or, you can do it for you.

Every decision you make doesn't require a jury, yet it's natural to feel like you need a board of advisors to weigh in before you come to a conclusion.

This habit is a slippery slope.

Each time you rely on outside opinions to make a decision for you, you trade your power for permission.

If you're considering a career change but can't make up your mind without dwelling on what your friends and family think—you're fixated on their validation over your ambitions.

If you're thinking about starting a side-hustle but hesitate after a few friends turned their nose up at the idea—you're sacrificing progress for people-pleasing.

What are you procrastinating on as a result of others' opinions? What would you do if it were *just for you?*

You love your friends and family, and they love you. But simply being a loved one doesn't always qualify them to get a vote.

This is *your* life. It's up to you to be the judge. Jury dismissed.

september

26

Acknowledge your fear so you can move past it.

President Franklin D. Roosevelt left us with these inspiring words for challenging moments of dealing with the unknown: "The only thing we have to fear is fear itself."

When you find yourself in the midst of the unknown, what is it that you're afraid of?

To overcome a fear, we first have to say it aloud. Something as simple as acknowledging your fear can give you the self-awareness you'll need to get it out of your way.

So, vocalize what you fear. See it for what it is and nothing more.

Remember, it's not the worries that keep us from greatness—it's the *power* we give them. That distinction is precisely what will make all the difference.

september

27

Go after the life you want.
It's never impossible when you remember who's in charge.

The life you want is yours—and yours alone—to define.

There's no instruction manual that'll tell you what move to make next. There's no gameshow bell to let you know what you've gotten right.

If you're ever in question or feeling like you've gone down the wrong road, call on those you trust. But remember that only one soul exists to be able to tell you what's right for you, and that's your own.

You decide what success looks like, even if you fail. You determine what feels good, even if it takes uncomfortable moments to get there. You know what you look forward to, even when there are challenges on the way.

Every day. Every decision. Every moment is reliant on you knowing what's best for you.

Listen.

Instead of feeling lonely because this journey is yours alone to make, lean into the joy of ownership. Stand tall. Be the boss. Have the final say.

september

28

Comparison is a fool's errand. Differentiation is a power move.

What are they doing? How do they live? What have they achieved?

Comparison runs rampant in our society. It drives unnecessary anger. It contributes to depression. It steals our joy. We lose the comparison game every time, yet we can't help but play.

The more you measure your life against everyone else's, the less yours will seem to measure up. Why? Because we can *always* find someone who's wealthier than us, smarter than us, doing more than us, or achieving more at a younger age than we have.

Comparing is destructive, but it sure is easy to do. The first step toward change is making it *harder* to do the thing that self-sabotages.

What contributes to a culture of comparison in your life? How can you stop allowing it into your space? Delete the app off your phone? Avoid watching that show? Take a break from speaking with that person?

Once you've figured it out, fill that void with something life-giving. Your best approach will be to channel that energy into what makes you different.

What do you love to do? What are you great at? These actions come from the higher self. Instead of looking for all the ways you could be more like others, celebrate the things that make you wonderfully distinct from the crowd.

The more you focus on all that makes you *you*, the less you'll feel the urge to compare.

september

29

Everyone will have questions when magic enters the room.
Let that magic be you.

You know the person.

The one you follow on social media, that teacher from your childhood, or someone you interact with on a daily basis. You see how they carry themselves, how they tackle what life throws at them, and how they honor their truest self.

"Wow," you think. "I wish I could be more like that."

When we have that thought, criticism usually isn't far behind. We want to be different, to stand out as our truest selves, but it feels…well…uncomfortable.

We think of all the people who know us to be a certain way, dress in a particular fashion, and speak the way they're used to. What would they think if we started letting our unfiltered personality show, sporting a new wardrobe, and asserting ourselves more?

You don't want to call attention to yourself, so you avoid stepping into something new. The fact is, people *will* notice. Because when you're going after the life you want, it's magnetic. It's attractive. They want to know more. They want to know how you did it. *They want to do it too.*

Be the person who dawns the red lipstick without any reason other than loving it. Be the person who leaves the party before it's over or the one who stays until the last song plays. Be the person who doesn't reply to text messages in the wake of a millisecond. And, when someone brings up what you know is coming, own it. Don't apologize or make an excuse. Share how you've evolved and how fun it is to venture into new territory.

If you really want to be bold, tell them how it *feels*. If you start a sentence with "It feels so incredible to be able to…[insert amazing new thing you're trying here]," no one's opinions can overpower your genuine happiness.

september

30

*Each moment that passes is one you could have done
something that matters to you.*

Time has a funny way of moving slowly when we wish it would hurry up, then zooming by when we're craving a chance to take it all in.

It's easy to lose track and forget to be present. We get consumed by our work, caught up in everyone else's expectations, and bogged down by all our responsibilities.

Every day is full of distractions. There's never going to be an opportunity to step away from everything. No one is going to hold your hand and escort you to the time, place, or mindset where you can brush off all the stressors and do what's important to you. It's on you to navigate toward that balance. That's just reality.

We make thousands of choices a day—many of them unnecessarily. Without thoughtfully planning for what's important to us (even if just for the few moments we can carve out in a day), we allow trivial stumbling blocks to steal our time.

How will you stop waiting and start making moments count?

Knowing no pause button is going to show up, it's time to spend your time intentionally. No excuses.

october

october

1

The only one who needs to approve of your path is you.

Have you ever wanted to go get a new job, even though it meant abandoning your old career? Or maybe you've entertained leaving a relationship even though you've given so much of yourself to it.

These critical decisions are challenging you for good reason. Your life experiences (combined with self-actualization) have given you a new perspective. This brand new lens is meant to help you figure out what's *next*.

There's just one catch: No one will fully understand it, except for you.

We know this, but still, we hesitate. It's hard to focus on what's best for us when our worries about how everyone else will react are just around the corner.

Think back to a time when you were being 100% yourself. Unapologetic, fully expressed, genuine *you*. How did that feel? In moments of pure authenticity, we don't stop to overthink. We feel present. We feel purposeful. And we're only able to access these positive feelings because we aren't hemming and hawing over others' opinions.

There's a reason those moments felt footloose and fancy-free. There was clarity of your *why*. And when you're living from that space, there's no room to worry about all the things others might say.

Whether you're grappling with a big life decision right now or simply want to try something new, dig deep for the reason you need it. The more connected you are to understanding yourself, the less you'll feel the need to explain yourself to others.

october

2

Give your best, and give generously.

Your wealth amounts to more than what's in your wallet.

The beauty of paying it forward is that you have the power not only to inspire others but also to generate *more* for them.

Think of the zillionaire who donates a spectacular chunk of change to charity. It might be difficult to make sense of the size of such a gift, but it's even more mind-boggling when you realize the sum they gave away is only a minuscule fraction of their total net worth. It's a drop in the bucket whose absence will hardly be felt.

Now, consider the person who donates $20 to a cause that they deeply care about. On paper, that $20 bill pales in comparison to the many zeroes on the zillionaire's check until you factor in the weight it holds to the person giving it away. Consider what this person might have had to say no to in order to have a spare $20 to give away.

It's not about the dollar amount but the willingness to give. This willingness is driven by more than just a surplus or convenience. Giving is especially significant when it *costs* something, whether that be money, time, energy, or effort. For what is a gift if it requires no sacrifice for the giver?

When you contemplate your wealth, look beyond what you've earned. Consider what you've given back.

october

3

*Productive permission can be granted in many ways,
even when saying no.*

We're so accustomed to getting what we want easily and quickly that we assume we must offer others the same luxury.

But when did the word "no" become the enemy?

Every yes you say is a no somewhere else. Maybe you had plans to be alone on a Saturday morning, and someone requested you help them move house. Maybe you've already taken on too much at work when your coworker asked for support on their own project.

We're so quick to trade future consequences with the momentary satisfaction of being an agreeable person. And yet, there are *so* many better things to be than agreeable. Wouldn't you rather be perceived as decisive, honest, or self-assured?

When you confidently say no in a situation when it's fitting, you give yourself (and others) the permission they need to move on from the issue immediately. There's no need to leave someone waiting in the wings with a half-hearted maybe.

Not to mention, you deserve every second of the time and energy you've reserved for the life you want. Turning others down is simply a byproduct of mastering prioritization and becoming the person you want to be.

Saying no isn't the enemy. When used wisely, it's a tool for empowerment.

october

4

Move your body to move your mind.

Sometimes the only way to get out of your head is to *step* out of it.

Many of us have a true talent for overthinking. Each time we go down that rabbit hole, we spin ourselves until we're completely stuck. After a while, you might be tricked into believing that where you are right now is where you'll be forever. In these moments, remind yourself that being mentally frozen doesn't mean you *really are.*

This goes for your writer's block, your late-night cram session before finals, or your lack of creative inspiration. Opting for a change of scenery can give your mind the wake-up call it needs.

The more you get moving, the more you encourage motivation to come back to you. Instead of hunkering down and forcing it, release the pressure. Get outside yourself and shake things up a little.

What you do to move will move you.

october

5

When you anticipate the day's inevitable obstacles,
you get better at ensuring they don't take you down.

No day will go perfectly as planned.

Read that again.

Say it aloud: *No day will go perfectly as planned.*

When we make plans, we're doing what's in our control to set ourselves up for success. Planning is vital to helping your dreams come to life while anticipating inevitable, uncontrollable events.

We're creatures of habit, so our triggers, frustrations, and moments of disarray have trends to them. When you track the similarities, you can identify ways to combat them ahead of time.

Notice what seems to send you into a frenzy. See if it's the same person, the same task, the same place, and so on. Are you always leaving the house in a panic because your keys have gone missing? Can you never seem to remember that one nagging (but essential) task? Is there one chore that always slips through the cracks, causing chaos later?

Most of the so-called plot twists that throw off our plans are actually pretty predictable. Once you know what they are, you can put systems in place that prevent them from happening.

Make a rule that you always put your keys in the same place the second you walk in the door, so you're never frantically looking for them again. Set a recurring reminder that takes the guesswork out of when it's time to pay that bill. Delegate that chore to someone who has more bandwidth to get it done.

When you count on the curveballs that'll come your way, you teach the Universe that you're ready for anything.

october

6

We are here to live a life. Not just a morning.

You've planned the perfect morning. You've set your alarm. You're ready to wake up with the best of intentions to start the day on your terms.

Except something happens.

Your coffee doesn't taste quite right. The kids wake up earlier than they're supposed to. You accidentally grab your phone a little too soon, and before you know it—your beautiful morning is out the window, never to be seen again. Or so it feels, anyway.

It's never ideal to have your morning routine go rogue, especially after how much thought you put into making it your safe space to start the day. But, of course, it still happens to the best of us.

In those moments, remind yourself that the real reason we care about a morning ritual isn't because we know it'll go perfectly. It's because we're proving that we get to be the leader of our life. It's meant to support us so we can be our best selves, even when those unpredictable moments arise.

Be careful when you put too much stock in your morning routine. Remember that it's supposed to support us, not stress us.

When things fall off the rails (and they will), pick them back up the next day. No need for a perfect streak here—just commitment to trying *again*.

october

Show your support system you appreciate them by leaning on them.

The best gift you can give to the people that love you is to *let* them love you.

Our network was made to support us when we feel the urge to flee. Over the years, you've carefully curated the people you keep close by. Those individuals are invested in your success just like you're invested in theirs.

Think about the times you've shown up on a friend's doorstep (potentially with wine/snacks/care kit in hand) to pick them up and remind them of their worth. Remember the days you wanted to do something kind for someone just because, and they graciously accepted your help.

When we feel lost, our friends rally together to remind us of our purpose. When we've forgotten the vision, they're there to bring it back into focus.

Allow them in. Let yourself rely on them when you feel completely at a loss on your own. Give them permission to carry you when you feel weak. Remember how good it felt the last time you were able to be there for them, and give them that same opportunity to be there for you.

Decide to rise together. Growth is always better with company.

october

8

You gotta do you, or it's not gonna come true.

This very well might be the simplest (yet hardest) advice you'll ever receive: *You do you.*

There's so much beauty in the simplicity of those three words. Best of all, two of the three hold all the power: *you.*

The decision is yours to make. Are you going to calibrate your life path based on the desires of someone else, or are you going to lead the only life that's yours to rule?

Being you means releasing the need for external validation. Being you means prioritizing your own integrity. Being you means taking actions that'll make yourself proud.

These aren't easy feats, but the rewards are considerable. Doing this work means achieving the life you want, emulating it every day, and never allowing yourself to settle for less.

The truest definition of "doing you" is nurturing the most important relationship you'll ever have: the one with yourself. When you stay true to this mission, you can make anything happen.

october

9

Embrace what you get to do today instead of what you have to do.

No matter what your life looks like, it's hard not to get stuck in a rut now and then. Life is made up of routine, which comes with both benefits and drawbacks. There's your job, your relationships, extra commitments, chores, and about a thousand other things all fighting for your attention.

There isn't a magic word that simplifies everything, but there's a way to thrive in the chaos instead of merely surviving. The more we look at our obligations as, well, *obligations*—the less fulfillment we get out of them.

Instead of always leading with *I have to,* try saying *I get to* instead.

I get to leave work early to take my daughter to the dentist.
I get to wash the dishes after dinner.
I get to wake up early tomorrow morning.

If that sounds silly to you, try it out and notice how it genuinely shifts your perspective. Our brains are constantly listening to what we tell them. It's a blessing to have a child to care for, clean dishes for each new meal, and time to start the day on your terms.

When we make a habit of what we *have* to do, we're focused on expectations. When we approach the tasks of life as things we *get* to do, we grow our gratitude.

Our lives, with all of their hassles and beautiful messes, are a gift.

october

10

You can't fail forever,
especially if you carry lessons forward with you.

Failure happens. And when it does—it hurts.

We're quick to console others when they feel they've fallen short, but we find it near impossible to offer that same grace to ourselves. Even though we *know* failure is necessary (and inevitable), it still feels personal when it happens to you.

Feel your failures rather than running from them.

There's not a single person that'll get through life without making many, many mistakes. It's just not possible. It's part of being human. Rather than holding yourself to an unrealistic standard that *no one* on this planet has ever reached, face your failures with ownership.

Henry Ford offered us this reminder: "Failure is the opportunity to begin again more intelligently." The key phrase here is *to begin again.* Failure isn't an indication you should quit. Quitting may be appropriate at some point, but right now, you have knowledge you didn't have before. You can use it to find out how to take another stab.

These will be some of the most motivating moments in your life if you accept them for what they are. The way you handle these shortcomings says volumes more about you than your failures ever do.

Decide to move forward with the abundance of wisdom you've earned.

october

11

The key to success is knowing yourself.

There are so many resources available on how to be successful. Self-development books. Digital articles. Motivating soundbites. In the sea of information, it's easy to forget the most important resource: you.

Is it a good thing to ask for help? *Absolutely.* Just be careful not to let your search for knowledge distract you. When you habitually look outside yourself for what you need to know about success, you risk getting so stuck in the research that you never move on to experience it yourself.

You could know all the tips and tricks in the world, but none of that will matter if you don't know yourself. You'll be missing the most essential ingredient.

True success looks different for everyone. Feel free to borrow from others' wisdom, but make sure you know what you're *really* after before you get after it. When you set the rules, the outcome will be that much sweeter.

What's attainable is yours to determine. It doesn't have to seem "realistic" to others. In fact, it shouldn't be. It should be an unrealistic, monumental, game-changing vision that makes you feel like a fully expressed version of yourself.

october

12

You can make a wish. Or you can do the work.

You know the story of the genie in the bottle: You get three wishes, no questions asked. It's a nice idea and all, but without requiring any real effort, it'd come with a fulfillment factor of zero.

Isn't it still so alluring, though? We're tempted to fall into a habit of wishing because it feels so…well…*easy.*

I wish I had a friend group like hers.

I wish I had more money so everything would be easier.

I wish I was more assertive.

The problem with a wish is that it's not a real manifestation. It takes something desirable and removes the responsibility it takes to make it happen.

You can wish to your heart's content, but you'll still be missing the inner work that's the real catalyst to creating your reality.

Turn your wish into a clearly defined dream. Imagine the result so vividly you can taste it. Emulate that result and ask for it to guide you. Look for what you should do next. You are the authority that'll take this idea and bring it into physical existence.

Instead of making a wish, have a vision. Then, do the work to bring it to life.

october

13

A new chance to begin is here.
Move into your day without hesitation.

Alarms are rarely music to anyone's ears.

We dread them. We grumble at them. We jump at the chance to silence them.

Putting off the day with one simple slap of the snooze button feels amazing in the moment. But when it sounds again five minutes later, it's a reminder that snoozing is simply procrastination from engaging in the only life you get to live.

Every morning is a new chance to begin again. Waking up is the invitation. You can decline it or push it off, but eventually, you'll need to make your appearance.

If you don't like the plans ahead of you, make a change. Today is your opportunity to do so.

october

14

The impact of your legacy is measured by feelings, not thoughts.

While the idea of leaving a legacy is a bit daunting, we can easily rattle off a laundry list of things we want to do in our lives to show our impact.

Writing a book. Volunteering our time. Contributing to philanthropic efforts. Children. These are just a few of the marks we might tally if we try to vocalize how we could leave the world better than we found it.

A legacy doesn't exist until we're gone. It's tempting to pontificate about how we'll leave one, though it hasn't even been lived yet. The only way for a legacy to be observed is by the individuals who've been affected.

In the words of Maya Angelou, "I've learned that people will forget what you said, people will forget what you did, but people will never forget how you made them feel."

A legacy isn't thought of but *felt*.

When someone asks you how you are, you might instinctively ask them the same question—but are you listening to their answer? You might notice someone who needs your seat more than you do, but do you just quickly insist they take it to alleviate any further interaction? Do you act on your instinct to compliment someone so they can feel your love as quickly as it appeared for you?

These are the actions that matter. By nature, they usually happen less with thought and more from your own genuine feeling. The true measure of your gift will be found in the hearts of those you leave behind.

october

15

*The roads paved by those who came before you are simply options—
not predetermined destinations.*

When we're young, we try to make sense of life as though it were a straight line.

We quickly internalize the equation we assume we have to follow: graduate high school, get a degree or two, find a secure job that pays well, and live happily ever after. Check all the boxes, follow the crowd, and all you've ever wanted will be yours!

Or...not? Just because someone did something similar before you doesn't mean you have to go down that same road. They paved *their* path, not yours. You get to determine the steps that are right for you, but you'll only know what those are when you shed everyone else's expectations. It's the only way.

What path would you be on if no one else pushed you in a certain direction? What pursuit would make your younger self proud? What would you do if fear wasn't a factor?

You have an opportunity to achieve *more* than your wildest dreams. Be more excited about the vision itself than you are rigid about the path to get there.

Surrender the need to follow the popular process and instead be open to all the good you could possibly receive.

october

16

Be careful how you say who you are.
What follows "I am" establishes how you represent yourself to the world.

Most of us are no stranger to self-deprecating thoughts.

You lock your keys in the car and immediately think, *Geez, I'm such an idiot.* Or, you forget an important appointment for your child and can't help but think, *Ugh! I'm the worst parent ever.*

In the moment, we feel like we deserve these words. It seems appropriate to punish ourselves at the get-go so we can get closer to moving on from our slip-up. But it's entirely unfair to negatively label yourself just because of an imperfect moment.

You are *human.* So allow yourself to be one!

Whenever you start a sentence with "I am…" you're making a connection to your highest self. Your best self. The co-creator of your life. Negative words following "I am" only manifest negativity that wasn't there to begin with.

Use this opportunity to announce what you truly deserve, even if it doesn't feel like it at the moment.

Try on a few positive labels instead.

I am a creator.

I am loved.

I am a good person.

I am who I am.

… and I love it.

Compliment your identity sincerely and often.

october

17

Small acts of service create big moments of connection.

There's no better feeling than when someone goes the extra mile for you, like when your significant other surprises you with your favorite coffee or your best friend gives you a pep talk right before the big presentation.

These are the moments that stand out. They help us acknowledge the good eggs we picked to join us in this life.

We're a summary of our actions. What we do each day for others cumulates into who we become. Set out to be the extra-mile person for the people you appreciate.

You might take notice of the book they mentioned they've been wanting to read or remember their favorite restaurant for the next time you meet up. You could silently vow to do that one chore your partner despises before they get home. All these small details (that would otherwise remain small details) are now given a new significance.

It all comes down to *attention* and *intention*. When you pay attention, you demonstrate your intention. Think about how you show up for the people that matter to you. Find the small ways you could show you care.

Be willing to go further than most. Stay late or arrive early. Remember birthdays and anniversaries. Offer to help. Follow through.

october

18

A calendar with something to look forward to is a sign of someone who makes time for what's important.

Okay, let's not pretend you've got an entirely blank calendar just waiting to be filled with whatever you choose. If we're being honest, right now, your schedule might feel more chaotic than compelling.

If seeing your commitments for the day sparks more panic than enthusiasm, you're not alone. Maybe doing the mountain of dishes, responding to endless emails, or making the 100th snack for your little one isn't necessarily something you just can't wait to tackle. And that's okay.

However, when too many obligations (with too little fulfillment) consume your days, you get burnt out pretty quickly.

Aside from your daily obligations, you have ambitions. That charitable project you've always wanted to launch still sits in the back of your head. The song in your head is itching to be recorded and unleashed on the world. If you want to see these dreams materialize, what you *want to do* has to get aligned with what you *actually do*.

When you look at your list of aspirations, compare it to how you spend your time. Is space being made for what you want to do? We'll always have more commitments that use up our finite amount of time, but they're merely obstacles—not full stops.

Learn to recognize what tasks must be done by you so you can give your full self to them when it's time.

Be a person who does what they say they'll do. Not just for others, but for yourself.

october

19

*Be so focused on what you want for yourself that the
only competitor you notice is a former version of you.*

We all play the comparison game, despite the fact that the odds of winning are abysmal (approximately zero, actually).

Everywhere you look, there's competition. The sports channel is spotlighting a long-standing team rivalry, social media offers us a never-ending highlight reel, and that's just the beginning.

Society has taught us that if we're not competing at *their* highest level, we're not worth anything. No wonder we're so emotionally fatigued, mentally drained, and confused about what we really want!

What would happen if we chose our own competition?

The key to winning the comparison game is stepping out of it altogether. How? We must recognize that we're not competing with anyone but ourselves. The people around us aren't our competition—they're our *motivation*. We're all here to lift each other up. The only way to see this, however, is by staying laser-focused on a more fruitful endgame.

Friendly reminder: The only person to be better than is the person you were yesterday.

When you compete at your own level, you'll move faster and see greater results. As for all the others you're worried about? They'll still be distracted trying to measure themselves against everyone else.

It's more than okay to look outside yourself to gauge what barriers can be broken—in fact, it's a brilliant idea. Just promise you'll challenge yourself to be great rather than assuming you're a failure in contrast.

When you compete with internal motivation, grace, and a desire to learn—it's impossible to lose.

If you want a morning routine that's right for you,
know what you really want for your life.

When the initial glow wears off from going after the life you want, you might be left feeling overwhelmed. You feel motivated, sure, but you also feel surrounded by goals on top of goals and a sense of uncertainty on how to begin.

First, evaluate the building blocks of your day: your habits, your accountability, and—you guessed it—your morning routine! These fundamentals are uniquely yours, so they'll look different than those of the person next to you. The core ideas are the same, but the details are all about you.

Take whatever big-picture idea you're amped about and reverse-engineer it. What needs to happen to get to that end result? What habits need to be in place to move the needle consistently? Start by being honest with your goal and realistic about what will get you there:

- You want to sit down and write the book you've had in your head for five years? Try Julia Cameron's daily practice of morning pages to clear your mental clutter. Commit to journaling a predetermined number of pages each morning.

- You're trying to make movement a lifestyle by reaching 10,000 walking steps every day? Commit to taking a walk around your neighborhood every morning, no matter how much or how little time you have.

- Do you daydream about your childhood wish of becoming a chef? Your morning could start with trying new breakfast recipes for your family to start mastering your craft.

To design a morning that serves you, imagine what you want your life to feel like. Commit to the one step every day that'll get you closer to that reality.

october

21

You're always remembered when you make a positive impact.

We all hope our presence has power. We want to matter to others the way they matter to us. However, being unforgettable doesn't have to be on a grand scale. It's far simpler than we think.

"It's the thought that counts" is a cliché for a reason.

Small, consistent gestures are the key to lasting impact. Remember the friend in high school who always offered you a piece of their gum? Or the neighbor at the coffeehouse who always asked how your day has been?

Making an impression doesn't require razzle-dazzle. It's as simple as seeing the person in front of you and caring about them: where they're coming from, how they're feeling, or what's important to them in the moment. That's it.

People want to be seen. People want to be heard. People want to be supported and appreciated. This is all it really takes to leave a positive legacy.

october

22

Being easy to work with is nice.
Being a strong advocate of your value is powerful.

Picture this. You've put in the work. You have years of experience to show for it. You've worked with loads of clients. Time and again, you've presented your best work, and it's led you to success.

What could go wrong?

Now, imagine working with a client that you feel is a perfect fit for you. Everything is going smoothly. Synergy is practically flowing through your veins, and everyone is on the same page—until the client throws a big ol' wrench in your plans.

They seemed like they trusted your authority, yet now they show up asking for a big, custom request. At times like this, you question whether you should allow it. Just this *one* time.

You say you want to be easy to work with, but you're really just worried they'll go elsewhere. You can't succeed when you operate from a place of fear. Deep down, you know you can't do your best work under those conditions.

So, you decline. You set a boundary. And, sure enough, it was worth it in the end. They stopped questioning you and go right back to following your lead. Crisis averted—only because you stood your ground.

Give yourself the benefit of the doubt that being the best doesn't always mean being the easiest to work with. Everyone will be much better for it.

october

23

How you think is what you attract.

Far too often, we assume our own thoughts are the one infallible source of truth.

Who can blame us? Our inner voice broadcasts to us 24/7, so of course, that voice seems like the ultimate authority on all things us.

Thoughts and feelings are valid—but they aren't facts.

The good news is that our minds are incredibly malleable. The *great* news is that once you realize this power, you can use it for *so much good*. Instead of letting every negative thought become canon, nourish the ideas that deeply support you.

When you train your mind to only accept thoughts that build you up, you'll soon develop a strong bias toward what's possible.

Stay fully present in the now. Focus on what you wish to attract. As you do so, you send a signal that you're open to receiving all the good coming your way.

october

(24)

Patience and consistency will show you the progress you desire.

You know the feeling of gym-time dread. You know you gotta put in the work, but all you can think about is the discomfort and soreness that comes with each workout.

Still, you muster up the discipline to get it done. You feel some of the things you were dreading, but it's not nearly as bad you imagined it. Mostly you realize you're capable of pushing through and feel pretty good about yourself when it's all said and done.

Will you see immediate results for your work? In some ways, yes. In the ways you crave, probably not.

Both inside and outside the gym, the effort you put in is critical to your success. Even when it feels like all that work barely moved you forward an inch, it's doing something. Even if you're not seeing an immediate result, know that you're taking an important step. You're acting instead of procrastinating. You're owning what you can do. You're showing up—and nothing else can happen until you do that.

Unbelievable patience and devotion is the only way to find out if your dream has real sustainability. Will you let yourself quit before you start? Or will you venture to see where beginning will take you?

october

25

When they say you dream too big,
remember you're working with a different scale.

Manifesting your dreams can feel weird for two reasons:

1. You haven't practiced it enough.
2. You share your visions with people who don't understand.

Yes, you must put your desires into the Universe for them to come back to you. No, that doesn't mean you need to tell everyone what you're thinking about all of the time.

It doesn't feel so good when others aren't as amped about your dream as you are (it is *your* dream, after all). Before you tell someone the latest thing you're jazzed about, drop any expectations you have. Separate your *feelings* about what you want from their *opinions* about what you want.

This advice is applicable everywhere, especially when it comes to money. Money is a complicated and uncomfortable conversation for most, even if you're working on building a healthier money mentality.

When you share a vision you have for your investments, your business, or your income only to be met with criticism—take a step back. Whatever they say is not about you.

The resistance someone feels is their story—not yours. Your success hinges on your own inner narrative.

Focus on manifesting the story you want to see come true.

october

26

Connecting with other people is a surefire way to expedite success.

We go further together. Full stop.

We need each other to get where we want to be. No one is an exception to this rule. And if you need more proof, ponder these teams that made more happen together:

- NASA's Apollo 11: While we all know Neil Armstrong and Buzz Aldrin, there were 400,000 others behind the scenes that saw this mission through. It took two years of focused teamwork to make their scientific dream a reality.

- Wikipedia: You've probably heard of this little website and likely even used it recently. It's one of the most viewed digital resources in the world, with an anonymous team keeping it going consistently. Without this crowd effort, it'd take a lot longer to answer the random questions that pop up in your head.

- US Women's Soccer: Beyond winning four World Cups and Olympic gold medals, they've redefined women in sports by raising standards and creating new possibilities for generations to come.

When you finish your marathon, graduate with your degree, or hit another major milestone—do you feel more fulfilled if you reached that achievement alone? Or does it feel better to mark your victory surrounded by those who supported you along the way?

Let people in. Appreciate their energy. Recognize the influence they bring into your life.

Find your team and go further together.

october

27

Find your light.

It's a fact of life—there are good days, and there are bad.

There will be days, weeks, and maybe even months that feel darker than the rest. They'll be bleak and heavy. They'll scare you and isolate you. But, most importantly, they won't be the end of your story.

Only you can truly know the weight those moments carry. In reminding yourself to find moments of light, you cannot ignore the existence of darkness.

The struggle is definitely real. Mental health takes an exhausting toll. In fact, when you're in it, it can feel all-consuming. It can be persistent. But, no matter what feelings are looming right now—you're just as persistent. Remember that.

It's challenging to feel powerful when faced with so much heaviness. In the moment the negativity is strongest (and you feel at your weakest), you must muster up the strength to look for the light. It may seem small, but it's there.

When the light feels too far beyond your reach, remember to question the validity of the darkness around you.

What if this feeling isn't a fact?

What if there's more to my story beyond this moment?

What do I know for certain?

When all seems lost, you know you'll have your back.

october

28

Empower your mind by prioritizing your own
original ideas before others'.

Your mind is a sacred space all to yourself.

Just like you'd do with any other space, you'll want to be respectful of how much room you have, what fits the vibe, and how much room you'd like to keep empty. Just like that empty drawer in your house, it can easily become a dumping zone full of clutter if you aren't careful.

We're all guilty of letting others' ideas influence us at times. The danger occurs when we forget to regulate what we let influence us at *all*. Not every opinion is worth adopting. Not every perspective needs to be internalized. But with so much chatter flying at us each day, it's difficult to gatekeep what gets into our heads.

For our well-being and sanity, we must prioritize supportive thoughts.

This can be as simple as avoiding your phone for the first hour of the day or as challenging as compartmentalizing others' opinions. But whatever you do, be protective over the time you have in your day to just *think*.

Form your own opinions, daydream about your life, and brainstorm new ideas. This is where the magic happens.

Make space for you and the ideas that light you up.

october
29

It's not the number of followers you have.
It's the integrity of your brand.

On initial assumption, we might suspect that brands are merely for big corporations or social media stars. In reality, everyone has a brand.

Your resume illustrates your brand. Your habit of showing up ten minutes early is your brand. It's the vibe you give off, the way you conduct yourself, and how you speak to others.

Jeff Bezos, the founder of Amazon, is widely credited with saying, "Your brand is what people say about you when you're not in the room."

When you think about the person you want to be, do you see your actions lining up?

While we can't control what people think, we need to have peace that we've done our part when we bring our authentic selves to the table.

Living life with integrity is about presenting your best self *without* compromising your principles. You'll have a greater impact when you own your decisions and accept that you won't be everyone's cup of tea.

Money is not the only indicator of value.
Only you can know what an opportunity is worth to you.

When we deal with problems in life, money is usually the easiest culprit to blame. We can't help but default to thinking that more money would be the solution to all of our problems.

Have you caught yourself saying any of the following?

If only I made more money...

I wish I had saved more when I was younger...

If I had just invested at the right time...

Of course, there are times when money *is* the solution. But, depending on where we are in our lives and what we're working to achieve, money isn't always the magic remedy we're hoping for.

Sometimes what we need most is access. It's experience. It's education. It's a portfolio.

Value shows up in different ways, and not all of them are numerical. One opportunity might offer you key relationships you'll need in the future. Another might fill the gaps in your resume before applying to the job you *really* want.

When you bring value, you reserve the right to receive it. You just need to get a little creative with what it might look like for you at this moment.

When you make the most of every situation and bring significance through your work, every opportunity becomes invaluable to your future.

october

31

You may find that sometimes you turn out to be the bad guy in someone else's story. This does not make it your whole story.

Our inner monologue never stops.

There are countless moments throughout every day that contribute to the thoughts we have about ourselves. Negative or positive. Self-concluded or externally-driven.

We unfairly believe more pessimistic things about ourselves because it's easier than challenging our own lifelong scripts.

Because of this inner pattern, you may have also trained yourself to avoid confrontation. You don't want another shred of evidence that you aren't held in the high regard you'd like to be, so you try to stay on good terms with everyone.

Except this is impossible. Not only are you unable to make everyone happy, but you can't sustain all the ways you'd need to keep up this image.

Maybe it's okay to be the "bad guy" in the story sometimes, whether you're telling your child they must pack their lunch instead of buy, refusing to help your inlaws plan a party because you just don't have the time, or telling your boss who's treated you well for so long that you're leaving for another opportunity.

What would it feel like to focus on your narrative first?

You have your own story to tell. From time to time, let go of the ego and let down someone else's narrative so you can do what you've set out to do.

november

november

1

When you wait for opportunity to come to you,
you actually give away your chance.

You do the work. You manifest. You go after the life you want.

When you take on an active role in your life, you'll see your desires with perfect clarity. The story of how they can come true flashes through your mind so frequently that it feels more like a memory than a dream.

You know you'll get what you deserve...*someday*. But why not today?

It seems polite to respect the process and wait your turn to get what you want. We assume the experts will know when the time is right. We hope they'll just let us know instead of taking on the pursuit of finding out for ourselves.

But sadly, those who wait for permission rarely get it.

You may not always remember the role you play in making opportunities happen for yourself, but you *must* be your own greatest advocate.

Opportunities cannot appear out of thin air without our first generating a signal to the Universe. It's on you to throw your hat into the ring if you want to be seen.

Waiting for opportunities to come to you is the same as refusing to take ownership of your one and only life. Forget waiting for someone else's stamp of approval and sign off on your own permission slip.

november

2

When you wish for the ways of the past,
you're not preparing for your future.

Look how far you've come!

Everything you've experienced to this point has brought forth the incredible human you are today, and that's worth celebrating.

You can probably point to many wonderful moments that got you here. As you recall them, you might find yourself nostalgically wishing for those times. When you do, remember that just because something aligned well back then doesn't mean it's a perfect fit now.

Maybe you once had a workout regimen that felt flawless. Not only did it help you feel stronger and have more energy—you sincerely enjoyed it! But now, it doesn't click the same way. Or maybe your old morning routine now feels more like a chore than a luxury you look forward to. You loved it so much that it became a nonnegotiable, but now it doesn't hold the same spark.

We can absolutely appreciate what was once beautiful, but we can't live in the past. Times change, and the only option you have is to be in the here and now. When you try to hold onto the way things used to be, you relinquish power over the present *and* your incredible future.

What once worked for you may not anymore, and that's *great news*! You don't need the same things you did before. You aren't the same person you once were.

You have lived. You have grown. You're brand new today, and the possibilities aren't restricted to the ones you once knew. Celebrate that!

november

3

You can't fully receive what you don't ask for.

When asked what you wanted as a kid, you always had a few things to rattle off (especially if your birthday was coming up). You were unafraid to share what excited you and declare what you'd like to receive.

Think for a moment: When did you stop making those wishlists? Or, more importantly, *why?*

For many, it has to do with being exposed to limitations. Everyone else's ideas of what's socially acceptable to *want* for our lives make us hesitate. In an effort to fit in, we shrink to a smaller version of ourselves. We learn to omit details about who we truly are. Gradually, we start to believe that craving things is bad and freely expressing what we want is even worse.

Regardless of the doubts that set in, the Universe never stops listening. You attract everything you believe. What finds you is what you think you deserve. If you're disconnected from your desires, you'll attract the limitations you've learned to accept.

Your desires always matter because they're a direct reflection of your higher self. Let yourself wish and open your mind to the opportunities available to you.

Ask for what you want by emulating the result. Make that wishlist.

november

4

If you're tired of being tired,
you're wasting energy on the wrong things.

For too long, you've tried to balance it all. So understandably, you find yourself straight up exhausted.

You're tired of the constant juggle. Tired of feeling the push to do everything and the pull to try something else instead. Tired of wanting *this* while knowing you should, could, or would have something else too.

There's no avoiding fatigue, but we need to be aware of whether our exhaustion is worth it. A long day of work you deeply love is very different from pouring all your energy into efforts that don't matter to you.

What you love in life will require sacrifice at times—some mental, some physical, and some emotional. The true test is if the momentary sacrifice is worth the payoff in the long run.

Feeling tired is okay. Recognize it for what it is. Reflect on where it's necessary and where you can pivot a little. Then, honor what it takes to energize yourself again.

november

5

The one thing more powerful than knowing what you're capable of doing on your own is realizing you don't have to go it alone.

Being in your flow state is incredibly empowering. The excitement of making real progress toward your goals is enough to fuel years of hard work. Naturally, we find ourselves craving *more*.

Finding your flow is precious, yes, but it can only happen when you actively seek it out.

Be careful not to hold yourself back from greatness by assuming you must endure what you don't enjoy (or aren't all that good at). If you don't thrive at it, you don't have to strive at it. Bring others in, ask for help, and strategize to make space for that savored feeling of flow.

In a culture that constantly tolerates, asking someone to do something you know you can do yourself can feel weird. But, it's a necessary step to reach your ultimate calling. Get comfortable allowing others the same opportunity. Know there are people who love to do the things you stress over and help them unlock their potential in the process.

You're bigger than the box you're playing in. Step beyond those confines, and you'll realize you're capable of greater things than you've let yourself imagine. Let people in and lift the entire vision up in turn.

november

6

If everything were "just right," there wouldn't be anything left to do.

We wait for the right time.

We wait for the right place.

We romanticize the day we'll finally wake up and feel *ready*.

And then, we wait some more.

Success is never a straight line. It's a scribble going up, down, forward, backward, and everywhere in between. Despite well-intentioned planning, you'll never know your story until you *experience* your story.

No matter how long we wait, our circumstances are never going to be perfect. If that sounds disappointing, remember this: If everything were already exactly the way you wanted, there'd be no reason to go after your dream in the first place.

Whatever your circumstances are, they aren't what gives you the courage you need to act. The only way to collect any confidence is to simply *move forward*.

If you're looking for a reason to wait, you'll find one every time. Instead, make the case for: *Why not now?*

november

Learning from regret is powerful. Fearing future regret is pointless. Own your path by accepting whatever comes your way.

Have you ever been in the middle of the hustle and paused for a moment, only to realize how lost you really were?

You find yourself holding a diploma for a degree that was everyone's dream but yours. Or you see yourself seated in the corner office with a skyline view doing work that doesn't ignite you.

But you succeeded, right? You did something important, something impressive. This is fine, right? *Right?*

Somehow, without realizing it, you wound up blazing down a path you never wanted to be on. When you take stock of your surroundings, you discover that everything isn't adding up the way you hoped.

If you're in this place, know that you have options. You always do. You can resign yourself to staying in the place you never wanted to be, or you can throw away the rulebook and vow to find the path that actually excites you.

Choosing to discover what's right for you will bring both joy and uncertainty. Staying stuck will be safe for a while, but only until the pain is too much. Only one of these choices will be worthwhile in the end.

Here you are, standing at the crossroads of possibility. What choice will make you proud? The decision is all yours.

november

8

If you're doing one thing better than yesterday, you're winning.

You're amped, energized, and ready to roll. You've got a list of a hundred habits you can't wait to tackle. You're taking on the world, one goal at a time, and no one can stop you!

Or, maybe you're struggling. You're exhausted. Even the bare minimum feels like too much to keep up with.

At some point, we've all found ourselves at both extremes. While they seem like polar opposites, they share a strong similarity: When you find yourself there, you don't need to take *everything* on at that moment.

When you've got endless motivation at your disposal, you'll be tempted to overcommit (and eventually fall from the high). Don't do it. Just promise to do *one* thing better than before, then build upon that thing when you've mastered it.

On the flip side, when you're feeling low and can't imagine taking on anything else—know that one baby step better than yesterday is still *better*.

Instead of dissecting your areas of weakness, take notice of areas of improvement. How far have you come from a year ago? A month ago? Yesterday?

Keeping score is helpful when you're competing with your former self. In fact, the you of the past is the only competitor that really matters. Give yourself the credit you deserve.

When you reflect on where you've been, you build the inner strength you're looking for. There's restorative energy in it, too.

If today is better than yesterday, make a note. If not, make it happen tomorrow.

november

9

You attract what you're ready to receive.

Before you can receive what you want, you have to show that you're ready for it to come your way.

If you've ever found yourself in the dating world, you know the struggle of going on not one, not two, but a *series* of disappointing dates. You've probably struggled to quiet the nagging voice in your head saying that there's something inherently wrong with you.

We get so caught up in whether someone else is right for us that we forget to make ourselves undeniably available to the destiny we want to attract.

The biggest thing you can do to attract someone new is to emit the energy of a present and loving person.

Whether you're searching for your perfect match or for a more promising future in another area of your life—the rules are the same. If you don't believe you're worthy of the good you want in your life, you'll attract whatever it is you *do* believe you're worthy of.

If you're subconsciously attracting undesirable results, figure out which belief is the culprit and question why you're still holding onto it. How is that belief keeping you from what you truly deserve?

What you think dictates what you manifest.

Think about how much you can build rather
than how little you have to work with.

An idea just hit you out of nowhere.

Something piqued your interest. You felt an initial spark of excitement until that familiar feeling quickly interrupts it.

Doubt.

You know what to do. You want to avoid disappointment, so you shut your idea down before there's any further damage. Crisis averted. You're safe from criticism, safe from failure.

But at what cost?

We too often stop short of making our boldest dreams viable realities. We do it in an act of self-preservation. Instead of trying and failing, we fail to even try. We question what's attainable by questioning the few resources we have.

How many times have you marveled at an idea in your mind only to stop it in its tracks because of your circumstances?

Your dream job opened up, but you don't put your hat in the ring because you only check 8 of the 10 requirements listed. Rather than leaning into the 80% you fulfill, you fixate on the 20% that isn't in your favor.

Focus on your advantages instead of fixating on what's missing. Successful people lean into their strengths. They're not worried about their weaknesses because they know the support for them is available.

You can apply for that position and *own* the boxes you check perfectly. You can remind them why you're the perfect hire by relying on your resourcefulness.

It's not about what shows up on paper. It's about how you show up in life. Focus your energy accordingly and exceed expectations along the way.

november

— 11 —

Give the time that you can. Give the money that you can.
Give all you can for the things you believe in.

When all is said and done, your actions are a direct reflection of your values.

Imagine that at the end of your life, only two documents remained: your monthly budget and your calendar. How you spent your money and how you spent your time. What would these items tell the world about you?

Our bank statements are an undeniable tell of our priorities. If you've ever met with a financial planner, this is one of the first exercises they'll walk you through. What's important to you? Do your transactions align?

Your calendar is another telling source. If there was a running tally of how you spent your time, where would most of it go? There's work, family, friends, hobbies, travel, and philanthropy—just to name a few. Is your most precious resource going to the things that matter to you the most?

If where your money goes doesn't speak to who you are, change your approach. If where your time goes doesn't match what you value, it's time to find the alignment.

It's that simple.

november

⑫

Balance is what you ask for when you actually wish for peace.

Our society has an incredible fascination with balance. It sits high on a list of "Things We All Want," yet no one seems to know what it would look like if they found it.

The word "balance" just *sounds* nice. It's the perfect pipe dream: insanely desirable and conveniently out of reach.

If I could create a balanced life, what would it look like? How would I know I achieved it? Visualize your ideal day. What kind of work would you focus on? How much leisure time would you enjoy? Who would be with you?

Aiming for balance without understanding these details is both an illusion and an unattainable goal. When we fail to define *what* balance even is, it causes us to settle for problems we could otherwise solve.

You can't balance a scale without equal weight. Your work. Your family. Your hobbies. Your many facets of life can never all have equal measure. The truth is that balance is only possible when all things equal *zero*.

Be honest with yourself about what balance really means to you. Is it less conflict with those close to you? Is it feeling present with your family when you spend time together? Or, do you simply wish for less time running around and more time being still?

Life will never be perfect, but we have the power to establish peace of mind for ourselves.

What could you do to create peace for yourself today?

november

13

When you create value for others,
remember that they determine how valuable it is.

We live in a society of instant gratification, where you can get any quick fix or answer you need in just an Internet second.

The wonderful byproduct of this is that (if you choose to) you can share yourself and your own message with an audience that relates to you. This is why it's so important to note the meaning of true value.

You can probably think of so many life lessons you believe would be interesting to your target audience. However, you won't know if you're spot-on until you've done the most important work in building connection: listening.

Your life experiences are invaluable to you, but their value to someone else is dependent on where they are in their *own* journey. Value isn't what you think it is. It's what *someone else* thinks it is. Ultimately, value is determined by those who have it offered to them, not by the person who creates it.

Whether your audience is thousands of followers on social media or a hiring committee you're pitching yourself to—think like them. Stand in their shoes. At *this* moment. What do they *need* that you have? Offer them whatever would move the needle for them today.

This is what it takes to build the greatest value for your journey: trust.

november

14

When you're present for it, every morning is perfect.

If you had to describe your mornings in one word, "perfect" probably isn't at the top of the list.

More often than not, our mornings invite a...*special* cocktail of chaos. Whether you've got kids, pets, significant others, alarms, or just the magnetic pull to stay in bed—any one (or combo) of these easily leads to morning anarchy.

It's normal to feel like a failure when your routine goes awry, but give yourself some credit for the circumstances in your life right now. The ones you wished for and carefully chose. The people you surround yourself with, even if they *are* a little noisy the moment they wake up. The fun you had last night, even if it meant you stayed up a little later than usual.

Instead of seeking out more *perfect*, appreciate the abundance you have and seek *presence*.

Show up with your (once hot, now ice cold) cup of coffee and a screaming toddler. Show up with bags under your eyes and a skipped skincare routine. Show up when you don't want to.

Embrace it all and show gratitude for the season you're in. There's no better way to start the day.

november

15

*When you feel compelled to explain why you're right,
instead look for evidence that makes it unnecessary.*

We all have our share of hills we're willing to die on. When we feel truly convicted, we can't help but offer our opinion. However, others may not receive our thoughts as well as we hope.

Even when you mean well, speaking up always comes with the risk of being misunderstood.

There's always something we can learn in these moments, whether it be about the current situation, the people around us, or ourselves. This moment may tempt you to prove your point, but the urge to convey just how *right* you are is another trick of the ego. The more you dig your heels in, the more you get wrapped up in the trap.

At a moment like this, someone has been sent to teach you a lesson (not the other way around). If you find yourself feeling defensive, you reveal that you're not really at peace. If you were, you wouldn't have armored up to go to battle in this discussion in the first place.

Notice the opportunity to discover something new when you're being tested. No need to prove your point. Get the most value from every interaction by asking yourself: *What can I learn from this?*

november

16

Be genuinely curious.

If we're blatantly honest, our lives might seem overwhelmingly ordinary at times.

Yes, there are those exciting transitional moments like graduations, new careers, and new arrivals to the family. But still, we spend a great deal of our time sitting in whatever season we're in and learning to embrace that moment for what it is.

This is why we need curiosity—it's the spice of life.

No matter what happens today, who you meet, or what new ideas appear, remain genuinely curious. Every extraordinary day started out the same as all the other ones. Who's to say there isn't something incredible on its way to you *right now*? If you decide you already know better than to expect something great, you foolishly chase away any opportunities for growth.

Allow the day to happen and as it does, think to yourself: *How can I use this knowledge to create something better?*

Every new day brings with it the opportunity to ask ourselves what *could* be. Welcoming curiosity gives us the power to create change. The power to be accountable for our lives. The power to wonder.

You're worthy of all the answers you seek. Keep questioning.

To be able to say who your friends are, you must be a friend.

Remember back in elementary school how being called someone's best friend was the greatest honor? Not only was it an envied status, but you also had the matching friendship bracelets to prove it.

As we get older, making friends becomes more complicated. It's less instantaneous and more intentional. Less formulaic and more nuanced.

How do *you* define a friend?

Some people seem to have a friend in every room they step into. Others take years to give someone that title (and even then, they might keep them at a comfortable distance).

Whether you call someone a friend, an acquaintance, or any other name—it's not the label that matters. What matters is how you show up for them and how they show up for you.

Great friendships will come and go in your life. You'll know you've found a lasting friendship when you can show love to them while staying true to your authentic, ever-evolving self.

november

18

Whether life happens to you or for you is entirely up to you.

The saying goes, "We're all heroes in our own story," and to some degree, that's true.

That said, we also play the role of the victim just as often (maybe without even realizing it). The victim doesn't always look like the damsel in distress in need of saving. You can easily recognize a victim by how they speak.

When they read their lines, you might hear them say:

That's not my fault. Ah, yes. A classic example of removing responsibility and lending blame.

I know I'm late, but I have a very good reason. Isn't overexplaining such an elegant approach to making excuses?

You would have done that to me too. A tit-for-tat approach that quickly extinguishes resolution.

Victims need a hero to save the day. Heroes are self-aware enough to recognize their own weakness *before* it takes them down. They do this by refusing to waste time on silly stories.

november

19

Your path is unclear for a reason: It's meant to be discovered.

Refraining from making decisions always stems from a place of fear.

The fear of making the wrong call. The fear of upsetting someone dear to us. The fear of heading down the wrong path. The fear of *regret*.

Ego-driven fear keeps us from our greatest potential and from connecting with our higher self. All the while, that higher self will love us unconditionally no matter what decision we make.

Having the agency to decide is a *good* thing, especially when we realize that there are no right or wrong decisions. There's only right or wrong *for you*. You set the rules.

Keep these two truths in mind:

1. The life you want is completely yours to discover.
2. Fear and love cannot coexist.

When we forget these, we struggle to be decisive. The reason your path is unclear isn't so you will fear it, but so you can discover it (and love the process along the way).

november

20

You always have the power to make a change.

One of the greatest talents you have is your ability to know what's good for you.

Maybe you're used to drinking a can of soda a day, but deep down, you know you'd benefit from upping your water intake. Maybe you've been shrugging off your body's plea for a little more movement each day.

Whatever the case may be, you probably already know the change that needs to be made. All you need to do now is *make it*.

Listen to what your body needs. Start responding to what it's asking for. Not only will you feel better physically—your mind and heart will thank you as well. They all work together for you to thrive, and it's up to you to get everyone on the same page.

If it all feels daunting, purposefully make small changes. Ease into drinking more water by sipping some when you wake up. Get back into dancing by stepping into your old stretching routine to remind your body of the feeling.

We get so wrapped up in the anticipation of making a change that we forget the rewards it'll bring. Once you've decided which adjustment is right, try it and see how it feels!

november

21

Invest in yourself.

Our minds just *love* to think in black and white. As our brains are pelted with millions of stimuli every day, it's no wonder we rely on shortcuts to process information.

For instance, we jump straight to dollars and cents when we hear words like "wealthy" or "abundance". We're quick to forget that wealth takes on several forms—many of them not monetary.

Where do you see wealth in your life today? It might take a few moments to notice, but it's there.

When you sit around a table of friends that make you laugh until your belly hurts, you experience wealth. When you soak up the wisdom of those who came before you through their books and podcasts, you experience wealth. When you protect space on your calendar and enjoy the feeling of freedom it gives you, you experience wealth.

Create more wealth in your life by recognizing all the ways it takes shape for you: your relationships, your inner peace, your mindset, and—of course—your wallet.

There are countless ways to invest in yourself, and only some of them will be worth it. You'll know what's right when you feel in your heart that you're energetically matched to that investment.

november

22

Yes, you can have it all. Go get it.

You deserve to have it all. To hold out until you get everything you want. To not compromise what you value most.

The idea of "having it all" seems like the ultimate achievement, but it can quickly become a pressure cooker of frustration if not approached the right way.

The only way to have it all is to enjoy every contribution along the way. Give yourself time to value having it all—one piece at a time.

The pieces will come together, and when they do, you'll find the full picture you uncover to be even more satisfying. Give space to each element as you discover it. Allow yourself to have a journey with each incremental desire.

You might find that "having it all" changes its meaning along the way.

november

23

The right thing is always the right thing.
The right thing is always the right thing.

We've all been there. We feel stuck. Unsure. We have no idea what to do next, much less how to get all the way to where we want to be.

In these moments, we're tempted to buckle down and think through it all again before moving forward. We forget how much simpler it is to just do the next right thing. Whatever that is. Try not to overthink it.

What is the next right thing to do?

The answer to this is probably also the simple, hard thing. The first thing you thought of. The far-too-obvious choice. The thing you initially overlooked because it seemed too straightforward to be the solution to such a big, complicated problem.

You've found it! That's the thing to go all-in on.

Choosing the easy, safe decision might feel good momentarily, but it'll veer you away from where you truly want to be.

If you're still unsure, consider which action you can proudly stand behind one year, five years, or even 20 years down the road.

You know the answer. Move confidently in that direction.

november

24

Generosity generates gratitude.

A lot can be said about a person based on where and how they offer grace to others.

There are times we hesitate to spread the wealth, most often out of fear. We worry there won't be enough to go around. We subconsciously believe that someone doesn't deserve a piece of what we've earned or that we're not responsible for bettering someone else's life.

It doesn't make you a bad person to feel that way. We're all human. We must simply rebuild our response. These moments of hesitation are nothing more than opportunities to act differently this time.

Giving isn't only about those who are receiving. Giving is about indicating that you know there's much more where that came from. It's about participating in the exchange of *abundance*. More for you, more for me.

What are you doing to create a thriving and inspired life—not just for yourself but also for those around you?

Give what you can at this moment. If you have money, donate it. If you have time, offer it. If you have experience, share it. Life isn't about what you'll get in return.

november

25

When you reconnect to your blessings, you reconnect to your why.

The noise of our daily lives can easily overpower the big picture. That noise is especially good at getting us so wrapped up in the little details of life that we lose focus on the vision.

All great goals are only as good as the gratitude you embrace them with. It's not just about the ultimate achievement, it's about the appreciation for the process along the way.

We're all on a journey to happiness. The gratitude that comes with achievement is amazing—no doubt—but it's also momentary. There will always be the next thing. The danger is that when we're too focused on *next*, we forget to check into *now*.

Before you achieve the next great thing, you must have gratitude for the great thing right in front of you.

Look around. What do you see that makes you feel thankful?

Listen to your surroundings. What do you hear that brings comfort?

Breathe in. What aspect of your life would your past self be elated to know about?

There is already so much to be grateful for. In order to keep your vision for the future top of mind, make gratitude for today a priority.

november

26

*Fulfillment comes from the love and
nurturing of relationships we keep.*

Life is ultimately about who you have by your side.

Every experience you have is influenced by who you share it with. Look down and see the person holding your hand on the tough days. Look out to see who's applauding you on the celebratory days. Look around and see those you can serve with your unique gifts.

Some might call it your support system, your tribe, or your network—the name doesn't matter. No matter what you call them, curating the circle of people in your life takes thoughtfulness and care. It's the ultimate VIP situation. The tone of your life depends on those you surround yourself with.

As you make your selections, remember to keep these questions in mind:

Am I being the kind of friend I'd like to have? How can I show more support to those I love?

Am I celebrating the people in my life? Who could I cheer on a little extra today?

Have I found the love I need? How can I seek out more of it?

As you reflect, make more room for the reciprocal relationships. Be thankful for those who lift you up and lift them up in return.

november

27

There is no blessing too small to show gratitude for.

Gratitude is exponential when practiced diligently. And yet, isn't it interesting how we find ways to limit something as *unlimited* as gratitude?

We often think things are too small, too silly, or too strange to show gratitude for—and what a shame that is.

There's always something to appreciate. All we have to do is notice it.

The things you love and value give your life meaning. When you practice everyday gratitude, you'll start seeing goodness in everything. Nothing is by accident, not even the smallest serendipitous happenstance.

Have gratitude for the hair tie you found in the bottom of your handbag at the exact moment you needed it.

Have gratitude for the bunch of sidewalk flowers that made your morning walk a little different than yesterday.

Have gratitude for the fact that you can eat dessert first if you want to, just for the heck of it.

Thank you, thank you, thank you.

Acknowledge the seemingly insignificant things as practice for the big and beautiful moments that are to come.

november

28

*What you want will come once you've proven
what you're willing to do to achieve it.*

All good things come in time.

As true as this is, it doesn't mesh well with our modern-day desire to receive things instantly. But it'll be worth the wait.

Meaningful success is always worth the wait.

When your moment arrives, everything makes sense in hindsight. The key is time. Putting your 10,000 hours in. Showing up (not just once, but over and over again). Even when you're the only one there.

Don't let others' success discourage you. In fact, seeing good things coming to fruition in front of you (even when not for you directly) is a good thing! It's a sign that you're manifesting this desire so well that possibilities are popping up all around you. They're reminding you that you're on the right track.

Take those signs as fuel for continuing to head in the right direction.

When you really want something, you'll stop checking the clock. You'll forget the clock is even there.

november

29

Forget perfection. Acknowledge excellence instead.

Our perfectionist recovery journey is not only about our own lives but also about the way we see the lives of others.

That presentation was just perfect!

She's the perfect mom. I don't know how she does it.

Your life is so perfect!

Each seemingly complimentary comment only worsens the underlying issues we have with perfectionism.

The next time you find yourself saying these words, remember that perfection doesn't exist. Anywhere, anytime, in any way.

Writing someone off as "perfect" might *seem* like a nice thing to say. In reality, it unintentionally minimizes their life experience and glosses over the work it took to achieve their success. They likely don't consider themselves to be perfect because they know the messy middle—not just the shiny end result.

Excellence, on the other hand, is the acknowledgment that perfection cannot offer. Excellence doesn't care about being flawless—it focuses on quality. It describes ownership. It admits adversity while still showing perseverance.

When we see excellence in action, we feel drawn into the contagious energy that leaves us in awe. Show respect to excellence when you see it so that you can immediately chip away at the old perfectionist way of thinking.

november

30

To know your why is to embrace the whole truth
of what you aspire to be.

Your real why is what gets you out of bed in the morning.

It's not the thing you say at dinner parties because it sounds good. It's not what you post because you know others will like it. And it's *certainly* not what you think you "should" do.

If you aren't sure what it is, clear the mental clutter. Throw everyone else's approval and expectations out of the window during this exercise. Instead, focus on a reality where the only milestones that mattered were the ones that were self-awarded.

What would you do if the only opinion you based your decision on was your own?

What would you do if failure didn't feel fatal?

What would you do if you stopped waiting to be ready?

Who do you want to *be*?

This is what matters. Give yourself the chance to experience it for real.

december

december

1

*Knowing where you want to be is the first step
to figuring out what to do next.*

We spend a great deal of our lives asking ourselves what's next. We know something needs to happen between Point A and Point Z, and we're eager to begin checking those boxes.

This mentality serves us well enough in our schooling when we live according to structured semester plans. The same might apply to rising through the ranks at a specific company, each promotional jump clearly laid out ahead of you.

…But what happens when those authorities fall away?

What's next is now multi-faceted. What's next is no longer hard and fast. What's next is, well, up to *you*.

If this feels terrifying instead of liberating, start by exploring your options to gain clarity:

Where do you *not* want to be? This can be as helpful (and as motivating) as knowing what you *do* want. Take note of where you've been that you wouldn't want to return to.
Who's someone you feel has it all figured out? What in their life is appealing to you? Read their book or ask them how they got there.
How do you want to feel? Close your eyes and think about who might surround you and what your days could contain. Illustrate a day in your future life.

Feel the freedom to let yourself daydream. Know that your map isn't set in stone. Just because you set off in one direction today doesn't mean that it must be your destination tomorrow.

The only way to find out is to keep moving forward.

december

2

What you seek is already on its way to you. Believe in its arrival.

There will be times when it seems like nothing is going right—when it feels like there's a new obstacle or a flashing sign titled "Not yet!" at every turn.

It's tempting to look outward to figure out why you're not getting what you want; still, instead of projecting, remember this is just part of the human experience. What will be will be. Nothing—not even the biggest obstacle—will be able to prevent what's truly meant for you from coming true.

Rewire the thought processes that falsely tell you interruptions are endings. Instead of stopping every time an obstacle appears, refuse to be surprised by them. You might not know what shape they'll show up in, but you do know they'll show up.

Your limiting beliefs are nothing more than distractions from self-trust. When they pop up, put on your best customer service voice: *Thanks for your input, but I'm not accepting feedback at this time.*

Enough said.

december

3

Release all expectations. Give for the sake of giving.

We all know what it feels like to cross our fingers and hope others will show up for us. We yearn for their connection and support. This is what it is to be human.

This becomes a slippery slope when those innocent hopes morph into uninhibited expectations. Usually, expectations are agreements we've reached only with ourselves. We've decided how someone should act, and that's the end of that. No matter what we think is obviously appropriate for another person to do or say, it's likely they won't be on the exact same page.

Ugh! I always drop everything for them, why aren't they doing the same for me?

Thoughts like this are a glaring reminder that we've been holding onto a one-sided expectation. If the entire point is to have real, meaningful connections with others, why are we keeping score?

We can't control others' actions. We can't control the decisions they make for themselves. Whether they're ignoring your email, refusing to support you, or simply turning you down when you ask for their time—accept them for who they are. Trust that they're making the best decision for themselves (as you should continue to do for yourself).

When you let go of expectations, you begin to give without any qualification. The abundance you share—especially the grace you give to others—will come back around.

december

2

A day is only planned well when there's time to rest.

For most of us, getting a consistent eight hours of sleep feels like a pipe dream.

Our physical health is often so focused on diet and exercise that we easily forget about sleep. Of course, we all *know* it's important—it takes up ⅓ of our lives! But still, when the chips are down, it's the first thing we sacrifice.

No matter who you are or how superhuman you may feel, your body needs rest to function fully. More than that, you deserve to feel refreshed and energized. Sleep isn't only essential to a happy life, it's one of the most productive things you can do!

When you give yourself the rest you need, you:
Reduce stress (Yes, please!)
Increase brain function (Everyone could use this one.)
Maintain a healthy metabolism (Bonus for those nutrition goals!)

Treat your body well. Rest when you need it. This is a non-negotiable.

december

4

Release all expectations. Give for the sake of giving.

We all know what it feels like to cross our fingers and hope others will show up for us. We yearn for their connection and support. This is what it is to be human.

This becomes a slippery slope when those innocent hopes morph into uninhibited expectations. Usually, expectations are agreements we've reached only with ourselves. We've decided how someone should act, and that's the end of that. No matter what we think is obviously appropriate for another person to do or say, it's likely they won't be on the exact same page.

Ugh! I always drop everything for them, why aren't they doing the same for me?

Thoughts like this are a glaring reminder that we've been holding onto a one-sided expectation. If the entire point is to have real, meaningful connections with others, why are we keeping score?

We can't control others' actions. We can't control the decisions they make for themselves. Whether they're ignoring your email, refusing to support you, or simply turning you down when you ask for their time—accept them for who they are. Trust that they're making the best decision for themselves (as you should continue to do for yourself).

When you let go of expectations, you begin to give without any qualification. The abundance you share—especially the grace you give to others—will come back around.

december

5

If you have the audacity to think of an incredible idea,
leverage that boldness to bring it to life.

Having an idea is only the beginning. When you feel that rush of adrenaline and inspiration, you know you're just getting started. The best is yet to come.

Daydreaming is the greatest, isn't it? It allows you to get fully wrapped up in possibility without being weighed down by any present circumstances. You can let your mind wander without any of the scary risks of pursuing an idea.

You can picture it clearly. You feel the excitement coursing through your mind. What more convincing do you need? How much more compelling does that daydream need to be for you to pursue it?

You are the only difference between what stays in your mind and what lives in the real world. If it's this fun to imagine, think of how amazing it'll feel to dive in *for real.*

Everything started as someone's daydream. Your computer, the lights in your house, the glasses you're wearing, the book you're reading, the painting hanging on your wall, the music playing through your speakers. That person took their daydream beyond just a passing thought, and now it's one of your daily luxuries.

The next time your imagination wanders somewhere great, let your mind linger on how it'll feel to make it a reality.

december

6

Remain a student for life.

There's always more to learn. This we know, especially in an age where information is more available than ever, and a single Google search offers billions of results at our fingertips.

When you have the mentality of being a forever student, you discover a beautiful paradox: The more you learn, the more you realize you *have yet* to learn.

It's a delightfully enticing truth. The ancient Chinese philosopher Confucius put it simply, "Real knowledge is to know the extent of one's ignorance".

There's just one appropriate response to such a statement, and that's an enthusiastic willingness to learn.

Take this attitude into every day. Pick up a book on a topic you've never heard of. Marvel at the random facts and figures of our world. Ask more questions. Listen to what others have to say.

Tap into the childlike curiosity that has no shame in asking *Why?* over and over, just to find out where it leads.

A richer, more fulfilled life awaits you.

december

7

Choose the way you want to feel.

Feelings come and go constantly. They can be so relentless and unpredictable that, at some point, it's easier to just let them take the wheel. Or, at least, that's how it feels.

Most of the time, we settle with one of two approaches when an emotion comes our way. We relinquish control completely and let our emotion take us where it may, or we grasp for control of it in vain. Either surrender or stuff it down. Neither option leaves us feeling our best.

Feelings seem out of our control, so we resign ourselves to being at their whim. While our feelings are valid and should be treated as such, we don't have to be at the mercy of their every shift. No matter what we're feeling, we retain the ability to choose what follows.

No emotion is wrong. We're allowed to feel how we do. What matters more than the feeling itself is doing right by our own mindset. If you're tired of being annoyed, disappointed, discouraged, enraged, or any other negative emotion—it's okay for you to choose a different one. It doesn't make your feelings any less important. It just means you're open to something *better*.

Be open to choosing the way you want to feel.

8

When we ask for help, we show our true desire to succeed.

Talk is cheap—especially if you don't say what really matters to you.

One of the most overlooked keys to success is the ability to ask for help. Most of us shy away from it; no matter how universal the need for help is, *asking* for it ourselves often makes us feel uncomfortable, vulnerable, or less-than.

Of course, this is even more challenging when we're taught that talking about money is rude. How are we supposed to learn anything new if the whole conversation has been taken off the table?

Your financial well-being relies on you being open to asking for help, both thoughtfully and honestly. It's not about asking people what their business is. It's about observing their ability to make their aspirations come true and borrowing the knowledge it took to get there.

If you can, bend the ear of someone who has the wisdom to offer. The best move in a conversation like this is to end with a personal question: *What would you do if you were in my shoes?*

This is how you remove any nosiness or inappropriateness from a conversation about money. This is how you'll learn real steps that'll pay off long-term—both in your wallet and in wisdom.

To get comfortable talking about money, sit back and listen first.

december

9

You can do this. Whether they say you can or not.

When something new or ground-breaking that we've been waiting for *finally* arrives, we get super pumped. This unbelievable, once-in-a-million opportunity just showed up for us, and we think: *This must be a dream. Is this for real?!*

Before we fully soak it in—BAM. Our second instinct kicks in. This is the voice that says, *Woah, slow down! Before you get ahead of yourself, take a second and see if this is real.*

The thoughts start spiraling. What do I need to do to keep this up? Will others think I'm worthy? How can I stay safe from criticism?

We do our best to give ourselves safety nets—emotionally, financially, and mentally— so that if everything falls to pieces, at least we're prepared! We tell ourselves, *It won't hurt so bad that way...right?*

Truthfully, there's no way to fully protect yourself when you're going after something that strikes a chord in your soul. Admitting that you desire something is vulnerable enough on its own, but going after it is even more so.

People are going to see what you're doing. People are going to comment. People will have their thoughts about whether you're too old, too young, educated enough, creative enough, smart enough, or whatever else to make it happen.

It's all irrelevant. The outside factors might seem as important, but they're only characters in a story you're telling. You don't need to justify your decisions to others to make sense of your actions. The only thing standing in your way is the decision to go after progress.

It's time to cut out the characters that don't contribute to your experience. It's not only possible for you to determine what's right for you entirely on your own—it's the first step to building the confidence you seek.

december

10

*The best way to tell someone your plans is
to show them your results.*

It's natural to want to share what's on our minds. It feels really good to let people in on our ideas and to enjoy their reactions in return. However, despite our excitement, sharing can come at a price.

Sometimes you're lucky and simply receive the enthusiastic reaction you're hoping for. Then there are also times the person on the other side might now feel invited to give their own perspective.

You excitedly announce to your family your decision to leave your 9-to-5 and grow your own business. They might feel responsible for protecting you and see an opportunity to point out what could go wrong.

You share your commitment to writing a book, and now you're constantly fielding inquiries about where your first draft is. You've added pressure to what was otherwise your precious creative space.

You tell your boss about the new workplace initiative you want to pursue but have nothing to show for yet. They may like the idea but wish you had come up with some concrete suggestions to go over.

When you share, you open the door for new expectations to creep in. This can be very useful, especially if you're asking someone to hold you accountable—just be prepared for the hit to your mindset.

There's something powerful in the sacred period of time before you let anyone else in. There's freedom sitting in solitude with the thing that excites you.

Savor that sacred space. Share thoughtfully (and only when you're ready). Walk the walk before you open up and begin to talk.

december

⑪

When you say what you're going to do, mean it.

We're all guilty of saying things we don't really mean. Maybe some of these sound familiar:

Yeah! We should totally do a road trip!...knowing full well it doesn't interest you in the least.

I can't wait for your baby shower!...when you're struggling to balance life as it is and you know you'll likely send a gift in your absence.

I really should start going to the gym every day...just the sound of an unrealistic "should" makes you shudder.

We make statements like this without realizing we're also making commitments. We hope if we say these things aloud, we'll be more likely to follow through on them. Many people think it works this way, so they give their best speech. It feels like the first step in the process.

The power of the words you use might help you take a step in the right direction, but they can't be the only measure you take. The more you do what you say you'll do, the more evidence you give yourself and others that you're capable of following through.

december

12

Realize the wealth you want, then observe those who have it.

There are a lot of people out there who will say they know what it's like to have financial freedom. The question is: What does financial freedom *mean* to them?

Pay close attention to the people whose advice you listen to and assess whether their actions match their words. If it's someone who's living the kind of life you want, then, by all means—hand them the megaphone and let the truth keep on coming!

But, if you notice their world doesn't match their story, you might want to take a step back and reassess just how good their guidance will be for you.

Don't look for the people who talk the talk—they're a dime a dozen. Find the people who walk the walk so well that they don't even need to talk at all. These are the thought leaders. These are the ones who will give it to you straight.

And, if you're still not sure, it's usually the quietest ones who know best. They're too busy focusing on doing what works to worry about making noise about it.

Make a point to follow those who emulate the results you want to see.

december

13

To live an unlimited life, critically assess the limits you've set yourself.

You were created to be a source of unlimited abundance. Let that sink in.

You were created to be a source of unlimited abundance.

This is easy to forget. As humans, we pay a lot of attention to what's right in front of us. And, if what's in front of us is telling a story of scarcity, we're quick to believe it's true.

When our limitations consume our thinking, how can we fully embrace what's possible? How can we foster a beautiful, abundant state of living—no matter what's around us?

It starts with being honest with yourself. Notice the times you're caught thinking small. Notice the temptation to silently criticize others for thinking big. What if you stretched your mind to find out there's more to the story...more to *your* story?

Start identifying your tendency to place limitations in simple, everyday moments. These mental statements are great indicators of just that:

That's impossible.

They'll never go for that.

Everyone will think that's stupid.

That's not the right way to do it.

There's no way I could do that.

You might call yourself a realist, or you might claim this is just how you are. Either way, remember that the limitations in your life will never change until *you're ready to see them change.*

Do you like your version of the truth? How's it working for you?

december

14

*Simply asking how you can help someone is
more significant than you realize.*

How can I help?

It's the simplest of questions but has an exponential impact.

We're all juggling a million things most of the time. Every last one of us has been at the end of our rope, needing someone to throw us a lifeline—not by solving all our problems, but by being willing to sit in them with us.

We get to take care of people in our lives just like we hope people will take care of us. That's the beautiful cycle of connection. We're all here to help each other, and a small gesture goes a long way.

So, just ask how you can help. Put the ball in their court, so you don't have to guess what they need. That's the beauty of it—they'll tell you!

Listen to the answer. Do what you can. Just because you offer doesn't mean they need anything other than the thought.

december

15

The difference between self-care and self-sabotage is the collection of choices you make daily.

The word "self-sabotage" carries a strong connotation.

None of us like to admit we're doing something detrimental to ourselves, but it doesn't always have to manifest in the extreme ways you might think.

You become the choices you make, and *every single choice* counts. Opt to care for yourself rather than restrict yourself.

If you don't sleep, you suffer. If you don't move your body, you suffer. If you eat nothing but junk food and never absorb the nutrients of a vegetable, you suffer. Every choice you make for your body influences your life and your ability to show up for it.

Go to bed just a few minutes earlier tonight. Plan to incorporate movement into your day, whatever that looks like for you. Assess the nutrition you need to take care of your body and extend your life. Indulge in some quiet time when you know you really need it.

True self-care comes from learning how to do the hard things. Each time you do them, you make the habit easier and easier.

Remind the only body you have that it can depend on you so you don't have to question whether you can rely on it.

december

16

Expectations are a prayer for disappointment.

We crave certainty. We want to feel prepared. We like to know what we're getting ourselves into. We don't like to get our hopes up.

Many of us rely on our expectations to gauge how excited, confident, or bold we're allowed to be *without* stepping out of the safe zone. We wouldn't dare risk coming across as *too much*, would we?

The result? We want to live on our own terms, but we end up spending our time wondering how others are going to react to our authenticity in action. All the while, someone else's actions (and reactions) remain far beyond your control.

Their standards are their own unique formula. You'll never have the complete solution, so why bother trying to crack the code at all? When we have expectations of how others should behave, we only set ourselves up for disappointment. Not because we should assume the worst from them, but because we cannot forget that we're all human.

Expectations are impossible to avoid entirely, but we can at least weed out the unnecessary ones. The rest will give us the perspective we need to stay grounded.

Instead of touting your high expectations (and ultimately manifesting defeat), keep your own standards in focus and give yourself grace when you show your humanity.

Even a morning gone perfectly doesn't equal a perfect life. Use the momentum of a great start to prepare you for what comes your way today.

The name of the game is *Good Morning, Good Life* for a reason.

Perfect mornings are hard to come by—and even if they happen, the magic won't last long.

This is why we must learn to see the potential in *good*. Good starts us on the right foot, so we have a better shot at winning the day. Good teaches us gratitude for a regular day instead of just the extraordinary ones.

A good morning helps you center your mind for the obstacles in the day ahead. It gives you a head start on feeling accomplished. No matter what happens the rest of the day—hey, at least you had that dedicated time for yourself in the morning!

And, when you're being tested, you can remember the inner work you did to start the day on your terms. Remember your studies and your journaling. Remember how you prioritized the important things.

The unpredictability of life might scare you into thinking you aren't ready to take it all on. But you've already trained for how to respond to confrontations and upheavals in your day. You've already decided that good is enough for you, knowing that perfect isn't an attainable goal.

Take solace in your mornings. This is your time to remember that you're capable of handling whatever comes your way.

december

18

*When you connect people to each other, you demonstrate
your power to listen, understand, and abundantly serve.*

Getting to know different people throughout life is magical.

You'll quickly learn that *everyone* has something interesting to share. This is pretty enticing on its own, but it's even more fun when you realize what you can do with these people you meet: You can connect them to *each other*.

When you see an opportunity for two people you know to benefit each other, you have a chance to initiate something new.

This is the power of becoming a connector, whether it's driven by love, business, or friendship. Watching people you know become closer to each other makes everything better. Not to mention, it speaks to your ability to tune into people so well that you make the people puzzle come together.

Sometimes we hesitate to introduce people to each other to avoid awkwardness or a personality clash. Or, we worry that if we share the love with others, we might lose it for ourselves.

Keep yourself from operating from a place of fear. You can't do this life alone—and even if you could, what fun would that be? The key to generating more success is encouraging others to enjoy the benefits alongside you.

december

19

Track your time to find your bliss.

Moments are fleeting. As quickly as we experience them, they're already on their way out the door. Time is our ultimate resource—yet we so easily lose track of it.

We find ourselves unhappy, distracted by what we haven't done, and annoyed with our commitments.

The culprit? *Letting time pass us by.*

You can only make the most of the moments you register. What would you learn about yourself if you documented every moment of your day today?

Without telling yourself a story about why things have to be the way they are, just look at the state of your life right now. Do you like it or not?

If not, ask the follow-up questions: What would you change if you could? Where would you spend more time if you had it?

You deserve the freedom that comes with looking forward to your life. Not all of what we spend our time doing will be sunshine and rainbows, but the challenges will be a lot more manageable if we've created a life we love.

december

20

Comprehension is good. Experience is better.

Learning a new craft is incredibly fulfilling.

In fact, we can get so caught up in the honeymoon phase of soaking up knowledge that we forget we're supposed to *do* something with it.

If you've gone out and read every book, listened to every podcast, and followed every person out there doing what you want to do—that's a great start! Just don't let the pursuit of knowing more keep you from trying the thing for real.

If knowledge is power, action is a close second. Following that knowledge with focused action will give you the level-up you're looking for. Getting stuck in the "prep" phase can be a vicious cycle (and a sneaky form of procrastination).

Pinpoint what's at the root of your procrastination. What's the thing you're waiting to "know" before you begin? If it's a practical skill or a question you need answered—great! You know what to do from here.

If you're waiting to know if you're capable or if it'll all work out the way you're hoping—the only way to find out is to try.

december

21

If a conversation is uncomfortable, it's not happening enough.

From a young age, we're trained to respect what is and what isn't "appropriate" to talk about. Money tends to fall in the age-old "Do Not Discuss" category.

When we grow up, we forget this isn't a rule we must abide by forever.

While it might not feel natural to discuss money, that doesn't mean you shouldn't try to. You simply have to flex the muscle after years of being conditioned not to. Breaking out of a generational mold brings discomfort, but it'll let up with time and (you guessed it) more uncomfortable conversations.

Knowing that dreams require money, realistically discuss your ideal life with your partner. What could you start doing now to prepare for your future?

Take stock of your financial life, whatever it looks like right now. Ask your budget-savvy friend if they have any tips for you.

Contemplate your worth at work and put a value on it. Bring your analysis up in a conversation with your boss to get their professional advice.

Challenge yourself to ask: *What's on the other side of all that discomfort?*

Find your answer. Then start talking.

december

22

*The confidence you wish for will come
from the collection of actions you take.*

The biggest mistake we make in the pursuit of confidence is looking outward instead of building inward.

You can't magically grant yourself instant self-confidence, but that doesn't mean it's out of your reach entirely. Your actions hold all the power, and luckily your actions are well within your control.

Narrow your focus on what you're missing.

If you wish you felt more confident in a conversation with someone you're attracted to, flex the muscle of approaching people and making small talk. If you wish you felt more confident at public speaking, give the next toast at a dinner party with your family. The steps you take are as big or small as you determine—you just have to *take* a step.

To be a true master of anything, you need to show up every day. This means practicing and honing your craft. It means committing over and over again until you achieve the result you want. It's a culmination of actions.

What will you do today to contribute to your confidence tomorrow?

december

23

Mindfulness is the most important habit of all.

We are our rituals.

For better or worse, the things we do time and again are the building blocks of who we become in this life.

Are your daily routines serving you? In order to create a life you can't wait to wake up to, you must be aware of what is (and isn't) working.

Break it down. Start by evaluating each of your routines.

Make a habit out of being mindful. Notice the parts of your day that light you up and the parts that drain you. Look for where you can relieve some tension. Find the path of least resistance for the things you want to do more of.

Why did I start doing this in the first place? Does it still make sense for me?

What does this habit do for me? What peace does it bring me?

What do I fear if I quit this habit? What do I have to look forward to?

Let these questions guide you to your answers.

Hold onto the habits that accelerate you, drop the ones that no longer serve you, and seek new ones that embolden you more.

december

24

Peace will come when you decide to emulate it.

Peace.

You can seek it. You can share it. Most of all—you can be it.

We get a choice in how we embody the energy we put out. One choice that always exists (whether or not our circumstances warrant it) is *peace*.

When you emulate peace, it radiates through you onto others. The more you send that feeling out into the world, the more it'll return to you.

Take a deep, slow breath in. Remind yourself what you know to be true. Make the choice to feel gratitude deeply right now.

Be the peace. Let the rest release.

december

25

It's not what we have but who we have.

We've all heard the saying "family first." Though we're all born into one family, we find our other family as we grow.

If you're truly fortunate, with time, you'll end up with a beautiful hybrid of both. The family we shape for ourselves is a representation of where we've been and what we value.

When we consistently love others the way we wish to be loved, we pour into these relationships. It doesn't matter what's going on around us when we have the *people* around us that matter.

Your family, however you define them, is your greatest mirror. Take a look at your inner circle. Recognize their impact on you and your impact on them in return.

Acknowledge those that surround you. Let their heartbeats remind you of what's truly important.

december

26

If you always rush to find what's next,
you'll miss the only thing you ever actually had: this moment.

Start today by taking your finger off of the fast forward button.

It's crucial to be in the moment when you can. We know this, but the shiny new thing vying for our attention typically wins out against the present moment. We can't help it, we just can't wait to find out how where our story goes! Still, what's next doesn't exist yet. It's much better to focus on what's here now.

Your dreams are valuable. Your sense of possibility is essential. You should indeed be excited to make your life all you believe it can be!

But in the midst of it all, don't forget the truth about what you have. This moment is passing whether you see it or not.

Everything you've been through and all you've done has led you to the here and now. Look around. Feel it. Take it in. Appreciate it.

What do I have now that I once waited for?

What good do I see in front of me that I can be grateful for?

What proof do I see in this moment that my life is already abundant?

When you acknowledge *what is* now, you look toward *what will be* in the future. To do both, you have to reflect. You have to be honest. You have to be present.

Be here now.

december

27

*Call on your relationships for the reminder
that you're already loved as you are.*

Relationships are a great solution to stopping the cycle of stress (at least for a moment) and getting reconnected to our highest selves. They're the reminder we all need when we feel the most lost.

When things in life get to be too much, many of us forget to reach out, and we turn inward instead. Step outside of yourself and remember you're not alone. Who can you call on? Who makes you laugh? Who makes you feel lighter?

Call on the person who gives you these much-needed reminders: You are enough. You are worthy. You *matter*.

These truths are undeniable, but they risk getting overshadowed by the noise in your mind. When you can't find the mute button, call on someone who will speak that truth back into your life.

Pick up the phone. Send some snail mail. And when life calms down a bit for you, take every chance to be the reminder for someone else who needs it.

december

28

Let the process be the process…and try to enjoy it!

Many of us are suckers for a happy ending—and who can blame us? We just love seeing everything come together nicely and neatly, so we can't wait to experience our very own formative moment.

How will it all turn out? Will it be just like I imagined?

The story might feel the most satisfying all wrapped up with a bow at the end, but that's not always the best part. All the really good stuff happens in the process. If you jump ahead to the finale, you miss all the moments that make the conclusion feel so sweet.

Happily ever after doesn't always take into account all that the "after" entails. Plus, it certainly speeds past the many happy "before"s.

You might get to the end only to realize you wish you could do it all over again. The anticipation, the experience, the figuring it all out along the way—those turned out to be the best parts.

What will be will be soon enough. No skipping to the last chapter. It's time to embrace every page.

december

29

It's always your day to move everything out of your way.

What if you woke up tomorrow and discovered that nothing was in your way? Picture it.

You miraculously wake up before your alarm, both rested and enthusiastic for the day. You hit only green lights on the way to work. The coffee tastes extra good, and you breeze through the day with zero obstacles. You get off work early at the end of the day and find you have lots of time to enjoy anything you want.

Go after *that* life. Begin by answering these questions:

- *What would I do if I had nothing but time?*
- *What career do I daydream about?*
- *What destination have I been longing to visit?*
- *What hobby have I always wanted to pick up?*
- *What person would I reconnect with?*
- *What does it mean to me to go after the life I want?*

The reality is you won't see a day where all your challenges have simply evaporated. However, a day full of enthusiasm is still attainable. Your perspective and your habits will be invaluable in creating a life you love.

No more hesitating. Make today your *yes* day.

december

30

If you're waiting for a sign, here it is.

Whatever you believe is what will show up for you.

When we wait for faith to show itself, we forget our role in bringing it about. We hold out for a billboard-sized sign. We wait for the "aha!" moment to hit us like a ton of bricks. But the sign we're waiting for is only possible when we put it out there for ourselves.

You can't wait for the Universe to tell you what's in store for your life. You need to tell it what you're available and ready for. Put the signal out. Alert the presses. Let it radiate from your mind, body, and soul. This is the only way to see the signs you wish to see.

You're pausing your dreams and waiting for permission, but the only person whose permission you need is *your own*.

Stop wishing and waiting. The sign you need is in your heart. The permission you need will come from your own mind. Step into your authority as the one who has the power to make it all happen.

It's time to set your sign out. What will yours say?

december

31

What you desire is created by your past.
What you do now creates your future.

Humans are the ultimate meaning-makers. As a result, we're constantly in a state of pursuit and constantly searching for understanding.

We see, feel, or experience something—anything—and instantly add our own cocktail of details and perspective. The stories we tell ourselves are heavily influenced by what we've experienced before. We draw from what we know, and those preconceived notions dictate our future. Whether we realize it or not, the things that drive us most can be linked back to old narratives we never fully outgrew.

Old stories matter, but they're not the *whole* story. Their significance comes from what you *do* with them. If a certain narrative causes you to assume the worst, give it a break to look at new ideas. If certain memories drive you to do whatever it takes to prevent your previous life from showing up again, they could be exactly the motivator you need.

Your past will always be your past. That said, it has nothing to do with what's to come. It only gets power if you grant it. Your beliefs and actions dictate who you have yet to become.

Keep the past behind you and step toward a future of your own making, led by actions you believe in.

conclusion

Mortimer J. Adler was one of the great contemporary classic thinkers of our time. Passionate about philosophy, he enjoyed reformulating the ideas of great philosophers to help the modern world understand life's big ideas. Adler offered this insight alongside writer Charles Van Doren in *How to Read a Book: The Classic Guide to Intelligent Reading*:

"In the case of good books, the point is not to see how many of them you can get through, but rather how many can get through to you."

You know the truth behind Adler's words. Reading can be a challenge, for any number of reasons. Many let those challenges stop them short from reading any more than necessary after their last final exam in school. But not you. You've chosen to be different. You recognize the power that words carry. You welcome their influence into your life.

While our book offers convenience with a page-a-day approach, it's not how many words you read or pages you turn that deems your reading a success. It's your choice to show up consistently and absorb content that feels aligned with you.

With each day, you've inched yourself forward from the life you live now to the life you're building. You've chosen to stay curious and remain open to new ideas.

The last day of this book is really another beginning. Whether you joined us for all 365 pages or dabbled throughout the year, count up all the ways you've allowed the principles to influence your life. How has your mind changed? What do you do differently? What would you go back and tell your younger self?

CONCLUSION

You hold the power over what tomorrow looks like for you. Be honest with what you see and keep applying what you absorb. Go forward knowing you can always open this book again and rediscover the pages with newfound wisdom.
The greatest compliment you can offer an author is to critically consume their words and test their theories on the constructive evolution of your own life. The pleasure of being a part of your journey is all a writer could ask for.

If even one page of this book does that for you, it will have served its purpose.

acknowledgments from Amy

I don't think you ever completely get the hang of writing a book. I find that it always presents me with new challenges, no matter how "ready" I feel going into it. Simply put, if not for the most amazing people surrounding me, there's no way I could have gotten through this process for the third time in my life.

To my husband, Vincenzo, thank you. For everything. There are not enough words in the world to convey my appreciation for all you do to support me in going after the life I want. It's a tall order, and I've never needed it more than I need it now. And now, you've surprised me once again as I see you fathering our first child. There is no one else in the world I could go on this ride with. I love you.

To my best friend forever and co-author Sara Mitchell McCain, we did it! Can you believe we're finally writing the acknowledgments? Bianca is to me what Roy is to you, and I can't begin to thank you enough for agreeing to write this book with me without hesitation, even after finding out you were expecting child #2. It all feels so perfect since your child #1, my goddaughter Grace, came to be while you were helping me edit *Good Morning, Good Life*. You're extraordinary at your craft, and I feel so lucky to work alongside you. I can't think of a greater privilege than to be a part of the first book you've put into the world as one of the most talented writers I've ever met. Thank you for pushing through all the challenging moments of this process, for supporting my vision with your exemplary genius, and, most importantly, for being my unconditional best friend. I love you.

To my daughter Bianca, this book may as well be your twin sister. It's funny how every time I sit down to write, I think I'm prepared. Then, something happens that not only makes the content better, it makes me better. You were that event for this book. Thank you for showing me how much more I have to learn. I love you.

To my family and friends, I am continually amazed by your support. The number of ways you show up for me—whether I ask or not—boggles the mind. I don't know what I'd do without you, but I know for sure it wouldn't be anywhere near as fun. I love you.

To Audrey Morabito, you are the unsung hero of this book. It's impossible for me to thank you properly for how you supported two pregnant women in getting our book to the finish line. When I think of the incredibly bright future you have ahead of you, I am blinded by the light. It has been an absolute pleasure to be a part of your beginning to an exciting writing career. I appreciate you bringing all of yourself to this process and helping us achieve our vision of 365 Days of *Good Morning, Good Life*. Thank you.

To Hannah Kahn, your ability to keep a multihyphenate's head on straight is nothing short of exceptional. As the chief of a creative staff, you have more than understood the assignment. You have leveled it up! Thank you for the plethora of tasks you took on to help the writing team get this book into the world. You have taught me so much about how I can better ask for the help I need by doing your best to stand in my shoes, and that means more than you'll ever know. Thank you.

To Kylie Lovsey, your graceful design efforts brought this book to life. I'm so grateful for all the passion and energy you've brought to our community. You bring so much light to your work, and that's what makes working with you so much fun. Thank you.

To Nancy Alvarado, it is always a pleasure to work with you on the design of our products and the experience for our cover art here was no different. I'm over the moon with the experience for our readers. Thank you for your brilliance and care for our brand.

To Andrew Lewin, you are the best audio engineer a girl could ask for! You are always ready and willing to help me get my words out into the earbuds of the world, and there was no shortage of your support when it came to getting this audiobook done. You are a first-class partner, and I love working with you. Thank you.

To 99Designs, you have been one of the greatest partners I've ever worked with. I can't imagine putting out another self-published book without your help and the incredible talent of your ebook designers. Thank you so much for always being there and ready to help me when it's time to put my words out into the world!

To my viewers, listeners, and readers, you have always been my North Star throughout my career. Everything I do is to serve you, and I have the deepest gratitude to you all, whether you're just getting on board this bandwagon or you've been around since the Savvy Sexy Social days. Thank you for showing up for me because I have never been more excited to continue this journey and show up for you. Thank you for changing my life.

Go after the life you want! Cheers!

acknowledgments from Sara

Life has shown me time and again that one core truth remains: It all comes down to people. The time you have to spend is given meaning by the circle you surround yourself with because, ultimately, it's about who you're with (and who they bring out in you) way more than where you are. Knowing this, it cannot be understated that this book would never have happened without my circle—the ones who have a way of constantly strengthening me and believing in me (especially when I lose sight of that myself).

First, no words would have been possible on any of these pages if not for Amy. Obviously, I mean this literally as she co-authored this, but more than that, I mean it emotionally and mentally. Amy, thank you for choosing me to embark on this journey with. I was honored to be asked and privileged to let the world in on what I see as our daily friend conversations. Having a best friend and confidant who sparks meaningful dialogue, sharpens my wit, and never stops encouraging depth has been transformative. Here's to many more long talks, constant transparency, and experiencing many more chapters together.

Every entry in this book was shaped to generate more and engage with whoever chooses to pick up this book. That said, the writing process was long, and perfectionist tendencies came out along the way. Nothing would have come together without the commitment of Amy's phenomenal team. Audrey and Hannah—your ability to dive in with us is what got us to the finish line. Audrey, thank you for your immense contributions—your perspective, capacity as an editor, and expertise was foundational to the final product we now get to hold in our hands. Hannah, you upheld the process seamlessly and undeniably kept us focused and on track, always maintaining the significance of the big picture.

ACKNOWLEDGMENTS

The process behind these pages meant many late nights after putting a toddler to bed, writing through a second pregnancy, and refusing to slow down during newborn months. It would have been impossible to strike this "balance" (Note: Balance doesn't exist, we just all find our own way to juggle and tap dance) without my husband, Kevin. Kev, your patience and grace with me made this happen. You know I can be stubborn and you love me through it. You take care of me even when I refuse to ask for help and remind me it's okay to take breaks (even if I say no ten times first). Thank you for going on this journey with me. Our partnership will always make me feel like I can achieve more, and that's because you always tell me it's true.

I said yes to this book for two reasons: Grace and Roy. You are my forever source of inspiration and my why in this world. There are not enough words in every language combined to describe the magnitude of what being your mom means to me. Grace, I love you around and around the world, my girl. Your first sentence was "I did it," and I hope you never stop yelling it. Roy, my boy, you came into our family with calm joy that has made us all more present and loving. The smile lines you've given me are my greatest badge of honor.

Simply put, I am the woman I am today because of my mother. Mom, you both gave me life and saved my life. You taught me resilience and tenacity when I needed it most, and on a daily basis, you keep me grounded. And, to my dad, the person who introduced me to my first love—words. Thank you for opening me up to the magic and wonder of endless worlds, believing in the power of the pen, and always being willing to meet under the poet tree. Because of you, I have found comfort, compassion, and hope on endless pages.

To my sister, Heather, you were the first friend I had in this life and my foundation for relationships. I don't know a world without our sisterhood, and know you will forever be my most excited advocate. Thank you for celebrating me even when I forget (or feel unworthy) of celebrating myself.

Rosemary and Dale, I am honored to be your daughter. Being part of your family helped me find my home. Thank you for welcoming me with unconditional love and reminding me that days spent with laughter and storytelling matter the most.

To the phenomenal women who hold me together more than they realize. Annette, thank you for seeing me and what I am capable of in moments I lose sight of myself. Our conversations about purpose and passion are unparalleled. Mallory, our friendship remains a North Star in my life. Thank you for never letting go of my hand and always holding onto life's beauty (and reminding me to do the same). Sam, meeting you changed me, and I wouldn't have it any other way. You show up and show me how to use my voice with pride and confidence without apology, and it has made me better.

ACKNOWLEDGMENTS

Shelby, if anxiety had an antidote, it would be you. Thank you for being a ceaseless reminder that we are stronger than our loudest inner critic—it has gotten me through more than you know.

And finally, to you. Thank you for reading this book, for choosing to challenge yourself and love yourself. Whether it helped you see your potential, stop a negative thought cycle or, heck, just get out of bed today—it was worth it. You are more powerful than you think, and I believe in you.

suggestions for further reading

Good Morning, Good Life: ***5 Simple Habits to Master Your Mornings and Upgrade Your Life***
by Amy Schmittauer Landino

The book you're holding now wouldn't exist without its predecessor, *Good Morning, Good Life: 5 Simple Habits to Master Your Mornings and Upgrade Your Life*. That book lays the foundation for all the themes we explore in this book, with a focus on customizing your morning routine. Not a morning person? Not a problem! I want you to wake up on your terms and no one else's. We'll talk about sharpening your decision-making skills, anticipating obstacles, discerning the habits that uplift you, defining your ideal morning, and taking purposeful steps to create a life you adore.

Vlog Like a Boss: ***How to Kill It Online With Video Blogging***
by Amy Schmittauer Landino

No matter what your end goal is—to market a business, get your dream job, or simply share your passion—video is one of the most powerful sources of information delivery that you can leverage today. Don't let Imposter Syndrome or lack of resources stop you. This is your time to thrive, so develop your creator mindset and unleash your gift to the world.

references

Adler, M. J., & Doren, C. V. (2006). How to Read a Book: The Classic Guide to Intelligent Reading. Simon & Schuster.

Akhtar, Allana, and Marguerite Ward. "28 People Who Became Highly Successful After Age 40." Business Insider, Business Insider, https://www.businessinsider.com/24-people-who-became-highly-successful-after-age-40-2015-6.

The Associated Press. "Apollo 11 Moon Landing Had Thousands Working Behind the Scenes." Bangor Daily News, 19 July 2019, www.bangordailynews.com/2019/07/19/news/apollo-11-moon-landing-had-thousands-working-behind-the-scenes/.

Axelson, Cloe. "The U.S. Women's Soccer Team Is All of Us. Come on, Ladies, 'LFG'." Cognoscenti, WBUR, 23 July 2021, www.wbur.org/cognoscenti/2021/07/23/uswnt-olympics-equal-pay-lfg-cloe-axelson

Baguley, Bonnie. "6 Famous Authors Who Once Faced Rejection." WildMind Creative, 15 Jan. 2021, www.wildmindcreative.com/bookmarketing/6-famous-authors-who-once-faced-rejection

Cameron, Julia. The Artist's Way: A Spiritual Path to Higher Creativity. Souvenir Press, 2020.

Castrillon, Caroline. "Why Personal Branding Is More Important Than Ever." Forbes, Forbes Magazine, 12 Oct. 2022, https://www.forbes.com/sites/carolinecastrillon/2019/02/12/why-personal-branding-is-more-important-than-ever/?sh=79bdda024085.

Dyer, Wayne W. Excuses Begone!: How to Change Lifelong, Self-Defeating Thinking Habits Hay House, 2009.

Dyer, Wayne W. Manifest Your Destiny: The Nine Spiritual Principles for Getting Everything You Want. Harper, 2008.

Gilchrist, Karen. "Media Icon Arianna Huffington Faced 37 Rejections Before Kick-Starting Her Career." CNBC, 25 June 2019, www.cnbc.com/2019/06/25/huffington-post-founder-faced-rejection-before-kick-starting-career.html

Groth, Aimee. "You're the Average of the Five People You Spend the Most Time With." Business Insider, Business Insider, 24 July 2012, www.businessinsider.com/jim-rohn-youre-the-average-of-the-five-people-you-spend-the-most-time-with-2012-7

"History of Wikipedia." Wikipedia, Wikimedia Foundation, 17 Jan. 2022, https://en.wikipedia.org/wiki/History_of_Wikipedia

Holiday, Ryan. The Daily Stoic: 366 Meditations on Wisdom, Perseverance, and the Art of Living. Profile Books, 2016.

Holiday, Ryan. The Obstacle Is the Way: The Ancient Art of Turning Adversity to Advantage. Profile Books, 2015.

Idol, Billy. "Dancing With Myself." Don't Stop, iTunes app, Chrysalis, 1981.

"Impostor Syndrome." Wikipedia, Wikimedia Foundation, 1 Oct. 2022, https://en.wikipedia.org/wiki/Impostor_syndrome.

Inc. Staff "How Sara Blakely Got Spanx Started." Inc.com, Inc., 20 Jan. 2012, www.inc.com/sara-blakely/how-sara-blakley-started-spanx.html

"Iris Apfel." Wikipedia, Wikimedia Foundation, 8 Sept. 2022, https://en.wikipedia.org/wiki/Iris_Apfel.

Kennedy, John F. "Inaugural Address." Little Brown Publishers, 1961.

"Maya Angelou." Wikipedia, Wikimedia Foundation, 13 Oct. 2022, https://en.wikipedia.org/wiki/Maya_Angelou#Chronology_of_autobiographies.

Michalski, Jennifer. "23 Successful Actors Who Dropped Out of High School." Business Insider, 4 Jan. 2014.

Newsweek Special Edition. "Michael Jordan Didn't Make Varsity—At First." Newsweek, 25 Apr. 2016, www.newsweek.com/missing-cut-382954

Roosevelt, Franklin D. (Franklin Delano), 1882-1945. Franklin D. Roosevelt's Inaugural Address of 1933. Washington, DC: National Archives and Records Administration, 1988.

Saju, Neha. "How to Cope with Rejection in Your Professional Career." The Daily Targum, 9 Mar. 2021, https://dailytargum.com/article/2021/03/how-to-cope-with-rejection-in-your-professional-career.

Zander, Rosamund Stone, and Benjamin Zander. The Art of Possibility: Practices in Leadership, Relationship, and Passion. Michael Joseph, 2006.

AMY SCHMITTAUER LANDINO is the bestselling author of *Good Morning, Good Life* and *Vlog Like a Boss*. Her work has been translated in multiple languages to serve her global audience and has been featured by media outlets such as the Tamron Hall Show, Inc Magazine, Entrepreneur Magazine, Business Insider, and many others. Amy hosts the award-winning YouTube series AmyTV where she is passionate about helping people emulate their vision and go after the life they want. With over 30 million views and counting, Amy is a known authority on getting digital attention. As an internationally-acclaimed public speaker, she travels the globe teaching the power of digital tools and how they help elevate a positive image and influential brand.

While her work has brought her purpose for over a decade, her greatest joy comes from outside the office. She recently celebrated 5 years of marriage to her best friend and business partner, Vincenzo Landino, and their family continues to grow with the arrival of their first child in 2022, Bianca. They share time between their home in Palm Beach, Florida, and residences in New Haven, Connecticut and Columbus, Ohio. Reach out to Amy directly on Instagram: @Schmittastic. Find more information at amylandino.com.

Photo Credit: Emma Low Photo

SARA MITCHELL McCAIN believes in the power of words - to connect, to create, and ultimately to transform. From a young age her passion to empathize ignited her love of writing, leading to her BFA in Writing, Literature, and Publishing and a career in communications. With over a decade of communications experience in the nonprofit and corporate sectors, she leverages the influence of storytelling to foster relationships and shape culture in the workplace.

Outside the office, Sara invests her time on Boards dedicated to mental wellbeing and community building. Based in Columbus, Ohio, Sara is a wife, mom, dog mom, and emotion advocate. At the end of the day, she is driven by the hope that stringing words together with love will lead to a better world for her children where their voices ripple beyond their imagination.

Photo Credit: Emma Low Photo

Take the next step toward enjoying your mornings with our premium content, including the *Good Morning, Good Life* 30-Day Challenge!

Tune in:
www.goodmorninggoodlife.tv

Made in United States
North Haven, CT
08 April 2023

35184640R00241